The Adventures of Sarah Ann Lewis
and the Memory Thieves

by

Joshua C. Carroll

Published by Telltales Publishing
www.TelltalesPub.com

© 2019 Joshua C. Carroll

All rights reserved. No portion of this book may be reproduced in any form without permission from the publisher, except as permitted by U.S. copyright law.

For permissions, contact:
help@TelltalesPub.com

Cover art by Ingvard the Horrible.

Print edition identifier: 20190706

ISBN: 978-1-7331547-0-3

*For Jadyn,
the first to show me
just how much love
a dad's heart can hold.*

AUTHOR'S NOTE

Several years ago, I received an unexpected phone call from my mom.

"We just bought a mountain!"

What she meant was that she and my dad had purchased a 142 acre lot that included what most people would call a hill or a mesa. In the part of western central Texas where I grew up, we call these "mountains."

Over the next couple of years, I spent much of my time hiking on that land. I found myself drawn to the mountain and explored it often. It was peaceful and mysterious and full of unknowable history. I would lie on the flat top watching buzzards circle overhead and wonder who else might have done the same before me. The neighbors told stories about the days when that region was wild and unsettled. Some of them had found arrowheads and other artifacts. They said that, according to one local legend, outlaws had stashed money in a cave in one of those hills. Until the summer before my parents sold the property, however, all I ever found were unidentified animal bones, names carved like graffiti into the sandstone wall beneath an overhanging ledge (some with dates back into the 1800s), and one angry and pungent turkey vulture who hissed warnings at me to stay away from his cave.

One of the last times I hiked on that land, I stumbled across an old lunch box half buried under some brush and loose rocks on the west side of the mountain. It was dirty and rusty, and the original Fraggle Rock artwork was faded and scraped. On the back, in the lower right corner, the name "Sarah" was still legible. Inside, I found a handful of pens and No. 2 pencils, a little notebook, a Coca-Cola pocket knife (rusted shut), a yellowed copy of <u>Nancy Drew: The Hidden Staircase</u>, and a folded dot-matrix printed letter addressed to a Sarah Ann Lewis from someone called Desjardins. Though many of the words were faded so that they were almost unreadable, I could see that it contained some personal details and the implication of danger. It sounded almost threatening, and I wondered if, perhaps, this was connected to an old crime.

Over the next several weeks, I dug through public records and scoured every internet resource I could find. I'm no detective, so it's possible I missed something, but I found nothing about Sarah Ann Lewis. Nothing. No birth certificate, death certificate, or obituary. No public school records. No tax records. The police were no help. The name was not familiar to anybody I asked. After a couple weeks with no results, I tossed the lunch box and its contents (except for the Coke knife, which I cleaned up and added to my collection) into a box in my closet and moved on with my life.

A few years later, I decided to attempt writing a short novelette for my daughter, Jadyn, who was only six years old at the time. I thought that Sarah Ann Lewis and Desjardins would make wonderful characters, so I started making notes about them and the sorts of situations that might lead to the strange letter I'd found in the lunch box. Nothing worked. I started over with fresh outlines for my story several times, but each attempt came to nothing. Though I never gave up on the idea, I only managed to write a few pages worth keeping.

Then one day, my wife sent me a text message while I was at work saying that I had received a package with no return address, only the sender's name: C. Carraway. I hadn't ordered anything, and I didn't know anybody by that name, but the package was addressed to me, so when I got home from work, I opened it. The first thing I found inside was a handwritten letter with my name on it:

Dearest Mr. Carroll,

We've not met, but I'm told you're the right man for this assignment. In truth, I'm not entirely sure you'll accept it. Lord knows you'll have little enough incentive. But yours is the name I was given, and I've chosen to trust.

It has been brought to our attention that you may already have some knowledge of a certain Sarah Ann Lewis, and you may have even heard the name Desjardins, though it's unlikely you've discovered much beyond the names. The particulars of these identities are, shall we say, inaccessible to the general public.

It is now, however, vitally important that Miss Sarah's story be told publicly, and we are counting on you to make that happen. Something important (the specifics of which I dare not disclose), something incredibly strange and dangerous is happening, and I'm unsure whether my colleagues and I will still be around to tell the tale ourselves when it's over. And if we are, we may not remember. But if our work is to be worth anything at all, this story, this tale of beginnings, must survive.

We are quite certain that the population at large won't believe a word of it, so unless you fancy being taken for a loony, you'd best publish the whole thing as a work of fiction. For that matter, take all the artistic license you like. I only ask that you keep certain names and events intact, which we will mark for you. Those who need the factual bits will find them; others will think nothing of them, and that's all the better for our purposes.

You'll find everything we could manage to collect for you in this parcel. I've included what maps and sketches I could gather along with a few notes of my own. Several of us have written out our experiences as best as we are able, and you'll find Miss Sarah's old diary enclosed as well. I hope you have all you need, and I do pray you'll accept this task.

I cannot guarantee that any of us will live to see your work published, Mr. Carroll, but if we do, we will do what we can to help it succeed. So much depends on this.

I will send what I can, when I can, if I can.

C. Carraway

Everything in the package was just as Carraway described it. The notes and the drawings were fascinating, and the stories in Sarah's diary were too exciting to ignore. So I accepted the challenge and started my story over from scratch.

Following Carraway's advice, I am releasing this story into the wild as a novel. I have, in fact, invented a lot of dialogue (though I was able to lift a bit from Sarah's diary), so it is fiction in that regard. And I have filled in certain points of the storyline where there are holes and allowed myself creative license regarding the descriptions of settings and the like. As the saying goes, however, fact is stranger than fiction, and in this case, it is much stranger and more fantastic than I could have imagined.

Some of the written accounts I received in that package seemed to be at odds with one another on certain details, and in those cases I have used the version that best fit the storyline. Although I was not forbidden to do so, I have chosen not to disclose any exact locations but, rather, to stick to general areas since I am not sure what's at stake.

To be honest, I am not convinced that I should have trusted Carraway in the first place. Who knows what I've gotten myself into? But, like Sarah, my own curiosity has landed me in this story, and for better or worse, I will see it through.

Enough about me, though. You are here to read Sarah's story, not mine. And so, whether you accept these stories as history or fantasy, I sincerely hope that you will enjoy the adventures of Sarah Ann Lewis and the Memory Thieves.

—Joshua C. Carroll

MARCH, 1988

The spies waited in the pickup line at Sarah's middle school. Blackwood peered out of the passenger-side window of a beaten-up Oldsmobile and scanned the crowd of departing students. The line of cars ahead of them inched forward. Murik eased off the clutch and followed, his eyes scanning the sky.

"Our friend, the hawk, is back," said Murik in a thick Russian accent.

"Shut up about the stupid bird," said Blackwood. "We are supposed to be watching for the girl."

"You watch for girl. I watch for Sentinels."

Blackwood rubbed his eyes and blinked. He squinted and scanned the faces of the students again. "You would think they could come up with something better for us to do than sitting here in the middle of…" He stopped mid-sentence and narrowed his eyes. "There. Near the sign. Red haired girl, walking alone. Give me the picture."

Murik reached into a leather portfolio and removed a small stack of blurry black and white photos.

Blackwood snatched the photos out of his hand and flipped through them. Then he squinted through the window again. "Yeah, that could be her." He laughed. "Of course they would hide her here, in plain sight. I'd bet anything that's the real Lewis girl. Pull up close, and I'll jump out and grab her."

"No. Wait. Could be shifter," said Murik. He leaned over Blackwood for a better look.

"Hey! Get off me!" Blackwood shook his head and pushed Murik away. "You worry too much about bogey men and phantoms."

"Is not joke," said Murik. "I have seen—" but he was interrupted by a loud rumbling noise.

A burly police officer on a white and gold motorcycle had pulled up next to the car and stopped. With one hand, the officer signaled for Murik to roll down his window; the other hand rested on his sidearm.

"Cop. Great," Blackwood mumbled. "Where did he come from, anyway?"

Murik cranked the handle to lower his window and spoke politely. "What is problem, officer?"

"Mind if I ask what you gentlemen are doing?"

"Certainly. We," Murik began.

"We're just here to pick up our nephew," said Blackwood.

The officer leaned down and eyed the men over the tops of his sunglasses. "Your nephew, huh?" he said. "Never seen you two before, and I know pretty much everybody around these parts. Small town. Who's the nephew?"

"Nicholas," said Murik.

"Johnson," added Blackwood.

"Uh huh," said the officer. "I don't know any—"

"He's new," Blackwood interrupted.

"Which one is he?"

"What business is it of yours?" Blackwood asked.

The officer pointed to his badge. "I see two strange men hanging around a school, I make it my business. Understand?"

Murik shot Blackwood a pleading look.

"Fine. We didn't see him with the other kids, okay?" Blackwood snapped. "Maybe he walked home. Maybe he left early."

"Mmhmm," said the officer. "Well, I think it's best if you gentlemen went on home too, then. Folks around here don't take too kindly to strange men lurking around their kids."

Blackwood growled and leaned toward the window, but Murik held up a hand and spoke first. "Yes, officer," he said. "We understand." The line of cars ahead of them had all picked up their students and left, leaving the road empty. Murik smiled at the officer, then he put the car into first gear and pushed the gas. The tires squealed briefly as it sprang into motion.

"The boss isn't going to like this," said Blackwood.

"Girl was already gone. We will come back."

"Not a chance," said Blackwood. "That cop will remember us. The boss will have to do it himself now." He punched the dashboard.

Murik sighed and said, "Is officer following?"

Blackwood turned and looked out the rear windshield. "No. The bike's still there. Don't see the cop anywhere."

"And hawk?"

Blackwood sighed. Then he rolled down his window, leaned out, and looked up at the sky. "Not a bird in the sky." He pulled himself back into his seat and rolled up the window.

For a few minutes, the men rode in silence, both checking their mirrors out of the corners of their eyes.

"Still no hawk?" Murik asked at last.

"You worry too much, Murik," Blackwood said. "This is the middle of nowhere. See? A deserted road. I could shoot you right here and bury you between those trees, and nobody would—"

The car screeched to a halt. Murik's face was white.

"What the—" Blackwood began.

"Silence!" Murik whispered. "Look. There."

"What?" asked Blackwood, straining his eyes toward the trees on the side of the road where Murik pointed. "I don't see anything."

"Is bear. Big black bear, hiding in trees."

Blackwood shook his head and snorted. "You idiot. There are no bears in this part of Texas."

"I know," Murik snapped. "This is what worries me."

1

THE PRINCESS

THE OLD WINDOW CREAKED AS IT OPENED, AND THE RARE SCENT OF fresh rain drifted into the bedroom. A bright patch of sun cut a path between the retreating clouds and the hills to the east, and a few bright rays flickered between the breeze-blown curtains and fell on Sarah's closed eyes.

"Mornin', Princess," said Grandpa Kirk. "Time for breakfast." He was entirely too cheerful.

Sarah groaned, scrunched her freckled cheeks up toward her eyebrows, and pulled the sheet over her face.

Grandpa chuckled. He ruffled her bed-messed red hair and left her to get ready. Sarah heard him whistling as he walked to the kitchen.

She hated being called "Princess." Especially on school mornings. Princesses were giggly and bouncy and popular, and Sarah wasn't any of those. A princess would dance out of bed with a smile and perfect hair. A princess would sing a song about how she couldn't wait for school to begin, and the birds and squirrels would talk to her and help her dress. Sarah didn't feel like singing or frolicking with wildlife. She didn't want to be bubbly or dainty. She just wanted the school year to end already.

"I guess being Princess Leia wouldn't be so terrible," she mumbled. Sarah forced herself to sit up, and then, with a stretch and a yawn, added, "but I'd rather be the Invisible Woman." She smiled at the thought of sneaking away from school unseen.

"Breakfast's gettin' cold," Grandpa Kirk called from the kitchen in a sing-song tone that reminded Sarah of her mother.

She pulled on some jeans and a tee shirt and stumbled to the dining table, drawn by the aroma of bacon and eggs. "Thanks, Grandpa," she said when she arrived.

"I was gonna eat anyway. Figured I might as well feed you while I was at it." He had said that every morning since she moved in three months earlier. "Hey, I've got one for you."

"Hmm?" Sarah slurped her milk.

He leaned forward, and his gray eyes twinkled at her over the thin rims of his reading glasses. "What do you call a pencil that's never been sharpened?"

"What?"

"Pointless."

"Grandpa!" Sarah rolled her eyes and giggled.

He smiled and picked up the newspaper. "It's good to hear you laugh, kiddo."

1987 HAD BEEN AWFUL. SARAH'S MOM HAD PASSED AWAY IN MAY. Cancer. The doctors had talked about how hard she fought, but all Sarah remembered was how tired her mom had been those last few weeks. The funeral was a blur of tears and thank-yous and strange faces. Summer drifted by in silence and loneliness. School, which she had always loved before, no longer seemed to matter. She would have failed every class that fall if her teachers hadn't been so gracious. And then, just before Christmas, her dad announced that he was moving away to take a job in a foreign country. He wouldn't say where he was going or what he would be doing. He only said that she couldn't come. Two weeks later, they silently loaded her clothes and a handful of keepsakes into the family car, and Sarah waved goodbye to the small apartment she had always called home.

Grandpa Kirk welcomed her with a smile and a bear-hug when

they pulled into his driveway. Her dad kissed her on the head and drove away without a goodbye. Grandpa never said a word about it.

He had already moved most of the furniture out of his enormous library and set it up as a bedroom for Sarah—leaving plenty of old-smelling books on the shelves for her to read. It was fantastic. He told her they could paint the walls any color she liked. She chose neon green, and she laughed for the first time in months when he splattered paint on his white beard. It took a week to wash out.

Sarah's new home sat in the middle of a 200 acre rectangle bordered by three flat-topped hills that she and Grandpa called "mountains." The land was rough and covered in thorny mesquite trees and prickly pear cactus, but Grandpa kept the yard around the house green and clear except for a few cedars. He took her on walks and pointed out the various species of birds and bushes as they talked. He taught her which berries were safe to eat, how to identify animals by their tracks, and how to handle a pocket knife without cutting herself. He sketched a map of the dirt roads that led to each of the three hills and the path to his small tool shed. Then he set her loose to explore. Sarah made it her goal to discover every hidden trail and secret path on the land and had marked half a dozen hideouts within a week. She was having fun again.

Sarah had always enjoyed Grandpa Kirk's visits when she was little. He had told the best stories about giants and dwarves and talking animals, always ending the same way: "Sure makes you wonder where all these stories come from." Now he was all the family she had. He drove her to school and back every day, helped with homework, and told corny jokes just to make her smile.

"STORM GAVE US SOME GOOD RAIN LAST NIGHT," SAID GRANDPA FROM behind his newspaper. "Says here they were expecting a quarter inch. I think we got at least that much."

Sarah nodded as she chewed.

"Won't be enough to keep ol' Smith from complaining about the drought, of course, but it's more than we got last month. I'd call that a blessing." Jack Smith was an old army buddy of Grandpa's who now ran the farm supply near Sarah's school. He always sent along something for Sarah whenever Grandpa visited the store—usually candy or a pen with the name of a feed manufacturer printed on the side. Last week he had sent her two old horseshoes bent into bookends.

Sarah swallowed. "Are you going up there today?"

"Aw, I might swing by later. Got to keep in touch. I don't get to see my friends every day like you do."

"Well, tell Mr. Smith I said hi and thanks for the bookends. They're great."

"Mmhmm." He paused. "Speaking of friends…"

Sarah took a deep breath and faked a smile.

"Did you make friends with that new girl yet?"

Sarah rolled her eyes. "I thought *I* was the new girl."

"Very funny. You know what I mean."

She knew exactly what he meant. Aubrey and her family, the Dvoraks, had moved into the house on the adjacent lot a month ago, and Grandpa Kirk seemed determined that the two girls would become best buddies.

"Aubrey?" Sarah asked with a smirk. "No," and then under her breath, "I don't think Princess Popular needs any more friends." She took another bite of scrambled eggs.

Grandpa Kirk raised one bushy eyebrow and opened his mouth as if he were about to say something, but he sighed instead and disappeared again behind his newspaper. "You'd better eat up if you want to brush that red mess on your head before we leave."

Though Sarah focused every last bit of her brain power on speeding up the clock, the school day passed with all the velocity of a sleepy slug. During her final class of the day, Mr. Litchfield, the new substitute math teacher, caught her daydreaming and asked her to explain the lesson he had taught. Sarah fumbled for a minute and then, embarrassed, admitted that she hadn't been paying attention.

"As I suspected," Mr. Litchfield sneered in his nasal voice. He seemed to be delighted at her misfortune. "Please plan to stay after school and review the lesson." A smile crept across his pale face.

"But sir, it's Friday, and—"

The teacher cut her off. "And what? If you object to staying late, you should consider paying better attention during class."

"But teachers are not allowed to keep us late on Fridays," Sarah whispered. "It's a school policy."

Mr. Litchfield closed his eyes and sniffed, jaw clenched tight. "Very well, then. Monday. I expect you to stay an extra hour."

"Won't our regular teacher be back by—"

"Monday!"

Sarah nodded, embarrassed, and wondered when substitutes started assigning after-school time anyway. When the three-o'clock bell rang at last, she flung her books into her backpack and sprinted out of the classroom.

GRANDPA KIRK MUST HAVE HAD SOMETHING ON HIS MIND BECAUSE HE didn't ask the usual hundred questions on the drive home, and Sarah was happy to keep quiet about the incident in math class. When they reached the house, Grandpa Kirk pulled a mechanical pencil and a small spiral-bound notebook from behind the seat and handed them to her.

"From Mr. Smith," he said.

Sarah thanked him and asked if she could go exploring.

"Do you have homework?"

"Nope."

"All right then, Princess. Be home in time for dinner."

Sarah ran inside, tossed her backpack into her room, and sprinted out the back door. She followed the dirt road behind the house over the little hill by the shed, cut through the trees to the gap in the brush near the eastern border, and followed the fenceline south. There was just enough room to squeeze between the barbed wire and the trees, and she had to be careful not to let her new notebook fall out of her back pocket. After a few yards, she came to a place hidden by brush where, years before, wild hogs had broken through the fence that separated the Dvoraks' property from Grandpa's. She peeked through for a moment and then turned around and ducked into one of her secret trails that led away from the fence, twisting and turning through the thicket. This was just an old game trail, but it felt magical. At the foot of the mesa, the trees opened up to reveal a winding stairway of loose stones and gnarled tree roots. She climbed these to a small ledge walled in on two sides by tall boulders and on a third side by the mesa itself. A scrawny cedar tree sprawled out from a crack in the rocks overhead.

This was Sarah's favorite spot on Earth. It was her secret mountain hideout. She had arranged the space with logs and rocks to form a small couch and covered them with an old picnic blanket. It was perfect.

Most days she would read, stare at the clouds, and daydream. Some days she imagined that this was her old apartment in the city. Mom was still alive and Dad was in the next room. She and her mother would have long conversations about school and TV shows and books and boys. Other days she pretended that she was a secret agent. The walls were futuristic control panels with flickering screens and glowing buttons. A stick was her high-powered telescope, an empty shotgun shell case was her camera, and she reported back to headquarters by speaking into her wristwatch. Today, though, she would sketch; today she was an artist.

Sarah opened her new notebook and tapped the eraser of her pencil on the first page. What should she draw? She looked around her hideout for inspiration. A horned lizard disappeared into the brush before she could get a good look at it. No good. Maybe a landscape. Sarah climbed to the top of the shortest wall, sat down, and began to sketch the skyline.

Then she noticed the smoke. A thick black cloud had sprouted from the side of the hill behind Aubrey's house, half a mile from where Sarah sat. She leaned forward, strained her eyes, and scanned the landscape as the smoke drifted out of sight. There was no fire that she could see. "I should have borrowed Grandpa's binoculars," she muttered to herself as she sat back and let her gaze fall to her notebook.

BOOM! CLANK! Bang! Rattle, rattle. Crash.

Sarah jolted upright. A large, gray thing bounced down the hill where she had seen the smoke. There was shouting, but the voices were too distant for her to understand. Sarah slipped down from the wall. She hid for a moment and then climbed on top of a log and peeked over the top. Silence. Then something moved. Some*one* moved. Sarah watched as a man in a long white coat stumbled down the hill, retrieved the thing, and then climbed back up the rocky slope. He stopped and looked around for a moment as if making sure nobody saw him; then he disappeared into the hill.

2

A CLOSE CALL

At dinner that night, Sarah told Grandpa Kirk about the smoke and the man. He laughed it off and told her the neighbors must be having some work done on their property and she shouldn't worry about it.

"But what would they be doing on the mountain?" she asked.

He didn't know.

"What if they're Communist spies or something?"

Grandpa said that was ridiculous and that she should mind her own business. That was that. They finished eating, did the dishes, read for a bit, and then went to bed earlier than usual for a Friday.

Sarah tried to forget the whole thing and go to sleep. She really tried. For what seemed like hours, she strained to think about something else—anything else. But Grandpa had left the window open, and it would be so simple to sneak out without waking him. After all, he had never told her she couldn't climb out the window in the middle of the night.

Moments later, she was outside in her rain boots and pajamas, following the beam of her little purple flashlight toward the eastern fence.

The night air was chilly. Branches creaked and rattled in the wind. The sky was clear, and the half moon cast a dull gray light onto the field below. Sarah clinched her flashlight in her teeth and climbed through the hole in the barbed-wire fence.

You're trespassing in your pajamas, she scolded herself. *Trespassing!* For an instant, she considered going back home, but then she imagined herself helping the police catch some really bad people, and trespassing no longer seemed so terrible. If she was right about them, this was more important.

Sarah squeezed through the web of tangled branches near the fence and stepped out onto a dirt road that ran between the tree line and an old sunflower field. She clicked her flashlight off and crept onward, keeping close to the shadows as she went. After a few minutes, the road veered to the right and rose toward the base of the hill. Mesquite trees crowded in from both sides and threw dark shadows across her path. Sarah inched her way to the middle of the road where it was smoother and she was less likely to trip. The road curved to the left as the line of trees thinned and then stopped altogether. Her destination loomed ahead, a black shadow against the stars. *Not much farther,* she thought and left the road. The ground here was sandy and dotted with patches of tall grass that swayed in the moonlight. As she reached the foot of the mesa, the grass gave way to boulders. Sarah stopped, lit her flashlight, and surveyed her surroundings. Long finger-like ridges protruded from the base of the hill, between which rainwater had cut rough trenches. Farther up, the slope was covered in gravel and loose dirt. Any attempt to climb straight up from this side would be too dangerous even by daylight. To her left, however, she found a little trail that led over a ridge. Sarah whispered a quick "thank you," turned the flashlight off again, and headed toward the trail. Her heart pounded in her chest. *If you get caught, Grandpa will ground you for life!*

A train whistled in the distance, and a pack of coyotes howled in response. The hairs on the back of Sarah's neck stood at attention. "Grandpa was right," she mumbled. "It was just a worker. He's gone now. I should go home too."

But as she turned to leave, something caught her attention out the corner of her eye: a dim, warm glow from behind a bush on the hillside. Sarah hesitated a moment and then grunted and h[...] source of the light.

It was a cave. The entrance was a little shorter tha[n ...] three or four feet wide. Sarah held her breath and s[...] inside. No sound. She sniffed. It smelled clean enough[...] shone from a large square hole in the wall several yards from the entrance, reflecting off hundreds of small shiny spots on the cave floor. Broken glass. Sarah tucked her flashlight into the pocket of her pajama pants, took a deep breath, and tiptoed toward the light with as much stealth as she could muster.

When she reached the back of the cave, she discovered that the square hole was a broken hinged window. A few jagged pieces of glass still protruded from its metal frame.

"Weird," she whispered.

Through the window she could see a cavernous, concrete-floored room lined with metal bookshelves and boxes. Fluorescent lights hung from chains that extended up into the darkness of the mountain. In the center of the room were two large steel desks topped with scribbled notepads, microscopes, spools of wire, beakers, and the like. Two old leather chairs, a matching couch, and a floor lamp were arranged to her left. In the far corner, next to a heavy-looking wooden door, a mangled metal contraption had been set beside a large waste bin. *That must be the thing I saw bouncing down the hill earlier,* she thought and wondered what it was. There was also a painting of an old, wrinkled basset hound standing on its hind legs and wearing a lab coat. It seemed so strange and out of place that she almost laughed out loud. A strange whirring noise came from somewhere on her right, but a tall cabinet blocked her view.

Sarah ducked out of the light and took a breath. Her brain spun. She lifted her head for another look. Across the room, a glass display case reflected a flashing red light attached to whatever was on the other side of the in-the-way cabinet. The whirring noise quickened to a chatter and then stopped, and the flashing red light was replaced by a solid green one. Sarah pushed her body through the window up to her waist, careful of the glass, and leaned in. Her neck stretched as she strained to see around cabinet. She wiggled another inch into the room and extended a leg behind her for balance. It was just far enough to see the source of the sounds. She squinted. White light illuminated something grayish-pink and glistening inside a glass box. Wires were attached at several points, and a black cone pointed down from above it. Sarah gasped. "Is that a brain?!" she heard herself say aloud. Horrified, she clapped a hand across her mouth, lost her balance, and toppled into the room.

Sarah's forehead hit the concrete floor hard. She froze. All was quiet. A few terrifying seconds passed, and then she forced herself to stand. She paused again to listen. Still nothing. She rubbed her forehead. It wasn't bleeding, but there was already a bump and, she was sure, the beginnings of a bruise she would have to explain. As she turned to leave, something in the cabinet by the window jerked.

Bzzzt. Bzt. Bzzzzt. Bzzzzzzzzzzt. Clunk. Bzzzt.

She glanced over her shoulder and then nudged open one door of the cabinet. Inside, she saw a large dot-matrix printer bolted to a shelf. Attached to it was a board covered in glass and metal bits that looked like the inside of Grandpa Kirk's old radio. She pulled both doors wide open and studied the contraption for a moment. In front, red numbers on a display that looked like her digital alarm clock read 23:10. Three small vacuum tubes were glowing softly in a row across one side. A bundle of black, gray, and clear plastic cables ran from the top of the device through a hole high in the back of the cabinet. Gray lines on a green circuit board formed a winding maze interrupted here and there by barrels, buttons, boxes, and dials of various colors attached by copper wire and solid pools of silver solder. A stack of perforated, green- and white-striped paper spooled through the noisy machine, coaxed along by gears that fitted into parallel rows of holes punched into the edges of the paper. Sarah twisted her head around to read the upside down words as the printer finished.

"No way!" she whispered and ripped the sheet from the printer. This is what she read:

TO SARAH ANN LEWIS:

Your mother's favorite perfume was White Shoulders. She was wearing it the day she died, and you still have half a bottle under your bed that you take out when you are lonely. Your father's nickname for you was "Sprinkles," and you regret that you rolled your eyes at him the last time time he used it. You want to be a detective when you grow up because you don't believe his reasons for leaving and you want to find out why he lied. You have a secret crush on Ben Booker.

I write all this in hope that you will trust me.

Your grandfather was right about your curiosity. It has gotten the best of you this time, and you are in very real danger. If you don't want to be caught, follow these instructions exactly:

Beside the sofa by the bookshelf in the corner, there is a small table with a pile of books on top. Hide underneath it and do not move. In a few minutes, two men will enter this room. Remain completely silent. After they leave, you will be able to climb back out the ventilation window you came through and go home. Don't forget your flashlight! It slipped out of your pocket when you fell. Move quickly and quietly. Avoid the road. Go the long way around the thick brush and pass through the gap in the fence near the easement. Say nothing about tonight and nobody will suspect you were here.

Exactly two weeks from today you will have a choice. You may either choose to come back to this room at 10:15 p.m. and begin the greatest adventure of your life, or you may choose to stay home and risk the consequences. You will not be safe either way.

Yours,

Desjardins

Sarah felt dizzy. "Who's watching me?!" she demanded in a hoarse whisper as she scanned the walls in vain for surveillance cameras. She tore the perforated edges from the paper nervously and folded the letter around them. The words she had read echoed in her mind. *Somebody saw me. How else would they know I dropped my...*She patted her pocket and realized that her flashlight was, in fact, missing. Disoriented and panicked, she turned in circles and looked for it. Sarah caught herself and forced her body to be still. *Relax. Take a deep breath and...what's that?* She stopped to listen. Voices. Someone was outside the door. Without thinking, Sarah dropped to the floor and scrambled behind the couch to the far end. As the letter had predicted, there was an end table covered in books that was just tall enough that she could hide beneath it. *Oh no!* she thought, *I forgot to close the cabinet!*

"No, no. Now listen," a scratchy voice with a funny accent—maybe Irish or Scottish, Sarah thought—said as the door flew open. "It's not the same thing at all. Not at all."

"How so?" asked a less scratchy voice with a British accent.

"What he was doing, well, it was practically kidnapping. It *was* kidnapping. And those people, they'll never be the same. People lost something in those chambers. Something they can't ever get back. He was *stealing*. We're not. Now here, hold this."

Sarah couldn't see what was going on, but she could could hear shuffling and then a creaking hinge and a whooshing noise.

"So what then? We're just *borrowing* these memories, I suppose?"

What did he say? Sarah thought to herself, biting her lip to keep from gasping.

"No, of course not. Don't be a goon. We're not giving anything back to 'em because nobody lost anything in the first place. We're just," the voice paused, "making copies and filing them away."

"I suppose so, but—"

"No. No more. Just you remember why we're doing this, you hear?"

"I know. I know. You're right."

Sarah peeked her head around the front of the couch and glimpsed two pairs of black canvas sneakers beneath two long white coats. The paper made a crinkling noise in her tightened hand. Sarah held her breath, but neither of the men seemed to notice.

"All right, then," said the scratchy voice. "Now, open the case. We're behind as it is with all your jabbering. If we don't get this thing into the flash freeze quick, we'll have to toss it and start all over. The old bear won't be happy about that."

Both men snickered.

"Indeed," said the voice with the British accent, "and Lord knows she's been cranky enough already without us giving her a reason."

Latches were released and then shut. "Why do you suppose she's so worried anyway? It's not like *she* has to do the reading."

"Aye. I think she's more concerned about you-know-who."

Sarah heard the door open, and exhaled in relief.

"Hey, who left the cabinet open?" the scratchy voice asked.

"Eh, must have been Michael. Still nothing, looks like, and we're the better for it. Come on. I'll close it up later."

"Aye. Later." There was a groan. "These new night hours will be the death of me."

"Well, we can't very well risk another—"

The door shut, and the voices faded out of hearing. Sarah took a deep breath. *Don't panic,* she thought. Gathering her courage, she stuffed the letter into the pocket of her pajama pants and scrambled to the window. She paused, shot a cautious glance at the door, and then climbed out the window and through the cave.

Sarah ran home as quickly as she could, navigating by feel and the light of the moon, and ignored the letter's instructions to keep along the fenceline. It wasn't until she was safely inside her own bedroom with the window shut and locked behind her that she realized she had left her flashlight behind.

3

SECRETS

An unwelcome parade of frightening dreams stole any chance Sarah had of real rest that night. In one, she was alone in the middle of a desert, searching for a way home. All around she could hear distant voices, but no matter how far she walked, she never found anything but endless sand and heat. When she stopped and reached for her canteen, it had turned into a slimy, pulsating brain. She dropped it and tried to scream.

Sarah shot up from her bed, heart racing and covered in sweat. She tiptoed to the bathroom for a drink of water, calmed herself down, and went back to bed.

Later she dreamed that her father had come to take her home. He was dressed in all black and held a sword, like Westley from *The Princess Bride*. It was the last movie they had seen together before he left.

"Daddy!" Sarah shouted and ran to hug him, but the harder she tried to reach him, the farther away he seemed to be.

"Sarah!" he called to her, "Come to me! Hurry! Run! Faster!" Sarah ran and ran, sobbing and yelling for him to come back. Just as she began to get closer, she tripped and fell, slamming her head onto a concrete floor. Her forehead throbbed, and she wanted to get up and run again, but she found that she could neither move nor speak.

"What's this?" said a scratchy voice. A man in a long white coat stood over her. "She won't be needing these." Hundreds of unseen voices laughed as a giant syringe approached her forehead. Slowly. Closer. Closer. "Now just you hold still. This is going to hurt."

Sarah woke with a start. The sun had not yet risen. She could hear coffee brewing and Grandpa digging through the pots and pans in the kitchen. She threw on yesterday's jeans and a fresh tee shirt, slipped on a pair of tennis shoes, tucked her hair into an Astro's baseball cap, and checked herself in the mirror. The bump on her forehead was not as noticeable as it felt, but she pulled the brim of her hat down and let a lock of red hair hang to cover it anyway. She emptied her lunch box and stuffed her spiral notebook and a handful of pencils and pens into it.

"Hey Grandpa, I'm going out to the mountain to watch the sunrise," she called across the house.

"You're up early! Sure you don't want to eat first? I was thinking of making pancakes."

"No thanks. I don't want to miss it." Sarah quietly pulled Grandpa's binoculars down from the top of the hall closet and slipped the strap over her head.

"All right then, Princess. Just be careful. I'm fixin' to head into town to take care of a few things this morning. Probably won't be back until this afternoon. You can make a sandwich if you get hungry."

She was out the door before he finished his sentence.

"Okay," said Sarah, "first I have to look at the evidence I have. What do I know?" She paced back and forth across the floor of her mountain hiding place, doing her best detective impression. "One: there's a laboratory inside that mountain." She stopped to write this in her notebook and then laughed and shook her head. She picked up the binoculars and looked at the hill again. Nothing out of the ordinary. "And I left my flashlight there like a moron," she muttered. In the margin of her paper she wrote MUST RETRIEVE FLASHLIGHT

TONIGHT and resumed her pacing. "Two: there's a brain in that lab. A *brain!*" She wrote this down with a shudder and forced herself not to think about it anymore. The memory made her stomach turn. "Three," she bit the eraser end of her pencil, "*somebody* knew I was there. Somebody who could *see* me. Somebody who knows things about me!" She gritted her teeth. "But why warn me about the guys in the lab coats?" Sarah wondered aloud. "What's their game?" She pulled the letter out of her pocket and read it again. It was still a mystery. She sighed, folded it, and put it back into her pocket. Sarah stared at the sky for a few minutes, wishing any of this made sense, and then twirled her pencil, tapped it against her forehead, and sat down. "Four: did they say something about stealing people's memories?"

They had. She was sure of it. But how was it even possible? Did they have to kill people first? Was that how they got the brain? Had they cut it from the skull of some unsuspecting person? Sarah felt ill. Maybe she had misunderstood. Perhaps they were talking about computers or something. Computers had memory, didn't they? No. No, that didn't make sense either. They would have said *memory*, not *memories*. And it certainly wouldn't explain the brain.

There was no other explanation she could see. The men in lab coats—probably assisted by Aubrey Dvorak's too-perfect family— were stealing memories from other people and "filing them away for later." But what did they want them for? And why *here?* This was nowhere special. Nobody important lived here, just a bunch of farmers and teachers and nobodies like Sarah.

A horrible thought struck her then. What if they had, somehow, already stolen her memories. The thought nauseated her. She couldn't imagine why anybody would want them, but it *would* explain how all those personal details wound up in the letter. She laid back, suddenly dizzy.

Then another, more hopeful thought occurred to her: even if somebody had stolen her memories, nobody could know what she would do next. Whatever game the Dvoraks were playing, Sarah could still win. She would have to be smart. She would have to find a way to spy on them without being noticed, and when she knew what they were up to, she would have to find a way to stop them. She daydreamed about taking piles of collected evidence to the police or maybe even the FBI. She would be a hero—a real life Nancy Drew solving a real life mystery. That was a much happier thought.

The rattling sound of Grandpa's old Ford pickup truck shook Sarah out of her fantasy. She climbed up onto one of the enclosing boulders, pulled the binoculars to her eyes, and watched Grandpa drive through the open gate, out onto the dirt road, and around the corner out of sight. As Grandpa's truck disappeared, a large black van came into view, traveling the opposite direction down the same dirt road. It passed their turn and stopped at the gate that led onto the Dvoraks' property. Sarah propped herself up on her elbows and focused the binoculars, gripping them with both hands.

From the far side of the van, a short, pale, bald man in a black suit walked around the vehicle, opened the gate, let the van through, and then hopped back inside. The van rolled toward the house. As it approached, Aubrey and her father came out to greet it. Aubrey carried a small green duffel bag. The driver stayed inside the vehicle, but the short man Sarah had seen at the gate exited. He opened the van's sliding door, and another man stepped out: dark complected and very tall—at least two feet taller than Mr. Dvorak and more than twice the height of his traveling companion. He wore a long, flowing, brown and tan tunic, matching pants, and a crimson turban adorned with what looked like a giant ruby high on his forehead. Aubrey and her father both made a strange gesture with their right hands and bowed. The tall man took their hands in his and bowed in return.

The four suspicious characters stood and talked for several minutes. Aubrey handed the bag to the short pale man who opened it and inspected its contents. Satisfied, he shook everyone's hands, loaded himself and the bag into the van, and rode away leaving the tall man behind. Mr. Dvorak pulled something from his pocket and handed it to the newcomer. It was too small for Sarah to identify until the tall man pressed its button and lit up his face.

"My flashlight!" Sarah gasped.

Aubrey pointed toward Grandpa's house as she spoke. Sarah froze with panic. The tall man stroked his chin and surveyed the landscape. He turned the flashlight over, seeming to study it, and then he looked straight toward Sarah. She dropped behind the rock. Her heart thumped so loudly that she worried they would hear it across all that distance.

Sarah spent the rest of the afternoon hiding behind rocks and sneaking around the mountain. She was certain that, at any moment, the giant man with the turban (who had grown even more monstrous in her frightened mind) would appear from around a corner and catch her. It wasn't until Grandpa Kirk had returned that she finally mustered the courage to sneak home, careful to keep trees and other obstacles between herself and Aubrey's house as she went.

"That's quite a sunburn you've got there, Princess." Grandpa remarked that night over a dinner of boxed macaroni and cheese. "Did you stay outside all day?"

"Yes. I mean, not *all* day. I just sunburn easy," she said with a sour expression. That last part was true—her red hair and fair skin did not do well in sunshine, and she had often complained about how quickly she burned.

"Mmhmm. And I see you've got a bit of a bump on your head."

Sarah bit her lip. She had hoped he wouldn't notice. "Ran into a tree."

"I see." He wasn't buying it. "And that's all you did today?"

"Mmhmm," Sarah mumbled as she chewed, trying to appear as natural as possible.

"You weren't spying on the neighbors again, were you?"

Sarah swallowed and shook her head.

"Hmm."

They finished their meal without speaking again. At last, Grandpa put his fork down and broke the silence. "Sarah, why don't you do the dishes and then come sit with me on the front porch for a bit?" It wasn't really a question.

Sarah nodded and obeyed.

After the last dish was dried and put away, she found Grandpa on the front porch swing where he was watching the sun set behind the western hills and puffing at his old straight-stemmed briar pipe. The fragrance was more than smoke; it was warm and sweet in a way that reminded Sarah of hot buttered waffles and made her crave a glass of milk. It was the smell of Grandpa Kirk. It was the smell of home.

"Sit down, kiddo," he said and patted the empty spot on the swing next to him.

She joined him and let her legs dangle as she watched a line of ants march single file beneath her.

"Sarah, I haven't said much about your dad since you moved in, but I'm going to say something about him now. I didn't much like him when we first met. He was reckless. His head was all full of stupid dreams; not the sort of man I had ever imagined would sweep my little girl off her feet. But let me tell you what: your mom was absolutely googley-eyed over that boy. She saw something in him that I never did. She saw potential. And you know what? She was right. There was more to your dad than I gave him credit for, and I didn't begin to see it until I saw him with you. The way he picked you up and swung you around. The way he would read to you before bedtime. The way he looked at you when you danced. That man absolutely adored you from the first time he laid eyes on you, just like I adored your mom. He was always a good dad to you. You know that, right?"

Sarah nodded and fought a burning sensation behind her eyelids. *Was*, she thought. *He* was *a good dad. But then Mom died, and...*

"He loved your mom more than you know," Grandpa continued. "I know you can't begin to understand all that he did for you two when your mama got sick. He was always with her, always cared for her, always did everything he could to protect you both. But when it came down to it, he couldn't save her. It tore him up. And there was more than that; things I can't go into." He was silent for a minute. Then he put his hand on Sarah's shoulder. "Listen, Princess, I know he hurt you when he left. I know it. But you need to know that he was trying to take care of you the best he knew how."

Sarah choked back a sob.

Grandpa Kirk set his pipe down on the side table and wrapped her in his arms. "I'm here, baby girl. I'm here." He stroked her hair. "You're all the family I've got left, and it's my job to take care of you now. It's my turn to protect you. But I can't do that if you aren't honest with me. You've got to trust me, Sarah. We've got to trust each other."

They sat together on the swing until she fell asleep in his arms and he carried her to bed. She never told him about what had happened.

4

"FRIENDS"

Sarah arrived at her English class Monday morning and found a note lying on her desk:

Dear SARAH LEWIS,

Attached is your revised class schedule, effective immediately. Please proceed to your new classes right away so your attendance can be recorded.

Thank you.

Principal Mooney's signature was stamped across the bottom of the Bluebonnet Middle School letterhead stationery. No explanation was given. The promised schedule was printed onto a sheet of plain white paper and attached with a staple. She read it over and felt her stomach sink. Every single class had been changed. Only her science class was still in the same room and with the same teacher, but it was now later in the day.

Sarah made her way to her new English class—same time, different teacher—and found Aubrey smiling at her from the second row as if she'd been expected. Today's lecture on verb tenses was already in progress.

"Excuse me, sir," she said when the teacher paused, handing him the note. "I'm Sarah. I'm in this class now."

The teacher grunted his irritation. He studied the letter and then pulled out his roll sheet to confirm. "I see," he said with a sigh. "Well, have a seat in the empty desk there, and open your book to page one hundred twenty-eight." He pointed to the only empty desk in the classroom—directly in front of Aubrey.

After English, Sarah noticed Aubrey following her to Art, and after Art, having waited for everyone else to leave first, she found herself following Aubrey to Texas History. This was not good.

During lunch that day, Aubrey sat at Sarah's table. Sarah pretended not to notice, and when several more popular kids filed in and took up the remaining seats, Sarah slipped away. She dumped what was left of her food into the garbage can and spent the rest of lunch in the girls' restroom.

Sarah hid in the stall, trying to understand what was happening. The idea that somehow Aubrey and her family could have rearranged Sarah's school schedule so quickly was both ridiculous and terrifying, but it was also the only explanation that made any sense. The question was: What would she do now? *I guess I could just ask her about the lab and the brain and all,* she thought. No. That was an awful idea. What would she say? *Hi Aubrey, I noticed there are some mad scientists working in an underground lair in your backyard. What are they up to? Stealing memories, you say? How interesting. And what, exactly, are you doing with mine?* No. Whatever else happened, she would have to be smarter than that.

The bell rang. Sarah hurried out of the restroom and made her way toward the gym for P.E., careful to take a longer route than necessary to avoid Aubrey. She was navigating a sea of seventh and eighth graders who were hurrying between their lockers and classes when she bumped into Mr. Litchfield, the substitute math teacher. He turned around, annoyed, and then smiled with evil glee when he recognized her. His oily forehead wrinkled as he raised his bushy black eyebrows.

"Well, well. If it isn't Ms. Lewis. I hear you found a way to get out of staying late in my class today. I hope, for your sake, that your new math teacher doesn't mind being ignored."

Sarah nodded and tried to duck around him.

"Oh no, Ms. Lewis. Not so fast. I have some questions for you. Which lucky teacher gets to put up with you now, I'd like to know? Hmm?"

Sarah couldn't remember. Math was after P.E. on her new schedule, and she hadn't been yet. She tried to explain her ignorance to Mr. Litchfield.

"Don't play dumb with me. Where's your schedule?" he demanded. "Come on, let's have it!"

Sarah was terrified. She dropped her backpack and had just unzipped it when the voice of Principal Mooney interrupted, "Mr. Litchfield, I'd like a word with you, if you don't mind."

The raven-haired instructor spun around and looked, but he could not find Principal Mooney anywhere. A few straggling students ran past. A janitor who was mopping the floor picked up his bucket and disappeared into a classroom.

"Come, Mr. Litchfield. I don't have all day," Principal Mooney's voice echoed.

The frustrated substitute teacher wheeled back toward Sarah, bowed close to her ear and whispered, "This isn't over, Ms. Lewis." Then he hurried off in search of his superior.

Sarah stood blinking for a few seconds as she watched him scurry away. A tug on her sleeve recalled her to reality. It was Aubrey.

"Come on, Sarah! You'll be late to P.E."

Sarah froze. If there had been any doubts about Aubrey's involvement in her schedule change before, they were gone now. But there was nothing else to do at the moment but play along, so she followed Aubrey down the hall toward the gym without another word.

The next hour passed without incident for Sarah, but it had not been so uneventful for Mr. Litchfield. By the time she arrived in her new math class, a rumor was already spreading that the substitute teacher had been arrested. Sarah overheard two girls at the back of the classroom say he had been hauled off in handcuffs for trying to kiss a student. Carey Dawson said that was all wrong. He said that somebody had found a bloody machete in Mr. Litchfield's desk drawer and that the police had taken him on suspicion of murder. But Jared Wheeler said that couldn't be right. He didn't know what it was about, but he saw Principal Mooney and two officers escort the irritated instructor to the parking lot just minutes before. There was a lot of yelling, but Mr. Litchfield had driven away in his own car. To Sarah's alarm, Aubrey shot a knowing smile her direction and added nothing to the discussion.

Oh my gosh, Sarah thought. *She had something to do with it!*

Sarah was grateful that Mr. Litchfield was gone, of course—he gave her the creeps—but she was all the more suspicious of Aubrey. What sort of influence did she and her family have? Sarah couldn't think straight. She had to get away.

"Mrs. Brown," Sarah called as she raised her hand, "may I go to the nurse's office? I don't feel well."

Mrs. Brown peered at Sarah over the top of her thick glasses. "Oh? What doesn't feel good, honey?"

"It's, umm, kinda personal," Sarah lied, feigning embarrassment.

"Oh! Well, all right then. Go on." She scribbled out a hall pass for Sarah and sent her on her way.

As Sarah walked through the hallway, she alternated between taking short rapid breaths and then exhaling all the air she could, waiting until she was dizzy before she inhaled again. She needed to be white as a ghost if the nurse was going to believe that she was actually sick. Her plan worked, and minutes later Grandpa Kirk was driving her home.

Neither of them said much on the way home, and once they arrived at the house, Sarah went straight to her room to rest. The stress of the day's events had left her feeling drained, and she soon fell fast asleep.

SARAH WOKE A FEW HOURS LATER TO A KNOCK ON HER BEDROOM DOOR. "Hey Princess, you have a visitor!"

"A visitor?" Sarah stood up, pushed her fingers through her messy red hair in front of the mirror, and walked to the living room.

There stood Aubrey.

"Umm, Grandpa," said Sarah, "can I talk to you in the other room for a minute?"

"Aren't you going to say hello to your friend first?"

Friend?! she thought, and then muttered, "Hi, Aubrey."

"Hi, Sarah. I brought your math homework." Aubrey smiled and pointed to a sheet of paper on the coffee table. "I guess you're in my science class now too. Weird, huh?"

You guess?! Sarah thought. *As if you didn't arrange the whole thing.*

"Anyway," Aubrey continued, "you didn't miss anything important. We just watched a video about the solar system."

"Thanks." Sarah faked a smile and then turned to Grandpa. "Can we go talk now?"

Grandpa Kirk grunted and apologized to Aubrey before he followed Sarah to her room.

"What has gotten into you?," Grandpa whispered. "That is not how we treat guests in this house."

"Why would you invite her into our house?"

"Invite? She knocked on the door. And she's our neighbor. Of course I let her in. Besides, it's about time you two got to know each other."

"Ha!" Sarah stomped. "Oh, she's getting to know *me* all right. You know why she had my math homework? They—the Dvoraks—they got my schedule changed! Now we're in all the same classes. All of them."

"That's great news!"

"What? No it's not! She's following me! Grandpa, they're *spies*. I know it. Or something worse. I saw—"

"Now Sarah," he began.

"But it's true! I saw them. They've got some sort of foreign guy staying at their house now. Showed up yesterday. Arab maybe, or Egyptian, or something. Really tall and suspicious looking, with a weird…hat thing." Her arms pantomimed a turban being wrapped around her head.

"And they have my," Sarah caught herself, "I mean, I think they know that I saw them—that I'm on to them. Now Aubrey won't let me out of her sight. Not even at home, apparently! And they got Mr. Litchfield fired or arrested or something. I don't even know why, but I'm sure it was them."

"Sarah Ann Lewis! I don't want to hear any more of that talk. You're being silly. They're just good people—"

Sarah cut him off again. "But they're not good people! Why would good people spy on me all day?"

"It sounds to me like you're the one who's been spying, young lady. I told you to leave well enough alone, and I meant it! I ought to ground you. That curiosity of yours is going to get you into a pile of trouble if you don't watch it. Especially with you jumping to all sorts of ridiculous conclusions!"

Aubrey's voice interrupted their whispered argument. "Mr. Kirk? I need to go home now. I have to do my homework before dinner."

Grandpa left Sarah alone in the bedroom and returned to the living room where he apologized to Aubrey again and walked her out.

"See you tomorrow, Sarah," Aubrey called as she left.

Sarah locked her door and didn't come out for the rest of the day.

5

SPY VS. SPY

"All right Duncan, place the sample of L-421 into the grippers. And move into starting position. Careful now!"

> "I've done this before, Michael."

"Yes, and then we all enjoyed a lovely little explosion that destroyed the containment unit and very nearly killed us all."

> "And whose fault was that?"

"Well, it certainly wasn't mine."

> "Are you suggesting I was the one who miscalculated the transmutational beta state mass of the Luxephorian alloy?"

"No. You're the one who rushed the approach and created excess interdimensional friction, which triggered—"

> "Gentlemen! Enough! Leave it in the past. Let's just focus on the task at hand. Shall we?"

Silence.

"All right now, five hundred microns. Three hundred microns. Steady. Two hundred microns. Benjamin, what's the radiation reading?"

"Six hundred thousand becquerels and rising."

"Heat?"

"Ninety-seven degrees Celsius."

"Okay, final approach now, Duncan. Slowly. One hundred fifty microns. One hundred microns."

"One hundred and ten degrees Celsius."

"Fifty microns."

Click. Silence.

Sarah ripped off her headphones and threw the tape recorder to the floor. "Almost two hours of silence, and then *this?!* Well that was a waste of fifteen dollars!" She flopped back onto the bed and closed her eyes.

ON THE MONDAY AFTER AUBREY LEFT, SARAH HAD BEGUN TO WORK ON a plan. She would no longer let Aubrey rearrange and invade her life without a fight. Two could play this game. She gathered all the money she had and began to put together her hatchling plot. If she was going to spy on the spies, she needed some spy gear.

Sarah remembered that Carey Johnson had bragged about picking up a portable tape recorder and microphone set from a garage sale for fifty cents. As far as she knew, he had only ever used it once: to produce an hour-long tape of himself telling terrible jokes and making fart noises, which, to Carey's humiliation, was stolen by an eighth-grader who swapped it with the tape of the National Anthem the assistant principal played over the school's P.A. system each morning. Sarah was sure Carey wouldn't mind parting with it.

So on Tuesday morning while Aubrey was busy explaining to several disappointed classmates that she had not, in fact, been selected for a minor role on the television show, *ALF* (a clever rumor, Sarah thought, that Mary Garzas, the gossip queen, was delighted to claim she had heard "from a reliable source")—Sarah managed to slip a note into Carey's hand without being noticed. In it, she made the following offer: if he would keep the whole thing a secret, and if he would ask no questions, she would pay him ten dollars for his tape recorder and some blank tapes. If he could bring it to her without anybody seeing, she would throw another five dollars into the deal. He delivered the merchandise the next day, wrapped in a brown paper bag passed stealthily under the lunch table.

Wednesday night, once she was sure Grandpa was asleep, she dressed herself in a set of his old army fatigues (sleeves and pants rolled up) and snuck out the window again, tape recorder in hand. She still had no flashlight, but the almost-full moon was bright in the cloudless sky, and she had no trouble finding her way back to the cave entrance. Her plan to hide the tape recorder under the couch in the lab was foiled when she found the window boarded up, so she improvised. The microphone fit tightly into a small gap between the plywood and the corner of the window frame. The cable stretched just enough to allow the recorder—loaded with brand new batteries and a blank cassette—to rest on the cave floor. She pressed record and slipped out with a prayer that it would capture *something* useful.

Thursday was almost too peaceful. Aubrey had kept her distance since Monday, but today she seemed especially pensive. Grandpa, too, had been quieter than usual. For dinner, he had driven her into town for burgers and fries, but he had barely touched his own food.

Once again, Sarah stayed up late and crept to the cave, this time to collect the recording. If she had known how little evidence it had collected, though, she would have left the machine there to record over the previous night's failure.

S<small>ARAH REPLACED HER HEADPHONES AND LISTENED TO THE END OF THE</small> tape again. Maybe there was something in it after all, even if she didn't understand. What was it they had said? She replayed the recording several times and wrote down key words in her notepad: *L 421, Transmyoo-tay-shun-al, Lux-uh-for-ee-un, Bek-ur-ells*. She glanced at the bookshelf and then at the clock. 1:37 a.m. Research would have to wait until tomorrow. First, sleep.

S<small>ARAH AWOKE</small> F<small>RIDAY MORNING TO BRIGHT SUN THROUGH THE</small> curtains. "What time is it?" She yawned and rubbed her eyes so she could read the clock. Then she saw the time. "I overslept!" Sarah jumped out of bed in a panic, threw on some jeans and a tee shirt, and ran to the living room, sneakers in hand. "Grandpa!"

No response. A rerun of *Magnum P.I.* was playing on the television, but Grandpa was not there.

She ran to his room. The door was open. He wasn't there. She rushed through the front door and onto the front porch, scaring off a bobcat that had been prowling the brush near where Grandpa usually parked. The pickup truck was gone. Sarah spun around, and then she noticed a note on the kitchen table.

No school today. I'll explain later. Running to town. Back soon. Make yourself some cereal. Love you.

She should have been excited about missing school, but instead, Sarah was worried. This was not like Grandpa. What was he up to?

Sarah tried to shake it off. If she was going to get a home day, she decided, she should make the best of it. She turned off the television, ate a bowl of generic raisin bran, showered, and then set her mind to research.

Neither the dictionary nor the set of old encyclopedias on Grandpa's bookshelves gave her any clues about *L-421* or the meaning of the word *Luxephorean*. She did discover that an *alloy* is a mixture of metals and that a *becquerel* is a unit for measuring radioactivity that was named for Antoine Henri Becquerel, a physicist who worked with the famous Marie Curie. Sarah didn't think that any of this information was very helpful.

Her study was soon interrupted by the sound of Grandpa's old Ford rattling up the driveway. Sarah slid her notebook under the bed, put books away on the shelf, and emerged from her bedroom just as Grandpa came through the front door.

"Mornin', Princess."

She folded her arms and leaned against the hallway wall. "I guess I'm playing hooky today?"

He smiled. "Well, I thought you'd want to be home for this, and I'm going to need your help. We have some work ahead of us today. Come on. I have something to show you."

Sarah followed him outside and saw, sitting in the bed of Grandpa's pickup, a huge white German Shepherd with black markings on his face and back.

"This is Duke. I brought him here to keep you company."

"You mean he's mine?!" Sarah squealed.

"Well, Duke's been staying with a friend of mine for a while, and now he'll be staying with us. But Duke belongs to nobody but himself."

"You brought me a dog!" she said, a huge smile on her face. "Oh, Grandpa! Thank you, thank you, thank you!" She ran to Duke who leapt down from the truck to meet her. The two rolled in the grass and covered each other with kisses. Then she jumped up and into Grandpa Kirk's arms with such force that she almost knocked him over. "He's the most beautiful dog I've ever seen!"

Grandpa and Sarah spent the rest of the day building a bed for Duke, pausing only to eat a quick lunch of bologna sandwiches. Duke drank some water and laid at Sarah's feet. Grandpa explained that Duke did not need a dog house because he would not live outside. Instead, they built him a daybed, which they painted neon green to match Sarah's walls and placed at the foot of her bed. For a mattress, they wrapped two spare pillows in a quilt Sarah's grandmother had sewn before Sarah was born.

Duke did not need a leash; he was happy to follow Sarah wherever she went and gave her no reason to fear he would run off. He did have a beautiful leather collar, though, with a curious blue-jeweled, silver ornament hanging from it. It was too fancy for any normal dog, but Duke was no normal dog, Sarah decided. He was special, and the jewel seemed somehow fitting on him.

To celebrate the new addition to their family, Grandpa grilled strip steaks that night and baked some potatoes. He pulled a silver platter down from the old china cabinet and placed the thickest steak on it for Duke. After dinner, Grandpa did the dishes while Sarah sat on the couch with Duke's head in her lap and watched The Jim Henson Hour.

FOR THE REST OF THE WEEKEND, SARAH FORGOT ABOUT HER PLANS TO spy on the neighbors. Grandpa patched the fence, replaced door locks, and drove back and forth to the hardware store in town. Sarah and Duke spent all their time together playing fetch, cuddling in front of the television, and exploring together. Sarah showed Duke all her favorite trails and her mountain hideout, and he barked happily at lizards and birds and rolled on his back to have his belly rubbed. For a little while, life was perfect.

That ended Sunday night after dinner, however, when Grandpa abruptly announced that he had withdrawn her from school early.

"Are you joking?" Sarah demanded. "Since when do you let me quit *anything* before I've finished?"

"Since when have you been upset about getting out of school?"

"But Grandpa, what about my classes? My teachers? My grades? Aren't you worried I won't get into a good college?" Grandpa always brought up college when she begged to skip school.

"Oh, don't worry about all that. It's fine. Your grades have been good, and there are only a few weeks left anyway. I talked to Principal

Mooney, and he agreed to let you skip exams this year. You're getting straight As."

He was lying. Sarah was old enough to know that was not how school worked. Besides, she was pretty sure that, after her last pop quiz, she was now making a C in math. She stared at her usually-honest grandfather for a few seconds, then asked, "Why?"

"Well, I was thinking we might travel a bit. I don't know where just yet, but I've got a bit of money saved up. We'll get a camper and visit some friends of mine, let you see some of this great country!"

Sarah hesitated. She was sure he was hiding something. "And this trip can't wait until summer?"

"Well...no!" He said, flustered. "Now, no more questions!"

Tears welled up behind Sarah's eyelids.

Grandpa breathed a sigh. "Sarah. The three of us—you, me, and Duke—we're gonna go on an adventure! There are a few loose ends I have to wrap up around here this week, and then we'll set out. It'll be great! And until then, you and Duke can hang out here at the house, or you can help me work on the fence if you want, or you can just sit around and watch TV all day. Whatever you want. Consider it an early vacation."

Sarah turned and stared out the window. She couldn't understand why he was lying to her. More than that, she couldn't understand why it hurt her so much.

Grandpa knelt down in front of her and rested his warm hands on her shoulders. "Sarah, you know I love you. Now trust me. What's done is done, kiddo. Everything's going to be fine."

EVERYTHING WAS NOT FINE. GRANDPA ACTED STRANGER AND WORKED harder every day. First, a delivery truck showed up with a brand new front gate. Grandpa stayed out past dark installing it, and Sarah had to cook dinner (scrambled eggs) for herself and Duke. She made a plate for Grandpa, but when he finally came home, he said he didn't feel much like eating and went straight to bed.

The next morning, Sarah found Grandpa cleaning his guns in the bedroom. They didn't talk about it. But later that day, she overheard him talking to somebody on the front porch. When she went out to check on him, nobody else was there. He was alone, installing a security camera above the front door. She asked him who he had been talking to, and he said, "Oh, just the birds and squirrels," and sent her to pack a box of plates and silverware. She could tell he was worried about something, and she suspected that Aubrey and her family were behind it.

That night, Sarah tried to sneak out and set up the cassette recorder again, but Duke would not let her. He barked when she tried to open the window, and she barely managed to hide her fully-clothed body under the covers before Grandpa peeked in to make sure she was all right. She assured him nothing was wrong, but she heard him double check all the locks before he returned to bed.

The next morning, Grandpa ordered Sarah not to leave the house. "It's supposed to storm, and I don't want you to get caught out in the weather." There wasn't a cloud in the sky the entire day, but he didn't budge. She spent the rest of the week indoors. "Just a couple more days, Princess," he reassured her, "and we'll get out of here. Then everything will be better. I promise."

He was wrong.

6

THE THIRD PATH

"Nine forty-five," Sarah whispered to Duke. "It's time."

And it was time. It had been two weeks to the day since Sarah had fallen into an underground laboratory and received a weird letter that said she would have to choose to either come back to the lab at 10:15 tonight or face some unknown danger at home. The letter had, in fact, said that she wouldn't be safe either way. She still had no idea why. For that matter, she had no idea who had sent her the letter, why they had warned her about anything, why Aubrey had been stalking her, why Grandpa Kirk was being so weird, or a good many other things. But of one thing she was certain: she would neither stay home nor return to the laboratory. If both of the obvious paths promised danger, she would find a third, less obvious path. Most likely, she assumed, the letter's writer was trying to scare her into returning to the lab so that they could...well, she didn't want to think about what they might do. Of course, if she did not go, they would assume she had stayed home, and they would look for her there. Sarah would give them no such satisfaction. No. She and Duke would pass the evening in her mountain hideout where they could keep an eye on both their own home and the neighbors'.

. . .

That morning she had explained the whole situation to Duke, who listened with almost human interest. As she spoke, she set aside several items that she thought she might need for a late night stakeout: a blanket and pillow (should she need to stay overnight), Grandpa's binoculars, a couple of plastic soda bottles filled with water, a box of safety matches, and a stuffed bear, which she had at first tossed aside, telling herself "I'm too old for stuffed animals," but later put back into the pile. She also packed her lunch box, not only with with some beef jerky and a pack of gum, but also with pens, pencils, and a fresh notebook to record anything she might witness, her pocket knife, a book to read by moonlight if she got bored, and the letter from Desjardins, which was now wrinkled and worn, having been toted in her pocket and re-read many times.

Grandpa, on the other hand, had spent the morning on the phone with his bank, arguing that he could not wait three to five more business days; he needed his money today. Eventually he had hung up the phone, cursed, and stretched the long twisted phone cord into his room, where he made more calls out of Sarah's earshot. At lunchtime, he came out and heated some leftovers. Then he left to "see a man about a camper trailer." Duke whined and barked at him when he left, but Grandpa ignored his protests and went anyway, instructing Sarah to stay inside while he was gone. But as soon as he had driven away, Duke ran to Sarah's room and brought out her backpack.

"Okay, smart boy," she said, laughing. "We'll get started."

They made several trips between the house and the mountain that afternoon. Each time they left the house, Sarah took a loaded backpack. When they reached the hideout, she exchanged the items inside with rocks and sticks for the return trip. They made detours, visited other spots on the land, stopped to admire some deer they happened upon, and played fetch. She wanted everything to seem as normal as possible to anybody who might be watching.

At around 6:00, Grandpa returned with a rickety old pop-up camper hitched to his pickup truck. He brought tacos and drinks since they had all but emptied the refrigerator at lunch. They ate together and then loaded the back of the pickup with the suitcases and boxes Grandpa had insisted they pack earlier in the week. He covered these with a tarp which he strapped down using bungee cords, and then he sent Sarah and Duke to bed. He would wake them before sunrise, and their adventure would begin.

Sarah lifted the window, and Duke jumped into the cool, dark night. Sarah followed, dressed once again in Grandpa's old army fatigues, and the two crept toward the mountain. The sky was overcast and the moon was almost invisible, so Sarah placed a hand on Duke's back and stepped carefully as he led the way through the dark.

They reached the hideout with some trouble, and the waiting began. For a while Sarah was alert and anxious, checking her watch and the binoculars every few seconds. However, as midnight approached without the least sign of anything out of the ordinary, Sarah's nerves calmed and she realized she was both tired and hungry. She plopped onto the ground and opened a bag of beef jerky. "Nothing's going to happen," she said as she fed a piece to Duke. The German Shepherd spun a circle and laid his head in Sarah's lap. She took a bite and laid back onto her folded pillow. Streaks of starry night sky showed through wispy gaps in the dark clouds. A pang of loneliness struck her, and she thought how much she missed her parents; how much she missed having a normal life. A tear ran down Sarah's cheek, and she closed her eyes.

BANG!

Sarah bolted upright. Duke leapt out from the rocks and sprinted toward the house.

BANG! BANG!

Grandpa!

Sarah tried to scream, but her lungs would not work. She could hear the muffled sound of distant shouting from the direction of the house, but she couldn't understand any words. She stumbled down the path that led toward the house, vision blurred by tears, feeling her way through the trees and rocks. At the foot of the hill she tripped over a tree root and bloodied her kneecap. She fell again a few steps later and gashed her chin. Then a patch of cactus caught her leg, and she cut her hand trying to free it. Branches scraped her neck and cheeks. Teardrops stung the scratches on her face. At last, bloody, bruised, and footsore, she reached the clearing near the shed and stumbled toward it.

Sarah wiped the tears from her eyes and caught her breath. Cautiously, she peeked around the shed at the house. Bright headlights illuminated the front door. *How could anybody have driven up without me noticing?* she wondered and felt suddenly ashamed at having fallen asleep. Light was shining through every window. Somewhere inside, something slammed against a wall and shattered. More shouting.

Sarah's mind raced. She wanted to run to the house, but then what? There had been gunshots. Someone was armed. All she had was a wristwatch. If she could get to a phone, she could call the police, but there were only two phones she knew of within running distance: one was inside the house she dared not enter, and the other was next door at Aubrey's.

Aubrey!

Sarah's face flushed with rage. Everything made sense. They'd come looking for her, and when she was not found, they went after Grandpa. That had to be it. She clenched her fists. "If it's me they want," she growled, "then it's me they'll get." She stepped out from around the shed and marched toward the house. But before her third step landed, something knocked her to the ground, and she found herself being dragged away by the collar of her shirt.

"Duke!" she whispered. "What has gotten into you?" The dog only whimpered and tugged more urgently. Sarah scrambled to her hands and knees and stared at him. Something in his eyes urged her to run and hide.

A door creaked behind her. Sarah jumped to her feet and ducked behind the shed. Duke pulled at her pants leg, and she followed him through the shadows into a patch of thick brush where she could lie on her stomach and peek out from underneath the gnarled limbs of an overgrown mesquite tree. As soon as she was settled, Duke vanished into the brush.

Two men, silhouetted by the headlights, emerged from the front door and walked to the far side of the house. When they came back into view, they were carrying another man, arms dangling, by the shoulders and feet. Sarah heard car doors open and shut as the two deposited their lifeless cargo.

One of the men hollered, "We've got him, Boss. Let's get out of here."

Muffled shouting.

"The old man says he sent her ahead. If she's already with them—"

More muffled shouting.

"All right, Boss."

The two men reappeared, swinging flashlights before them. One followed the drive that led to the gate and the other took the path to the shed, shining his light one direction and then another as he called, "Come out, little girl! I've got some candy for you!"

While he poked around the old sheet metal structure and tried the lock, two more figures emerged from the house. One held a handgun. The other had his hands tied behind his back and walked with a limp.

"All right, old man, I've had enough of your games. I know she's around here somewhere. Call her back now, or I swear to God, I'll—" The nasally voice sounded familiar. *No, it can't be. Mr. Litchfield?*

"What are *you* gonna do, coward?" Grandpa's strong voice mocked his captor, and Sarah's heart leapt in her chest. "They sent four of you, with guns, in the dark, to nab an old man and a little girl." Grandpa spat. "You must be real proud that I only took out one—"

The butt of the man's gun slammed across the back of Grandpa Kirk's head, and he sank to the ground. Sarah gasped.

"Murik!" the man who sounded like Mr. Litchfield called as he stuffed his weapon into the back of his trousers. "Come help me get this old badger into the van. Bring the gasoline with you. Blackwood, you keep searching." As he waited, he pulled a pack of smokes and a flip-top lighter from his coat pocket and lit up.

Blackwood, evidently, was the name of the man who had just given up on the shed and was now probing the thickets beyond. "Hey, little girl! It's all right. We won't hurt you," he sang. Then, with a chuckle, "but we will hurt your granddad if you don't come out!"

Sarah's lip quivered. Her heart pounded in her ears. He was getting closer. Already, he was too close for her to sneak away without being heard.

Across the grass, Sarah saw Murik return to the front porch and hand a sloshing metal can to his boss. The boss disappeared into the house with the can for a minute. When he reappeared, he tossed his lit cigarette through the open front door into the house, and the two hefted Grandpa toward the van.

"Little girl! Come out, come out wherever you are!"

Blackwood was right in front of her. Beyond him, flames licked the curtains in the living room window. Sarah felt as if she might vomit.

Then something happened that she did not expect. From all around her, Sarah heard shouts. Duke was barking. It seemed every coyote and wild thing for miles around was howling and calling in the darkness.

Blackwood's face went white. He cursed and turned to flee, but before he had the chance, Duke was on top of him, attacking the man with terrifying ferocity.

The van's engine roared to life just as someone or something enormous and hairy—like a bear, or a Sasquatch, or a very large person wearing a fur coat—leapt onto the hood and, with one mighty blow, smashed the passenger side window. The tires spun, kicking up gravel and dirt, and the vehicle sped backwards in a tight turn that threw its furry attacker to the ground. Another engine, deeper sounding and louder than the van, could now be heard approaching from the road.

Duke's victim had flopped and crawled all the way back to the shed and was now pinned against it where he cried like a frightened child, his neck caught in the dog's muscular jaws. The others, it seemed, had given him up and were now racing down the drive toward the gate at full speed.

Sarah crawled out of the brush and ran into the clearing. "Grandpa!" she screamed. "No! Stop! Bring him back!"

She would have chased that van until her feet bled, but just then, an enormous hand gripped her shoulder, and a deep, thickly accented voice spoke: "Sleep now, little one."

The world went black, and Sarah fell into a deep sleep.

7

TREASURE CHEST

"It's all right, Doris. I'll sit with her a while. She'll be awake soon, and then we'll need to dress these cuts. Bring the iodine and some bandages, would you? Better grab the tweezers too. Looks like she got into some cactus."

Sarah felt a work-roughened hand clasp hers. She was lying in a soft, cozy bed, but her whole body was in pain. She tried to open her eyes and squinted in the bright light. "Grandpa?"

"No, sweetheart. It's me, Jack Smith, from the farm supply store."

"Where's Grandpa?" Sarah pushed herself up onto her elbows and winced in pain as the horrible memory played again in her mind.

"Whoa now, take it easy. You've had a rough night."

"Mr. Smith," she whispered as she layed back down. "They took him. They took Grandpa. I saw them hit him. He fell, and…" A lump grew in her throat. "And they—"

"I know. I know." Mr. Smith rubbed her eyebrows. "Don't you worry about your Grandpa. Bo's an ornery old soldier. I've seen him in rougher scrapes than this. He'll be all right." He smiled, but Sarah was sure she saw worry in his eyes.

A gray haired woman entered carrying a basket of towels and a first aid kit. When she saw that Sarah was awake, she handed it all to Mr. Smith and rushed to sit on the side of the bed. "You poor thing," she said as she stroked Sarah's hair. "Jack, hand me that washrag hanging over the side of the basket." Sarah had never met Mr. Smith's wife, but she recognized the kind, round face from the photo he kept behind the counter at the store.

The smiling lady dabbed a warm, damp cloth onto Sarah's cheeks, gently pulling away dirt and dried blood. "Perhaps we should get you bathed first. Do you think you can stand?"

"I think so," said Sarah. "But, Mrs. Smith" she glanced around the unfamiliar room, "where am I?"

"Call me Doris, dear. This is our home, and you are very welcome here. Jack and I expected you and your grandpa to stop by and pick up a few things on your way out of town this morning, but it seems… Well, I guess the circumstances have changed. Ol' Samuel carried you all night long, and that sweet dog of yours never left your side. He only just fell asleep on the couch."

"Old Samuel?" Sarah asked.

"Oh, honey," Mrs. Smith began, "there'll be plenty of time for questions later. Let's get you cleaned up and bandaged first. You'll feel better."

A bathtub was filled with hot water, and Mr. Smith, unwilling to let Sarah walk, carried her to it. Doris offered to stay and help her, but Sarah insisted that she could bathe herself.

As soon as the door was shut, Sarah began to cry. Her mind was filled with questions, mostly of the sort she couldn't put into words. But it didn't matter. She couldn't focus on any of them for long; the pain was too much. Her entire family had been taken from her, and it was more than she could process. Sarah sat in the bathtub and sobbed until her fingers were pruny and the water had gone cold.

When at last she was able to compose herself, Sarah dried off, wrapped herself in a spare bathrobe, and walked out to the little sunlit kitchen where she found her hosts sipping coffee and conversing in whispers. Duke, who had been sitting next to Mr. Smith, ran to her side, wagging his tail furiously. She squatted to pet him, and he licked her face.

"Welcome back," said Mr. Smith, smiling. "Feel better?"

"Yes, sir. Only, my leg hurts a lot," Sarah stood and pulled up the hem of her robe to show them her left ankle.

"Mean ol' cactus. No problem. We'll fix you right up."

Doris directed Sarah to take her seat at the small dining table and proceeded to whip up some scrambled eggs and toast while Mr. Smith addressed the injured leg with a pair of tweezers. He was as gentle as anybody could have been, but the process of extracting so many tiny thorns was slow and painful. Mr. Smith apologized after each one. A few minutes later, Doris returned with Sarah's breakfast and examined her scrapes and cuts. "You're gonna hurt for a while," she said as she rubbed iodine onto Sarah's elbow, "but I expect you'll be gettin' into trouble again before too long." Sarah frowned at that—she was not a trouble-maker—but she nodded politely anyway. By the time she finished eating, both of her knees and both of her elbows had been wrapped in strips of stretchy fabric and a shiny plastic bandage covered her chin.

"Thank you so much," Sarah told them both. She looked at her shoes. "Can I..." her voice quivered, "I mean, would it be all right if I stayed with you for a while? My mom had a cousin in Florida, I think. Maybe if we can find a phone number for her, she'd let me live there."

Doris knelt and held Sarah's face in her hands. "Oh, honey, don't you fret. You've got a lot more folks who love you than you know. There's already a plan for taking care of you until they find your Grandpa. And they *will* find your Grandpa," she said. "But no. I'm sorry. I wish we could keep you here. It just wouldn't be safe."

Duke whimpered and laid his head on Sarah's lap. A tear ran down her cheek. "So who's taking me?"

Doris looked at Mr. Smith. He took a deep breath and answered, "Friends, sweetheart. Very good friends of your Grandpa's and mine."

Sarah sniffed and wiped her eyes on the sleeve of her robe.

Someone knocked on the door. Mr. Smith disappeared into the front of the house and returned a few seconds later with Sarah's suitcase in one hand and an old wooden trunk in the other. "They found it, Doris!" he exclaimed and then turned to Sarah. "I bet you'd like to put on some of your own clothes." He handed the suitcase to her. "And this—" he dropped the heavy trunk in front of her and patted its lid.

"Well, your Grandpa asked me to make sure you got this if anything ever happened to him. He'll be back, I'm sure, but I suspect he'd want you to have it anyway. Now, you're gonna need a key, and I happen to have a copy."

Sarah followed Mr. Smith to the living room. He removed a painting of cowboys on horseback from the wall above the large console television. Where the painting had been, she could now see a dusty, gray wall safe. He spun the dial back and forth, muttering numbers under his breath. The door swung open, and he removed a large, ornate, golden key, which he handed to Sarah. "You can have the guest room. It'll be a couple hours yet before they're ready for you, and there's plenty in that trunk to keep you occupied until then." He carried the trunk and led Sarah back to the room where she had awoken. "We'll be here if you need anything," he said and left her to change.

Sarah inserted the key into the keyhole and twisted until she heard a snap. Carefully, she lifted the lid. It felt like opening a pirate's treasure chest. The hinges creaked, and she inhaled the fragrance of dust and leather and old things. On top of a pile of papers and smaller boxes was an envelope with Sarah's name written on it in Grandpa Kirk's scrawly handwriting. She opened it and read:

Hey Princess,

If you're reading this, then I'm not around anymore. So before I write another word, I want to tell you how much I love you. Having you come to live with me has been one of the very best parts of my life. You've been a ray of sunshine that I've been allowed to hold for a while, and I'm so grateful. You've given an old man an awful lot of joy. Thank you for brightening my heart and my home.

When you were just a little girl, arrangements were made for your future so that, no matter what, you'd have a place and a family. With me gone, the privilege of raising and protecting you passes to my dear friend, Samuel Bin-Pereldoroth. You actually saw him recently when you were spying on Aubrey, though I couldn't tell you that's who it was. He's the tall, dark man with the "weird hat thing" you described as "suspicious looking." Took everything I had not to laugh. Aubrey and the rest of the folks next door work for him, as do I. And you were right, you curious little thing. There have been strange things going on, things you'll begin to learn about now. I'm sorry that I couldn't tell you about any of it sooner. Your parents wanted you to be sheltered from all this business until you were old enough. Whether you are or not, there's no keeping it from you now.

Samuel is very old and very wise. He is also very powerful, and he commands respect from people in a way that you've probably never seen. But most importantly, he's a good man. He'll take good care of you.

I first met Samuel during the war. Jack Smith and I crossed paths with him during the London air raids, but that's another story. The short of it is that, when your mother was little, I separated from the Army to go to work as a researcher, under Samuel's supervision, for an ancient and secret organization called The Sentinels of God. I've worked for The Sentinels in different capacities ever since. I only picked up that part time job at the University in recent years to keep myself occupied now that I'm "too old for field work."

Anyway, your father's family has been involved with The Sentinels for generations, and he worked with Samuel all his life. It is through Samuel that your parents first met. He loved them both very much, and when they made out their wills, they made him your godfather. You can trust him. Listen to him. Obey him. Learn all you can from him. He knows more than you can imagine. Any questions you have, he can answer, though he's a little particular about answering things only when he has decided it's time, so be patient. He's usually right.

All the things in this chest belong to you now. Most of it is from your mother. There are some photo albums that she put together before she died and a box of letters she wrote for you to read on certain days of your life. I've taken the liberty to include your mom's diary from when she was your age as well as a brand new blank diary for you, so you can record your own adventures. There are a few other items of your mom's in here that served her well during her time with The Sentinels. Yes, she worked for them too. In *particular, she wanted you to have her old jewelry. It's good for more than just making you look fancy.*

Your father also left a couple things for you: a dagger and sheath that have been in your family for hundreds of years, and the red and gold box that's in the bottom of this trunk. He didn't tell me what's in it, but he did say that, when you're ready, you'll be able to unlock it. I wish I could tell you more.

And finally, you'll see that I've included a brand new flashlight. I know you lost yours. Be more careful with this one.

The house, everything in it, and the land it sits on will become yours when you turn eighteen. Until then, they are in the care of Jack and Doris Smith. They'll make sure everything is in order for you.

I love you, Princess.

Grandpa

Sarah read the letter twice before she folded it and returned it to its envelope. Tears filled her eyes. There was so much to wrap her mind around. Why hadn't she known that Grandpa and both her parents had worked for the same people who were stealing memories? Had they known about the brain and the laboratory? Were they in on it?

"The Sentinels," she whispered. The name felt familiar. Surely, she must have heard it before, if only in overheard conversations between her parents, but she could not remember for sure.

Carefully, she unpacked items from the crate. Near the top, she found an old photo album. She flipped through the pages, but stopped when she reached a photo of her family in front of a sign for the *Tarrant County Courthouse.* Sarah had been a little baby in this picture. She read the caption aloud: "Jacob, Elizabeth, and Sarah Ann Lewis." She sniffed and wiped a tear from her cheek. Her mother was so beautiful. Sarah had always adored her mom's straight, dark hair and unfreckled, tanned skin. She had always told Sarah that red hair and freckles were adorable and rare and that she should be proud of them, but deep down, Sarah had always wished she looked more like her mom. Then there was her dad. He looked so happy in this photo—his big, brown eyes beaming under curly locks of black, unkempt hair. He didn't know about Mom's cancer yet. He didn't have a care in the world.

Sarah closed the book and returned it to the trunk. A bundle of envelopes were held together with a rubber band. Each was labeled with words like, "To Sarah, on your graduation day," "To Sarah, on your wedding day," or "To Sarah, on the day you become a mother." None of them were labeled for the day she lost Grandpa, so she left them all unopened.

She rifled through a shoebox full of yellowed newspaper clippings: THIRTEEN U.S. SOLDIERS KILLED IN LONDON RAID, HISTORIC STATUES DESTROYED IN BOMBING OF GUILDHALL, LOCAL FAMILY SAVED FROM FIRE ATTRIBUTES RESCUE TO MYSTERIOUS "GOAT MAN." Sarah giggled at this last headline despite herself and put the stack aside.

Next, she removed a lovely cedar jewelry box. Her mother's initials were engraved into a silver placard on the lid. Inside were a set of earrings—silver studs set with blue jewels that seemed almost to glow—and a hefty silver ring surrounding an oblong pearl. Sarah couldn't remember a time she had seen her mother that she wasn't wearing them. She pulled the ring from its velvet-covered holder and slipped it onto her index finger (it was too big for her ring finger).

Sarah found her mother's diary—covered in scribbles and doodles, even on the cover—but she couldn't bring herself to read it. Not yet. She also found the blank diary and the flashlight from Grandpa, and she placed both into her suitcase.

At the bottom of the trunk, underneath everything else, she found the two gifts from her father. The dagger looked very old, indeed. Its leather sheath was simple and worn, but when she removed the knife, she found its blade highly polished and razor sharp. The handle was gold, encircled by bands of red and black. A strange swirling design was etched into the length of the blade, ending in an angled basketweave pattern near the hilt. She replaced the knife and removed the box. It seemed cold, made of some sort of metal. It was taller than it was wide and surprisingly heavy. All around, the surface was painted red with swirls and interwoven lines of gold. She couldn't find a seam between the box and its lid, but one surface (which she assumed must be the top) bore a set of nine dials, each covered in letters and numbers that could be rearranged by spinning them, and a gold plate with the following riddle inscribed on it:

> *All of the shower, but none the storm*
> *Enhances sweet beauty, regardless of form*
> *Insignificant to one, Indispensable to another*
> *The laughter and love of a father and mother*

"What *is* this thing?" Sarah said to herself as she turned the box over. There were no other words or clues on it. She shook the box. Nothing. *What did Dad mean, I'd be able to open it when I'm ready?* she wondered. *And why would I want anything from him anyway? If he wanted to give me something, he should have given it to me himself when he had the chance.*

Sarah dropped the box back into the trunk. It landed with a strange, hollow thud. "That's weird," Sarah said and knocked on the bottom of the trunk. She measured its inside depth with her arm and then did the same on the outside. "It's got a false bottom!"

Sarah dumped out the remaining contents. She tapped all over the inside floor of the chest. Solid here. Hollow there. She pushed and prodded. Nothing moved. She turned it over and pushed from the bottom. Then she turned it on its side and pressed her hands flat against the underside to see if she could slide it. It held. She flipped it the other way and tried again. It budged! She could see a tiny slit between bottom surface and the edge. Sarah snapped up her father's dagger and inserted it into the gap, prying and twisting along the length of the trunk. It hit something. She pressed harder and felt a tiny latch give way. At that, the false bottom slid another quarter of an inch and then came loose. Underneath, within a hollow compartment, she saw the last thing she expected: her dad's old puzzle cube. It worked like a Rubik's Cube and was about the same size, but instead of plastic, it was made of black wood, and instead of nine colored squares per side, it had seven different sorts of symbols etched into the forty-nine tiny black squares on each side. She must have seen him play with it hundreds of times, and whenever she asked if she could have a turn, he had always told her that it was tricky and that he would teach her when she was older. Now, Sarah supposed, she would have to figure it out for herself.

8

FLATLAND HALL

Samuel was the strangest person Sarah had ever met. First of all, he was gigantic. He had to duck to fit through the Smiths' front door when he arrived, and the top of his scarlet turban brushed the ceiling where he stood. Second, though it was obvious Samuel was from another country, Sarah could not tell which one. His accent was strange. His skin was a dark olive brown. And she could not decide how old he was. From his appearance, Sarah decided that he couldn't be as old as Mr. Smith and Grandpa Kirk, but if they'd met him in the war, he couldn't be much younger either. His black hair and beard were short and spattered with gray. Lines showed on his forehead and beneath his eyes, but his skin did not sag. His nose and ears were too large for his face, and he had the brightest, most translucent green eyes Sarah had ever seen. He was thin but broad-shouldered and muscular, not like a bodybuilder, but like the hard working farm hands who frequented Mr. Smith's store. His clothes were long and flowing, and on his monstrous feet he wore leather sandals that looked as if he might have made them himself.

Samuel bowed to Mr. and Mrs. Smith and then embraced them both at once. Sarah sat on the couch, kicked at the shag carpet, and watched his every move.

"Won't you stay for lunch?" Doris asked. "It's been so long, and I'm sure this girl," she patted Sarah on the head, "would like to get to know you a bit before you head out."

"Ahh, Ms. Doris. How I wish that I could. But alas, we are in a great rush. Already we have been delayed, and I cannot risk it." Samuel's voice was deep and rich.

He turned and knelt before Sarah. Her stomach tangled in knots and her heart jumped into her throat. Samuel did not introduce himself as she expected, but instead spoke as one who had known her all her life. "Miss Sarah," he said, "You are full of apprehension. You do not trust me. That is understandable. But do not fear, little one. I give you my word, as I gave it to your parents, that I will protect you and keep you from harm, as far as it is in my power to do so. For as long as we both have breath in our lungs, you will be as my own daughter." He stared into her eyes and smiled. "Are these all your things?"

Sarah nodded, too frightened to speak. She had packed her suitcase and the trunk just minutes before Samuel arrived. The trunk's false bottom had given her some trouble, but she was able to reattach it at last after she gave up fitting the puzzle cube back into its place and tossed it into her suitcase instead.

Samuel carried Sarah's things to the box truck in the driveway, and Mr. Smith held her hand as they crossed the yard. The man Sarah recognized as Aubrey's father smiled and nodded at her from the driver's seat. Her stomach sank. She wanted to run, but there was nowhere to go.

Mrs. Smith ran after them. "Wait!" she called. "I packed you some sandwiches for the road."

Samuel thanked Doris and took the brown paper bags.

"We must ride in here," Samuel said as he motioned toward the cargo space, "but we have not far to go."

"Hey now, don't go spoutin' off more than you should," Mr. Smith interjected. "The less we know the better!"

"Indeed," Samuel replied. "Will you not allow me to leave a guard with you for the evening?"

"Aww, that's all right. We can take care of ourselves. Besides, we're havin' the sheriff over for dinner tonight, and Doris is making her famous pecan pie. If I know him, we'll have an armed guard sittin' in our dining room and eatin' our food until all decent folk are sawin' logs."

"I do not need to remind you that the people who concern us are not decent folk."

"Go on! We'll be just fine."

Doris hugged Sarah. "You be careful out there, sweetheart. And make sure Ol' Samuel lets us know when you make it safely to wherever it is you're going."

Sarah climbed into the truck, nerves on edge, and sat on her trunk in a corner. Duke curled up next to her feet. He, at least, seemed to be at ease, and that was some comfort. Samuel seated himself with legs crossed on the floor. The door swung closed.

All was dark. The air was hot and stuffy. Sarah's seat slid unsteadily beneath her as the truck pulled into the street and changed directions.

"Mr. Bin-Per—" Sarah began.

"You may call me Samuel, little one. What is it?"

"Where are we going?"

"Flatland Hall. There, you shall meet the rest of your surrogate family."

For a few minutes, Sarah remained silent.

"Is there anything else you wish to know?" asked Samuel.

Sarah fidgeted. Of course she had questions, so many questions, but how could she trust the answers Samuel would give her? "No," she whispered. "Not right now."

"All right, then," Samuel said. "You should eat."

"No, thanks." Food was the last thing Sarah wanted.

THE DOOR SWUNG OPEN. SARAH COVERED HER EYES WITH HER FOREARM and stooped as she followed Duke out from the back of the box truck.

They had parked in the middle of a single-lane gravel road between two freshly plowed cotton fields. In the distance, Sarah could see a line of hills she thought might include those on Grandpa Kirk's land, but here, all was flat and brown for miles in every direction.

There were no fences, just dirt. A clump of distant trees and a small windmill to her left indicated the presence of a farmhouse on the horizon, too far away to be heard or seen.

A horrible thought struck Sarah. Her heart almost stopped. Warily, she turned toward the gigantic man beside her. "Are...are you going to kill me now?" This would be the perfect place to hide a body.

Mr. Dvorak, who was busy unloading Sarah's things burst into laughter. Samuel silenced him with a motion and put a hand on Sarah's shoulder. "No, little one. Did I not give you my word that I would protect you? You are safe. This is where we will meet our friends."

"Now, where is the—" Mr. Dvorak mumbled as he kicked the dirt beside the road. "I can never find the stupid thing." He wore Wranglers, cowboy boots, and a shirt with FRED'S MOVING SERVICE embroidered across the back. Duke ran alongside him and sniffed at something in the brush. "Ah! Here it is." Mr. Dvorak squatted, grabbed what looked like a dandelion, and pulled it to his face, roots dangling to the ground. "We're here!" he shouted into the plant. "Password is Bullroarer."

"That was yesterday's password," Samuel corrected him.

"Oh right." Mr. Dvorak seemed annoyed and muttered to himself. "What was it this time? Oh yeah," then to the plant, "Sorry. The new password is Artaxerxes."

The ground began to shake. Sarah flinched at the loud, scraping roar that came from around the box truck. Mr. Dvorak dropped the plant. It zipped back into its original position as if it had never been touched.

"Here you go, Beeb," Mr. Dvorak called and tossed the truck keys. A short, stout man with a white beard and navy blue coveralls appeared from the far side of the vehicle. He held two wooden poles slung with leather straps in one hand, and with the other he caught the keys. He grunted, irritated. Samuel bowed to the short man as he waddled around to the driver's side of the truck, climbed into it, attached the wooden poles to his feet with the leather straps, slammed the door shut, and started the engine.

Samuel turned to Sarah. "Come, little one."

Sarah rounded the truck and saw what had caused the disturbance: a section of the road had sunk into the earth and formed a long ramp. Duke brushed against Sarah's leg and led the way into the gaping hole, tail wagging. Samuel, Sarah, and Mr. Dvorak—who was whistling and carrying Sarah's things—descended the ramp into the darkness followed by the box truck. When they had all reached the bottom, Mr. Dvorak shouted "Roverandom," and the road rose back to its original position.

The box truck rumbled into a bay on their right. The engine stopped, and the headlights went out. All was dark and silent. The air was cool and smelled of earth. "This way," a gruff voice called, and the short bearded man who had parked the truck appeared with a flashlight. "Watch your step."

They walked through the blackness, descending steadily along a winding, rocky path. The beam of the flashlight that bobbed ahead of them seemed to be swallowed up by the darkness and gave little light to their surroundings. The longer they walked, the colder the air became. Then, suddenly, they stopped. Sarah heard the sound of jingling keys and then of a lock being opened. Golden light and a wave of warm air greeted them as a pair of tall wooden doors swung wide into a cavernous hexagonal chamber.

Sarah's fears were overwhelmed by wonder. A roaring fire blazed in a stony fireplace at the center of the room encircled by cushioned benches and small tables. Walls of bare earth were supported by large wooden beams onto which were mounted no fewer than two dozen lanterns. A pair of wooden doors was set into the center of each wall. Each door was carved with swirling and cross-hatched patterns that matched those on Sarah's knife, and high above each doorway hung a banner.

The banner directly across the room from Sarah showed a many-sided silver star on a field of dark blue. To the right of that hung a jagged yellow circle over a banner of brown. Next was a golden lion on green fabric. Above Sarah's head, a swirling red pattern adorned a white banner. To her left, a purple banner was emblazoned with a silver winged man holding a silver sword, and on the last wall, a black banner bore a twisted and winged red serpent.

The stone floor, Sarah noticed, was set in a pattern: nine concentric circles at intervals from the center. Bisected by the edge of each circle was another, smaller circle, made of a polished white stone. It looked vaguely like diagrams of the solar system she had seen in school textbooks, with the fireplace at the center in place of the sun.

Samuel walked to the fire and stood warming his hands. "Please send for Madam Sardar," he commanded. "I desire to speak with her about this evening's agenda." At this, the short man whom Mr. Dvorak had called "Beeb" bowed and disappeared through a door on the left. "Duke, would you join us as well?" he added. Duke trotted forward and sat next to Samuel, wagging his tail. "We will be only a few minutes, Miss Sarah, and then we shall return him to you."

Mr. Dvorak entered last, still carrying the suitcase and trunk. He stopped next to Sarah, who stood just inside the room, turning circles, mouth open and eyes wide.

"Welcome to Flatland Hall," he said. "Follow me."

He led her through the double doors under the green banner at the far end of the room. As she left the great room, Sarah glanced back at Duke. He barked and wagged his tail enthusiastically. She forced a brave smile and then followed Mr. Dvorak through a long corridor with doors on either side and finally into a room on the right. The walls of the small dormitory were covered in wood. At the far end of the room, a lit oil lamp sat on a nightstand next to a bed that was covered by an ornately embroidered blue and silver quilt. Matching pillows leaned against the wooden headboard and partially covered a pair of angels that were carved into it. Another suitcase had already been laid on an identical bed near the door.

"You'll bunk with Aubrey tonight," Mr. Dvorak said as he entered. "I'm not sure what the plan will be after that. Someone will come to get you when dinner's ready. I'd bet there will be a long meeting tonight, so you might want to get some rest." He set the suitcase and trunk in the middle of the room and left Sarah alone.

9

THE SENTINELS

THE SCENE THAT GREETED SARAH'S EYES WAS LIKE SOMETHING OUT OF A fairy tale. A row of long tables had been set end to end at the far side of the room, near the blue and black banners, and were topped with an elegant white table cloth. A dozen or more short men and women hustled about as they brought out wooden chairs and placed silver dishes and platters of food onto the table. A lovely, elderly, onyx-skinned woman held a clipboard and stood on a chair, counting dishes and shouting orders to the others. Mr. Dvorak was chatting and laughing with a bobcat and a hairy-faced man who had short horns that grew from the top of his head. Samuel stood in a corner of the room and appeared to be in the middle of a serious discussion with a black bear who stood erect on its hind paws and stroked its chin. A whitetail buck and doe strolled near the doorway where Sarah stood, and she could have sworn she heard them speak to each other.

"Have I died and gone to Narnia?" Sarah whispered. She rubbed her eyes and pinched herself. This was no dream.

"Oh no. Nothing so fantastic," replied Aubrey, laughing, as she closed the doors behind them. Aubrey had shown up at Sarah's door a few minutes earlier to bring her to dinner, all smiles and cheer, and Sarah had been fighting to keep suspicion and distrust off of her face. Now, those feelings were replaced with dumbfounded wonder. "These are The Sentinels," Aubrey continued. "Well, a few of us anyway. There are lots more of us, all over the world."

Sarah took a deep breath. All of Grandpa Kirk's stories about giants and dwarves and talking animals rushed into her mind and suddenly took on new significance. Perhaps, she thought, they hadn't been mere stories after all. Even so, her brain refused to accept what her eyes were seeing. Duke licked Sarah's hand and leaned against her.

Just then, the woman with the clipboard noticed the newcomers. She stepped down from the chair, took a small silver bell from the table, and rang it. Everyone stopped what they were doing to look at her and then followed her smiling gaze to Sarah.

Samuel crossed the room and stood next to her. Then, placing a large hand on Sarah's shoulder, he addressed the group in a loud voice. "Welcome my friends, and please welcome Miss Sarah Ann Lewis, daughter of Mr. Jacob Alexander Lewis and the dearly missed Mrs. Elizabeth Ann Lewis." Cheers and applause erupted.

Samuel silenced the crowd with a wave of his hands. "Some of you have worked alongside Miss Sarah's grandfather, Mr. Marion Beauregard Kirk. For those of you who are unaware, he was most unfortunately captured and taken late last night by comrades of Les Luminaires. Miss Aubrey and Dr. Nita," he motioned toward the black bear with whom he had been conversing, "pursued the captors bravely and tirelessly throughout the night but were ambushed this morning." There was a quiet gasp from several in the room. Sarah stared at Aubrey, eyes wide. "As you see, they have returned to us unharmed, and we are confident that Mr. Kirk shall be safely recovered soon.

"However, until she is rejoined by her family, Miss Sarah is under my protection. She will be treated with the utmost hospitality. Anybody who causes her trouble will answer to me." All was silent for a long moment. "Also, I beg you to be *mindful of your tongues.*" He spoke the last four words slowly and with emphasis. "This is Miss Sarah's first introduction to The Sentinels, and indeed, to many of your noble races. There is much she does not know, even about her own family. Let us be wise with our words." Samuel shot a knowing look around the room. "And now, Madam Sardar, I turn over the festivities to you."

"The table has been set, and the food is ready," called the woman who had rung the bell. "Please, come and eat."

All was chaos for a moment. Sarah found herself being whisked to the table by a short man, no more than four feet tall, with a bushy black beard and a clean shaven upper lip. "Come, Miss Sarah," he said, "you can sit by me!"

Before she knew what was happening, Sarah was seated between Aubrey and the short man who was busy piling her plate high with fried chicken, mashed potatoes and gravy, fried okra, black eyed peas, corn on the cob, a green onion, and a slice of white sandwich bread.

"My name's Boarsmash," said the man with the black beard as he ladled more gravy onto Sarah's potatoes. "I'm usually on tunnel maintenance during the dinner shift. Didn't think I'd get to come to the feast at all, but here I am seated next to the guest of honor! This is my sister, Bellouise." A squat blonde lady on the other side of Boarsmash leaned forward and bowed her head to Sarah. "Highly trusted by Madam Sardar, this one. She pretty much runs the hall. And I think you've already met my elder brother, Beebleboddum—Beeb for short." Boarsmash pointed across the table to the white bearded man who had led her through the cave that morning. Beebleboddum, whose mouth was already full of chicken, grunted and nodded. Sarah could not help but smile at the funny sounding name. "Ehh, he's not much of a talker," Boarsmash continued. "More of an errand boy." Boarsmash laughed raucously at this. Beebleboddum scowled at him from across the table but kept his silence.

"Boarsmash, Bellouise, and Beebleboddum," Sarah repeated.

Aubrey giggled. "Dwarves," she said to Sarah. "They have a thing for alliteration."

"We *prefer*," said a bald, clean-shaven dwarf who sat on the other side of Aubrey, "to be called Fodinarans, if you—"

"And that," Boarsmash interrupted, "is my youngest brother, Bonk. Don't mind him. He's been acting as personal assistant to the Watcher since he arrived, and now he thinks he's too important for a beard, much less being called a *dwarf*." At this, several nearby dwarves broke into laughter.

"The Watcher?" Sarah asked.

"That's your Samuel," Aubrey's dad, Mr. Dvorak answered with a mischievous smile that made him look somehow younger than he had seemed before. Beebleboddum froze mid-bite and stared at Mr. Dvorak as if he expected lightning to strike at any moment. "It's his title—the Watcher—and the only name most of us use for him. Highly honored. Only his closest friends ever call him by his first name. It's all *mister* and *miss* and proper titles with him. All respect. All formality. No familiar names here, Miss Sarah, unless you're one of the special ones. You must be *very* special."

A long, awkward moment passed. Sarah felt her face burning.

"Well, Mr. Fred," said Boarsmash, breaking the tension, "I don't care what you or anybody else calls him. I'm just glad he picked the menu. The Watcher sure loves to eat like a Texan when he's in Texas! Here, try this brisket. House recipe."

"And you must try the salad," said the hairy-faced, horned man who sat beside Mr. Dvorak. "It's delicious." His plate was covered in undressed leafy greens and alfalfa. "I'm called Tellurak—just Tellurak—by the way. Almast. Red River division." He reached across the table and shook Sarah's hand. His arms, she saw, were also covered with dark brown fur all the way to the tops of his knuckles. "I'm honored to make your acquaintance."

Sarah sipped milk from her silver goblet and glanced up and down the table. At least a dozen more dwarves sat eating and laughing. Dr. Nita, the black bear, was seated on the floor next to Samuel, who sat at the head of the table. She demonstrated near-human dexterity and manners as she cut and lifted pieces of meat into her enormous mouth using a fork and a knife. Next to them, Duke and a bobcat both sat on all fours atop platforms near the table and lapped water from large silver basins between bites of brisket and chicken served on silver platters. A hawk was perched atop the table near them nibbling something that looked raw. The two deer stood at the other end of the table and ate corn and greens from a long white plate. The buck said something to the dwarf next to him, and the doe nuzzled her head into his neck. Throughout the room, The Sentinels laughed and smiled and slapped one another's backs or placed hands on each other's shoulders. It was a strange bunch to be sure, but Samuel had not been wrong to call them a family. Sarah's heart felt almost warm again.

The feast continued merrily, and Sarah ate until she thought she might pop. Indeed, Boarsmash did not stop putting food onto her plate until Madam Sardar rang the silver bell and called for dinner's end. In a flash, the dishes were cleared, and the table and chairs were whisked away. Boarsmash bid Sarah farewell. He and most of the other dwarves who, Sarah learned, lived and worked in the tunnels connected to Flatland Hall, had been dismissed to resume their duties or—in the case of those who needed to be up early for the morning shift—go to bed. Only Bonk stayed for the meeting.

"Perhaps we should begin this meeting with introductions since Miss Sarah has only met a few of you," Samuel said.

One by one each of the creatures introduced themselves. Madam Sardar was the director of the Mulberry Canyon facilities unit, which included Flatland Hall, the lab Sarah had discovered, and several other structures all connected by an elaborate system of underground tunnels. All of the dwarves and other creatures who lived here reported to her. Aubrey and Fred Dvorak turned out to be siblings rather than father and daughter, and both were agents for The Sentinels. They had been recently assigned to the Mulberry Canyon unit specifically to protect Sarah. This was Aubrey's very first field assignment. The hawk, the bobcat, the black bear (Dr. Nita), and the two whitetail deer introduced themselves. The hawk, the deer, and the bobcat worked security and surveillance around the Mulberry Canyon facilities. Sarah wondered if she had ever seen them while hiking on Grandpa's land. Dr. Nita—it was *Doctor* now, she reminded everyone—was a high ranking science officer among The Sentinels and had been overseeing laboratory operations. It had taken quite a miracle for her to complete her doctorate unseen, and she was proud of the accomplishment. Everyone else, though, was so accustomed to calling her *Ms.* Nita that they kept forgetting her new title. Tellurak, the horned man, had come that morning from the Red River division to deliver a message. He had been invited to attend the feast and the meeting upon his arrival. Duke did not speak as Sarah had hoped, but was instead introduced by Samuel as "Duke the ancient, high psuchamora of the pentrafax." Sarah had no idea what any of this meant, but the bows the others gave him and the looks of awe on many of their faces told her that there was more to her faithful dog than she had imagined.

With introductions completed, Samuel called for a status update from the director.

"We have a lot of work ahead of us here," Madam Sardar replied. "Now that Les Luminaires are aware of our presence, all traces of facilities and entrances near Mr. Kirk's home must be destroyed. The laboratory is being cleared out as we speak. The flash freezer and less sensitive equipment were relocated this morning. Our maintenance crew has been working with Ms. Nita's, I'm sorry, *Dr.* Nita's, science personnel to properly remove and store sensitive equipment all day. The tunnel construction crew have already sealed all of the exterior ventilation ports. One door remains, and that will be sealed tonight. Once everything has been extracted, the cavity will be filled from our reserves and tunnel access will be cut off. A new laboratory site will be selected, and construction will begin as soon as possible."

"Dr. Nita, I believe it is your desire to remain here and oversee this effort?" Samuel asked.

The black bear nodded.

"So be it," Samuel confirmed. "We must, however, relocate the scientific special task group to another laboratory. We cannot afford more delays to their work. Madam Sardar, would you please assign a team to help them pack required equipment and procure transportation for it?"

"Of course."

"And what of Mr. Kirk's estate?" asked Samuel.

"Unfortunately, most of the house and its contents were destroyed in the fire," Madam Sardar replied, casting a care-filled glance at Sarah. "However, thanks to the efforts of Mr. Fred Dvorak, we were able to recover a few items. I believe Miss Sarah has already taken possession of her things? Wonderful. I'm told Mr. Fred put on an outstanding performance. FBI Agent, I believe?"

Mr. Dvorak stood up and bowed like a stage performer, silently mouthing "thank you, thank you" and pretending to wipe tears from his eyes.

"Yes. Thank you, Mr. Fred." Samuel said, a hint of agitation in his voice. Fred stopped his pantomime and sat down. "It seems your impressive skillset will be required here for a few days more. Miss Sarah's and Mr. Kirk's public records must be removed. I trust you'll have no trouble procuring her school records. You must also ensure that her classmates retain no lasting memory of her. Are you ready to take on such a task?"

"No sweat," Fred replied with a smirk.

"You may have a little trouble with a couple of the boys," said Aubrey. "I think Ben Booker and Carey Dawson have become, umm, emotionally invested." Aubrey winked at Sarah, who blushed.

"Oh don't you worry about that," Fred responded. "I'll give them something else to think about."

Sarah's timid voice broke as she asked, "What will you do to them?" It was the first time she had spoken since the meeting began.

"Well, most of the kids will be no problem. No offense, but you didn't really make much of an impression." Fred paused and glanced at Samuel, then continued. "For those who do remember you, well, let's just say—"

The doors under the green banner swung open and Beebleboddum appeared leading three men in lab coats.

10

ANSWERS & QUESTIONS

Sarah's pulse quickened. The feelings of warmth and wonder drained from her heart. She had imagined coming face to face with the men in lab coats at least a hundred times since she discovered the laboratory. Now they were here in person. They were arguing and appeared to be oblivious to everyone else in the room.

"Gentlemen!" Dr. Nita's thunderous bear voice roared. She had risen from her seat and scowled at them with a terrifying expression.

They froze.

"Oh! So sorry! We didn't realize you'd all still be, umm, around." Sarah recognized the voice from the recording. He bowed respectfully. "Begging your pardon Doctor, Madam Sardar, Mr., er, the Watcher."

"Be at ease, Dr. MacPherson," Samuel replied. "Madam Sardar has already informed us of your efforts. Please, join us."

"Are you gentlemen hungry?" asked Madam Sardar.

"Starving!" the scientist replied. "And parched. I don't suppose you have any Dr Pepper about?"

Madam Sardar sent Beebleboddom with instructions for the kitchen, and in a moment two dwarves emerged from beneath the brown banner with trays of food left over from the feast, glasses, a pitcher of ice, and a two-liter bottle of Dr Pepper. The three newcomers took seats and joined the circle, thanking their servers and greeting the others.

Sarah listened to their voices and made mental notes. The tall, pale blonde who had spoken first had to be Michael. She recognized his accent from the tape recording. He wore glasses and talked more than the others. He was the only one of the three who had been absent the night she hid behind the couch. The gruff voiced, black man with the graying five-o'clock shadow would be Duncan. He was the one who had justified stealing memories, and his voice had most often haunted Sarah's nightmares. That only left the brown haired man shuffling his feet and chewing his thumbnail. Benjamin. He looked younger than the others. The feelings of fear and anger Sarah had felt toward these men, these memory thieves, resurfaced in full force.

The room quieted. Fred Dvorak, who had been tapping his foot impatiently since the scientists appeared, opened his mouth as if he was about to continue where he had left off, but before he could begin, Samuel spoke.

"Miss Sarah, allow me to introduce the respected members of our scientific special task group."

Respected? Sarah thought. *Does he even know?*

"This is—"

"That's Duncan," she interrupted. The sharp tone of her quiet voice surprised Sarah as much as anyone else, but the look of surprise on the scientists' faces emboldened her. "He rushed an experiment and blew up the...the containment...unit...thingy," she continued a little louder, "and he almost killed everyone. Too much dimensional friction or something." *Well, you've gone and played your ace*, Sarah thought. *No going back now.*

"How do you—" Michael began, but he was interrupted by Sarah.

"That's Michael. He miscalculated the trans...the trans...the thing with the alloy," she blurted. "And this is Benjamin. He's..." Sarah paused for a moment to blink away sudden tears. She knew her mouth was taking off without her, but she couldn't seem to do anything about it. "He's the only one of you three who knows that what they're doing is wrong! Memories are private! Taking them from people is stealing! But I don't even care. I don't care how you're getting them or why you're storing them or anything. All I want to know is, if you were going to use my stolen memories to trick me with that stupid letter anyway, why didn't you tell me to take Grandpa with me?" Sarah choked. "Now he's gone, and it's all your fault!" She hadn't known she was going to say most of what had just fallen out of her mouth. She wasn't even sure it had made sense.

All the wide eyes that had been fixed on Sarah slowly turned to stare at the three men in lab coats. They were frozen. Michael was still holding a fork-full of mashed potatoes halfway to his open mouth, elbow in mid air.

Samuel laughed. "Well, little one, it seems you know more than we imagined!" Sarah looked at him, confused. "Duke told me of your adventures sneaking into our laboratory, and he warned me that you had formed some suspicious theories." Duke, who sat next to Sarah, barked and wagged his tail. "I can assure you," Samuel continued, his voice gentle and full of sympathy, "that neither these gentlemen nor any in this room knew that you had so successfully surveilled us, and we were, likewise, all surprised and upset by last night's events." Then, changing his tone, "It seems Mulberry Canyon's security measures may be in need of evaluation if they were so easily infiltrated by a thirteen-year-old spy and a band of Les Luminaires thugs in a van." The hawk, the bobcat, and the deer all bowed their heads.

"But the letter," Sarah protested, "it told me exactly when to leave the house so I wouldn't be there! And whoever wrote it knew all about—"

Samuel held up a hand and stopped her. "That, Miss Sarah, is a matter of great importance about which I have many questions. We must discuss it later. Privately. For now, little one, all you need understand is that these are good and trusted men who have worked very hard doing important research and development for us. Their current assignment is part of a plan that was designed by your father, and it is not at all the horror that you have imagined. I give you my word."

The mention of her father's involvement did not ease Sarah's suspicions, but there was something calming in Samuel's tone that caused Sarah's racing heart to slow a little. She nodded, and he continued.

"These gentlemen are Dr. Benjamin Allen, Dr. Duncan Connolly, and Dr. Michael MacPherson. Originally members of our Edinburgh scientific division, Dr. Connolly and Dr. MacPherson met and recruited Dr. Allen while on assignment at the University of Southampton. They have contributed to several major scientific advancements that have been beneficial to The Sentinels and to the world."

Sarah nodded again. She still did not understand how stealing memories could be a good thing, but what could she do? She hung her head and fidgeted with her mother's ring. Sarah hadn't paid much attention to it since she put it on at the Smiths' house that morning. Now, its pearl inset swirled with various colors. *Weird*, she thought. *Must be some sort of mood ring.*

The meeting continued. A few field reports had come in, saying that the kidnappers had headed northwest to Lubbock where they had abandoned their van and taken a nondescript cargo truck. Grandpa Kirk had been spotted, walking between the vehicles. Knowing he was alive and well enough to walk gave Sarah some comfort. From Lubbock, it was speculated that they might take him to one of several Les Luminaires properties in the Texas panhandle, Oklahoma, or beyond in Kansas or Colorado.

Sarah asked why they didn't call the police, and Tellurak explained that, since an investigation into the kidnapping could lead to an investigation of The Sentinels, it was best to conduct the search on their own. "Besides," he said, "we have less red tape to deal with."

Plans were made to send the scientists and their equipment to another laboratory near Denver early the next morning. Tellurak agreed to join them as far as Amarillo at which point he we would split off and return to his home base. Sarah would be escorted by Samuel, Duke, and Aubrey as they followed the scientists at a distance. Many agents and friends of The Sentinels along the route and in suspected enemy destinations would be alerted and their help enlisted.

"It is our sincerest hope and expectation," Samuel said, "that Mr. Kirk will be rescued from his captors quickly and reunited to Miss Sarah. However, I must remind you all that this is not our only mission. We must, of course, protect our scientific special task group and their equipment. Their research must continue. And we must keep Miss Sarah safe. She is not, after all, on assignment as we are; she is the assignment."

All agreed. Madam Sardar sent Bonk away with instructions about the sort of transportation that would be required.

"And now, Miss Sarah," said Samuel once the room had quieted, "I believe you may have some questions for us. We may not be able to answer everything you wish to know tonight, but as far as we are able and prudence allows, we will satisfy your curiosity."

Sarah's mind spun. There were so many things she wanted to know. Questions about stolen memories and the letter from Desjardins seemed to be off limits, and with the pain of losing Grandpa Kirk so near, she didn't feel like talking about her family. So she asked the first thing that came to her mind: "What *are* all of you? Where do you come from?"

Samuel smiled. "We are of many different sorts and from many places on this beautiful Earth. As you may have guessed, Madam Sardar and our esteemed scientists are human, like you. The rest of us are not."

"What do you mean, not human? What about Aubrey and her da... I mean, her brother, Fred? Aren't they human?"

Fred smiled wryly. "Why don't you show her, sis?"

Aubrey shot a questioning look at Samuel who nodded. "Okay," she said, "well, we're agents for a reason. We have a special, umm, talent, I guess, that makes us suited for the sort of stuff we do."

"What sort of talent?" Sarah asked.

"Well," Aubrey took a deep breath, "this." With no apparent effort, Aubrey transformed herself from a slender young girl into the towering form of the man she called "the Watcher." She was every bit as large as Samuel, the color of her hair and eyes matched his, her clothing was now identical, and when she asked Sarah what she thought, her voice even sounded like his.

"How did you do that?" Sarah gasped, slack-jawed and blinking.

Aubrey shrank back into her more familiar form. The turban disappeared. Her hair lightened to an auburn hue and grew to touch her shoulders. Her skin smoothed and lightened to its usual tanned complexion. Her clothes seemed to melt into the hot pink skirt and blouse set she had worn before. "Well, I'm a Taborian, a shifter, not a human, so I—"

"You mean you're an *alien*?"

Everyone laughed except for Aubrey.

"No." Aubrey replied. "I am from Earth, same as you. American, in fact. From the great state of Oklahoma." This was pronounced with an air of bravado. Or was it irony? "My *ancestors* came here a very long time ago from Malemorphos, which is…" she paused, trying to find the right word, "somewhere *else*, and things don't work the same there —or here—for my people. I'm here now, of course, but I'm also there in a sense, and—"

"Picture it this way," Michael interrupted. His voice was high pitched with excitement, and combined with his thick Scottish accent, it might have made Sarah laugh under different circumstances. "Imagine that you're one of the bubbles on the surface of this fizzy drink," he lifted his Dr Pepper, "and everyone you've ever known was a bubble just like you."

"Here he goes," Duncan muttered.

Michael continued, undeterred, and snatched a ballpoint pen from Duncan's lapel pocket. "Aubrey there is a bit like this pen." He poked the tip into the liquid. "Right now, it produces a circle in your bubble's flat world, approximately the same size and shape as any other bubble. But if I do this, ahh," he inserted the pen up to the shank, "her circle is much larger now. Do you see? And if I tip it to one side a bit, it becomes bigger still, and oblong, no longer a circle at all. Understand?"

"But she didn't just change shape and size," Sarah objected. "Her hair! And her clothes!"

"It's a terribly insufficient analogy," Duncan objected. "If we were talking about another of the cosmic dimensions, it might work, but—"

Michael cut him off. "It's good enough!" Sarah got the feeling Michael was trying to impress somebody.

"Well," Aubrey interjected, "it *isn't* a fair explanation, but that is sort of how it feels. There's just more to me, to us, than you can see."

"I don't believe it," Sarah said and shook her head. "It doesn't make sense!"

At this, Samuel spoke up. His voice was quiet but strong with a calming authority. "It has ever been the way of humans to assume that the whole of reality can be perceived and understood from within that reality." He shook his head. "All of our combined knowledge about the universe, little one, makes up only the smallest splinter of all that could be known about it. And even if we knew and understood it all, this universe is one of many. Aubrey's ancestors came from a different universe, as you might call it; she's an Earthling by birth, an otherworlder by descent. Do you understand?"

"No, but...are you saying there are aliens from other universes, not just other planets?" Sarah asked.

Samuel nodded.

She scrunched up her face and tried to imagine another universe.

"According to legend, long ago, six other universes met, each in their turn, with this one," Samuel motioned toward the six banners that hung around the room, "and all seven were swept up into the same current. Eventually, they became so intertwined that they began to collide. That initial meeting of realms is known as the Intersection, and it forever changed all our worlds. This universe, with its relatively simplistic laws of physics, was habitable by many forms of life, and this planet had such a hospitable and life-sustaining environment that it became a sort of terminal for them all. Beings from all seven realms wandered this world together in peace for hundreds of years."

"But you said 'according to legend.' Does that mean it's just a made-up story?"

"No," Samuel replied. "I believe the stories are true."

Sarah thought she saw Fred roll his eyes out of her peripheral vision, but when she looked at him, he appeared to be listening intently.

"Evidence of otherworlders and their histories can be seen not only in the persons seated around you, but also in your own history, religious texts, and literature, if you know what you are looking for. Even today, echoes of The Intersection may be observed in the miraculous, in the magical, in the mystifying moments that convince men and women that they are only a small part of something much larger. Some humans have been caught up in revelations of other worlds. Some have found glimpses of their own reality reflected from another perspective in dreams or visions. Others found themselves walking right out of this world and into another. Conditions are much stabler now. But for many years following The Intersection, all was turbulent and unsettled, and the overlapping of realities was frequent and unpredictable. There are stories from that era of people from other worlds who, without warning, found themselves stranded on this one, with no way to return. In time, however, as understanding and chance aligned, portals were opened so that passage between worlds was possible. For a glorious age, Earth was a meeting place for the exchange of thoughts, ideas, and wonder."

"What happened?" Sarah asked.

Samuel raised one eyebrow. "Humans."

"What do you mean?"

"It is a long story. We must stop for the night so you can rest. Tomorrow will be a long day."

"But—" Sarah objected.

"No, little one. Answers calm our hearts, and questions stir our minds, but a good night's sleep is the fertile soil for both."

11

STEPS

THE GIRLS RETURNED TO THEIR SLEEPING QUARTERS FOLLOWED BY Duke. When they entered, Sarah saw that the bed she and Grandpa Kirk had built for Duke now sat on the floor against the foot of her bed. It was blackened on one side and smelled of smoke, but the white German Shepherd curled up in it as happily as he had done that first day.

Sarah changed into a nightgown that had been packed in her suitcase and crawled into bed. Aubrey was already under the covers in the other bed, so Sarah reached over and turned the dial on the oil lamp. The flame flickered and went out.

"Aubrey?" Sarah whispered.

"Yeah?"

"Did you really chase down those guys who kidnapped Grandpa?"

"Yes." There was sorrow in Aubrey's voice. "I'm sorry we couldn't get him back, Sarah. It's my fault. I...I took a stupid chance."

"What happened?" asked Sarah.

"I chased them east, toward Dallas. When they exited, I pretended to lose them, and then I shapeshifted to look like a cop. I caught up and pulled them over. But they were ready for me. As soon as I was off my motorcycle, four other cars surrounded us."

"Wait. You can ride a motorcycle?" Sarah was impressed. She rolled onto her side to face Aubrey in the dark and propped her head up on one hand.

"Yeah! I have an '82 Harley. Thirteen-hundred cc. White with gold trim. Well, it's not mine, really. It belongs to The Sentinels, but I'm the only one who ever uses it, and I love it! Usually, anyway. Today wasn't so fun."

"Rad! But you're only…How old are you?"

"Seventeen."

"No way! Seriously? I guess I shouldn't be surprised. How did you get away?" Sarah sat up and scooted to the edge of her bed. She heard Aubrey's bed squeak as she sat up too.

"That was the weird part!" Aubrey replied. "A woman got out of a car that had pulled over behind me. She held her hands up to let me know she wasn't armed, but she said that I should stand down before something bad happened. And she knew my name. It was totally weird. She said, 'Aubrey, look around you,' and when I did, there were guns pointed at me from two of the vehicles. Then I saw Ms. Nita with her paws raised back by the trees off the side of the road. I guess they'd caught her farther back and brought her there. She looked scared. There had to be a dozen men in the trees around her, all in camo, with guns pointed at her. It's like they knew we were coming! Anyway, I thought we were goners for sure. They made us walk back into the trees and lay down on our faces. We were waiting for them to start threatening us and demanding information—that's what they usually do when they catch one of us—and I was preparing my mind in case they, you know, decided to torture us or whatever. But then they just left. They didn't even say anything. They left us with my bike and disappeared."

"Wow!" said Sarah. "Do you think someone tipped them off? Would any of The Sentinels do that? Who are these people anyway? Do they have shifters too?"

Aubrey giggled. "You're funny, kiddo. Let me see. No, I don't think they were tipped off. Not by one of us, anyway. We're like a family. None of us would do that. Maybe they're just getting better at spying. Or maybe security's getting lazy. Anyway, it doesn't matter. They let us go. God only knows why, but they did. And no, they're all human. Les Luminaires, the ones who know what they're really about anyway, they hate otherworlders and halfies and all. I think they'd kill us all if they could."

"Do you think they'll kill Grandpa?" Sarah whispered.

Aubrey was silent for a moment. "No. I mean, maybe. If they get all they need from him, but…" she paused. "Well, that will take more time than they probably think." She paused. "I can promise you one thing, though: we'll do everything we can to get him back. Your grandpa and the Watcher are friends. He's not going to let this go."

Sarah laid back onto her bed and stared into the black. For several minutes she was silent. Then she whispered again, "Hey, Aubrey?"

"Yeah?"

"I'm sorry I was kind of a jerk to you before."

Aubrey was quiet for a moment. "I'm just glad you're safe."

Duke woke Sarah early the next morning. Aubrey was already gone. Sarah rubbed her eyes, and memories of the feast and the meeting flooded back into her mind. She looked at Duke.

"So, I guess you're kind of a big deal, huh?"

Duke looked at her with his big eyes.

"High something-or-other of the whatchamacallit?"

Silence.

"Is it still okay for me to pet you like I did before I knew you were more than just a dog?"

He jumped up, put his front paws onto her lap, and licked her face.

Sarah giggled and scratched behind his ears as she buried her nose in his neck. "Don't ever leave me, Duke," she whispered. Then she sat up and took a deep breath. "I don't guess there's a shower around here?"

Duke barked and ran to the door. Sarah grabbed her suitcase and followed him down the hall to an empty room with several shower stalls. She found some towels in a cabinet, removed her bandages, and took a long, hot shower.

By the time Sarah finished, the hallway was buzzing with life. Doors were open, and Sarah could hear voices all around her. She found Duke waiting for her near the door and followed him back toward their room. Before they reached it, though, Beebleboddum appeared, leading Michael in from the main hall.

"Oh, there you are!" Michael exclaimed. "I have something for you." He handed Sarah's backpack to her. "Night before last, when we surprised those goons, the Watcher, he didn't want the three of us in the scrape, so he had us out searching for your things. Duke there told him where you left it all, but we had a terrible time of it. Anyway, I'm afraid we owe you an apology. We had to take the long way out of there in case we were being followed, and Benjamin, well, he was carrying the lot of it, and not being the most coordinated human ever, and what with it being dark and all, and us trespassing on unknown land...Well, the short of it is, he lost your tin."

It took Sarah a moment to figure out what he meant. "He lost my lunch box?"

"Yes, I'm afraid so. And your pillow and blanket were soiled and torn. Anyway, I'm sorry I didn't bring this to you sooner."

Sarah unzipped the top of the bag and peeked inside. It was empty except for one of the bottles of water she had packed and the last of the beef jerky. "Thank you," she said.

"Don't mention it," Michael replied. "And while you're not mentioning things, I'd appreciate if you didn't say any more about how I messed up those transmutational calculations." He smiled and winked.

Sarah nodded and ducked into her room, followed by Duke. She shut the door, closed her eyes, and let out a long sigh. Despite Samuel's reassurance, Michael and the other scientists still gave her the creeps.

"Where have you been?" Aubrey asked.

Sarah started, unaware Aubrey was in the room. "I...I was taking a shower."

"Well, come on! The Watcher's been by twice already looking for you. We need to be packed and ready in ten minutes."

Sarah added her new diary, her mom's old diary, the flashlight, and her dad's puzzle cube to the backpack and slung it over her shoulders. Then she grabbed her suitcase and started for the door. But just as she was about to leave, she changed her mind. Sarah opened the trunk and pulled out the old dagger and a belt from her suitcase. She put the belt around her waist and through the loop on the sheath so that it rested against her right hip. Her tee shirt was long enough to cover the whole thing if she left it untucked, so she did.

Someone knocked on the door, and Aubrey opened it. Samuel smiled and bowed before he entered. "Miss Sarah," he said, "may I have a word with you?" Then, over his shoulder, "Mr. Bonk, would you be so kind as to take Miss Sarah's bags to the loading area?"

Sarah latched her suitcase and handed it to Bonk along with the trunk, then she left, taking the backpack with her.

Samuel led her across the main hall and through the double doors beneath the black banner with the red serpent. Beyond the doors was a long, dark, earthen tunnel. Samuel had to hunch over to keep his head from touching the ceiling. After a hundred yards or so, they reached a row of locked wooden doors. Samuel unlocked one, and they descended a set of stone steps on the other side. Flaming torches hung in brackets along the wall. The air was cool and damp, and the sound of dripping water could be heard echoing at the bottom.

Samuel grabbed a torch from the wall and led Sarah to a small wooden table with two wooden chairs. "Please sit," he directed as he placed the torch into a bracket on a nearby beam.

Sarah hesitated and then obeyed.

"Here we can speak privately for a moment, and then I have something to show you. I am sorry that we have not had more time to acquaint ourselves with one another. I am hopeful that we will have more time for that soon. Right now, however, I need to ask you a few questions alone. It is a matter of some urgency."

Sarah nodded, trying to look calm and confident.

"Duke tells me that, on the night you snuck into our *secret* laboratory," his lips curled into a faint smile, "you took away a paper from a printer you found there. He says you told him about it the day your grandfather was taken. What was on it?"

Sarah looked at him, puzzled. She wondered how Samuel and

Duke had such detailed conversations, but it seemed like a silly thing to ask, and she did not want to sound silly, so instead she said, "You didn't ask Duke?" her voice trembling. She cleared her throat.

"He thought it would be best if it came from you."

"All right," she replied and took a deep breath. "It was a letter. To me."

"To you? Are you certain it was intended for you?"

"Yes, sir. It said 'To Sarah Ann Lewis' right across the top." Then she added with an ironic tone, "I would show it to you, but it was in my lunch box, and Michael said they lost it." That helped. The sarcasm made her feel stronger.

Samuel stroked the stubble on his chin. "I see. And did this letter say who had sent it?"

"Someone named Des-jar-dins," Sarah pronounced the name phonetically.

"Desjardins?" Samuel asked, using the proper pronunciation (which sounded to Sarah like *day-zsar-duh*). "Most interesting." He paused. "The word is French. It means *gardener*. Or, to translate it literally, *of the gardens*. Most interesting. Might I ask what Desjardins wrote to you?"

Sarah resumed her sarcastic tone. "I thought you already knew. Or, if not you, one of the others."

"How could we know?"

Sarah considered making something up, but there was something about Samuel that made the thought of lying seem silly and useless. "Well, it had a bunch of stuff in it about me," she began, her voice softened somewhat, "personal things nobody could know unless they had been inside my head. And while I was hiding in the lab, I heard Benjamin and Duncan talking about how they were taking people's memories or something. So I thought one of them, or I guess, one of *you*, had somehow gotten my memories and printed the letter while I was there so I'd get it."

Samuel said nothing for a long time, his fingers steepled in front of his closed eyes. At last, he looked up and asked, "Did Desjardins give you any instructions?"

"Yes," said Sarah. "Well, actually, no. Not exactly. The letter told me that I could either come back to the lab in two weeks or stay home, but it said I wouldn't be safe either way. It seemed like someone was trying to trap me. I figured it was stupid to go and maybe stupider to stay."

A smile crept onto Samuel's face. "And so you chose to do neither."

"Yes, sir," Sarah replied. Now that things had gone so badly for Grandpa Kirk, she doubted that this had been the right decision. Her brow knitted and her head drooped.

"Ahh, little one. You are so much like your father." Samuel smiled at her for a long moment before he continued. "Desjardins has sent us letters before, of course."

Sarah raised her eyebrows.

"Oh, yes. And like yours, none of them contained any direct instructions. Instead, they contained information we could not have gathered on our own and set choices before us. Until now, though, they have all been addressed to Dr. Benjamin Allen. I find it interesting that Desjardins has now chosen to communicate with you."

"Who is Desjardins?" Sarah asked, careful to pronounce the name correctly.

"Ahh. Now, that *is* the question."

"You mean you don't know?"

Samuel did not respond.

"So it could be anybody? Anybody could have my memories?" Sarah felt panic rising in her chest.

"Be calm, little one. Nobody has stolen your memories. Consider: How could a person with only your *memories* know about something that would not happen for two weeks?"

Sarah opened her mouth to argue, but realized she had no answer.

Samuel stood, grabbed the torch, and walked to a panel mounted onto the wall. He opened it, removed a small electronic device, tapped a series of glowing buttons, and turned to Sarah. "Please do not be alarmed at what I am about to show you. You are in no danger. I only need to know if you recognize this man."

Sarah swallowed and gripped the bottom of her chair.

Samuel laid the device on the ground and pressed a button. There was a thumping noise followed by a hum, and a bright light beamed up from the device onto a man who floated in mid air with his back to Sarah. He was stiff as a board and turned slowly, as if weightless. Sarah crept forward for a closer look. The man's face came into full view in the bright white light, and Sarah shrieked. It was Blackwood, the man who had hunted her two nights before.

12

OUBLIETTE

"It's him!" Sarah cried and stumbled backward into the table.

"Do not be frightened, little one. He is not here." To demonstrate, Samuel passed a hand right through the man's torso. "This is merely a projection, a hologram. What you see is a three-dimensional snapshot taken just before he entered the oubliette. He cannot harm you."

Sarah caught her breath and reached a shaking hand out to where she should have felt a jacket but instead felt nothing. She yanked it back. "The oubliette?"

"It is an old word for a place of forgetting, a sort of narrow dungeon cell with a door in its ceiling. Prisoners were locked away to be forgotten, unable to even sit down. Ours is nothing so inhumane. Whenever we decide it is safe to release Mr. Blackwood, it will be for him as if no time has elapsed at all, and he will have experienced no pain."

"What do you mean?" Sarah asked.

"I am afraid we do not have time for explanations now. I can see that you recognize this man. Yes?"

"Yes. The night they took Grandpa, I was hiding in the brush, and Blackwood was looking for me. If it hadn't been for Duke, he would have found me." Sarah felt tears well up behind her eyes. She swallowed and tried to stay calm.

"Ahh, yes. Duke has been a great friend and protector to you. If it had not been for him, we would not have known anything was amiss, and the situation would be much more dire now. And it is thanks to Duke that we captured Blackwood."

"I'm surprised he survived." Sarah forced a laugh. "I thought Duke was going to tear him apart!"

Samuel smiled and placed his large hand on Sarah's back. "Yes. I'm sure Mr. Blackwood would not have been so fortunate if he had laid even one finger on you. As it is, it seems Duke frightened him speechless. We have been unable to persuade him to give us any information." He took a deep breath. "Had you ever seen him before that night?"

"No. I don't think so. But I think maybe I knew one of the others, the one they called Boss."

"You recognized Mr. Litchfield then? Very perceptive."

"It *was* him?"

"Yes. Miss Aubrey suspected him long before he revealed his hand. As soon as we were certain, we had him removed from the school."

"*You* had him removed? How?"

Samuel smiled. "Miss Aubrey and Mr. Fred have been very busy at your school. They are quite talented."

"Fred was at school too?"

"Yes. And you should be grateful. He has a talent for believable impersonations. Very difficult. He made quite a useful double for your principal on several occasions."

"Was he the one who changed my schedule?"

"Indeed, to keep you under Miss Aubrey's watchful eyes and out of Mr. Litchfield's reach."

"And all that time I thought they were spying on me."

"On you? Do you believe yourself so important that someone needs to spy on you?"

"Well, no. I guess not. I just thought I knew too much."

"And now?"

"Apparently, I don't know very much at all."

Samuel laughed. "Come, little one. We are late already." He switched off the hologram and hurried Sarah toward the stairs.

"Samuel?" Sarah began when they reached the door at the top.

"Yes?" he replied as he closed the door behind them.

"Do you think they will hurt Grandpa? I mean, really hurt him?"

Samuel stopped working the key in the lock and looked at her. "Yes. I think they might."

Sarah's eyes fell to the floor.

"We will do everything in our power," said Samuel, "to get him back as quickly as possible. Perhaps they would be willing to make an exchange for Blackwood, though I must admit I find that unlikely." He finished locking the door and pocketed the key. "But you must remember, little one, that your grandfather would wish for us to protect you even at the cost of his own life. If it comes to it, we will honor that wish."

A FEW MINUTES LATER, SARAH FOUND HERSELF STANDING WITH SAMUEL in a dimly lit bay at the end of a long tunnel. All around her, people hurried, carrying boxes and bags. A forklift beeped as it backed up and loaded a crate into the back of a semi-trailer. Grandpa's old Ford pickup and the camper trailer he had bought were parked at one end of the bay next to a white and gold motorcycle. Tellurak appeared and told Samuel in hushed tones that the decoys had been deployed.

"This way, Miss Sarah," a voice called.

"Oh! Good morning, Boarsmash." Sarah replied when she saw who had called her. Samuel's words still weighed heavily on her, but her new friend was so excited that she couldn't help but smile.

Boarsmash led her into the cargo area of a long delivery truck and slid open a panel near the front. Her trunk and suitcase were inside, along with some pillows, a blanket, and a cooler.

"It's a smuggling compartment that we usually use for equipment," Boarshmash explained, "but we've tried to make it comfortable for you. I'm afraid it will be a little cramped."

"I have to ride in here?"

Boarsmash nodded and continued. "See here?" He pointed to a vent in the top of the compartment. "We've run air conditioning from the cabin. You can adjust the airflow by opening or closing it like this." He slid a lever next to the vent. "I'm afraid I don't have a light for you."

"It's okay. I've got one," Sarah said and pulled her new flashlight from her backpack.

"Already prepared then? Wonderful! You'll find food and drinks in this cooler. I had the kitchen make up some brisket sandwiches for you since you enjoyed it so much last night." He smiled at her with pride. "Oh, and one more thing. It's going to be a while before we can stop, so you should use the restroom before we go. There's one just around the corner. If you need to go once we're in motion, I'm afraid you'll have to use these." He handed her a bag that contained a green plastic bladder with a screw top, a funnel, and a small roll of toilet paper. Sarah wrinkled her nose at the thought.

"Can't I just sit up front?" she asked.

"Oh no," Boarsmash replied. "It's much too dangerous. After the ambush yesterday, we have every reason to believe Les Luminaires will be watching for us. But don't you worry! *I've* been granted special permission to be your driver." He beamed. "And Duke will be up front with me. I think he really wanted to ride with you in here, but he's too big. Bonk will be with the Watcher in a van that will stay close to us the whole way. And Miss Aubrey will be right here." He slid open an identical panel on the other side of the truck. Sarah saw Aubrey's suitcase inside. "If we stop, you just stay quiet. It's unlikely anybody will find you, especially after we load the truck, but if they do, she'll be right here to defend you."

Sarah took Boarsmash's advice. Duke ushered her to the restroom and back, and then he stayed with her until she was settled into her tiny compartment. The door slid shut, and she was surrounded by darkness. The truck bounced and shook as boxes and crates were loaded, and she knew she was blocked in. A few minutes later, Sarah felt the engine rumble, and they began to move. She strained to keep her weight off the sliding door as the truck ascended an incline.

It was difficult to find a comfortable position. She shifted the trunk and the cooler so that, if she kept her knees bent, she could lay on her back across the top of both. She surrounded herself with pillows and managed to doze for a while. When she woke, she was hungry, so she dug around in the cooler and pulled out a cold brisket sandwich and a Coke. *The breakfast of champions,* she thought to herself. While she ate, she pulled out her mother's diary and read a bit from the beginning, squeezing the flashlight between her legs to illuminate the pages.

The first entry was silly. Her mom had introduced herself to the diary like it was a person she was meeting for the first time. She was fifteen, her favorite color was purple, and she was hopelessly smitten with some boy named William from her school. The edges of the pages were covered in flowers and hearts she had drawn. It was strange to think of her mother as a teenager with crushes and silly schoolgirl concerns. In Sarah's mind, her mother had always been a wise, caring adult. She tried to imagine what her mom would have looked like in high school, but all she could picture was the tired, careworn expression her mother wore in the days before she died. Even then, Sarah thought, she had been beautiful. Sarah closed the book. She told herself that she would get carsick if she read anymore, but in truth, it hurt too much to think about her mom for long.

She slid the diary back into her backpack and tried to think about something else. When she found that she couldn't, Sarah pulled out the puzzle cube. She turned it in her hands and examined it up close for the first time. Now she recognized the symbols carved into the black wooden squares. They matched the banners in Flatland Hall: a lion, a jagged circle, a man with a sword, a serpent, a star, and a swirl. There were also some squares with simple circles engraved into them and others that were blank. She began to work the cube. If she had ever expected it to be easy, she would have been mistaken. It seemed that the puzzle would turn in some directions but not others. Sometimes a row would turn clockwise but not counter-clockwise. Some rows would turn either direction but only if she pushed hard. Other times, a row would spin freely, and it was hard to keep it in the position she wanted. After a while, she noticed that there were not equal numbers of symbols. There was no way to make a complete side of lions, for example, because there were only thirty-seven of them, but she would need forty-nine to cover a side. *What's the point, then? Couldn't you at least have left me some instructions for this stupid thing?* she thought and threw the puzzle back into her bag, frustrated.

Sarah slumped back onto her pillow and pressed her palms into her eyes. Her parents had kept secrets from her for her entire life, and now that she knew, neither of them was around to explain why or to answer her questions or to tell her whom she could trust. She screamed at nobody and punched the wall of her container, her own personal oubliette. In a way, it was more than just a place to hide for a while; this was her life now: alone, in the dark, unable to escape. And there was nothing she could do about it.

13

DEEP IN THE HEART

THE ENGINE STOPPED. SARAH WAS AS STILL AND SILENT AS A STATUE. She heard the back door open and the sound of crates scraping against the floor. Sarah put her hand to the dagger on her hip. Footsteps. The door slid open, and there, silhouetted by the bright day behind them, stood Duke and Boarsmash.

"Come on, Miss Sarah!" said Boarsmash. "We're here."

Sarah followed Duke out into the hot, humid air. The sun blazed overhead. Beneath her feet was a white gravel road. Crates were stacked on one side next to the white and gold motorcycle she had seen before. A large oak tree cast its shadow over a green lawn. Somewhere in the distance, she could hear the neighing of horses. The aroma of meat cooking over a wood fire filled her nostrils.

Aubrey hopped down from the trailer next to her. "Ahh! I love this place."

"Where are we?" asked Sarah.

"San Antonio."

Actually, Sarah discovered later, they were a few miles outside of San Antonio, in a green, hilly stretch of country. This was, of course, almost due south of Sarah's West Texas home—the opposite direction from where she had been told they would go. They had arrived at the home of Alfonso and Rita Alvarez, a sweet couple in their fifties who had been long-time supporters and friends of The Sentinels. After everyone's luggage was unpacked and distributed into rooms inside the Alvarezes' pueblo-style mansion, Tellurak—the hairy, horned man Sarah met at Flatland Hall—explained the change in plans to Sarah.

It turned out that the message he had delivered to Samuel further confirmed what Aubrey and Doctor Nita had seen when they were ambushed. Large numbers of people and resources from Les Luminaires had deployed from various locations and were gathering in groups along every major northward route away from Sarah's home. And since they had known Aubrey's name, there was increasing suspicion that Les Luminaires were working with someone inside The Sentinels. So the meeting was held, and a general plan was made. Overnight, though, five different northward routes were planned in detail and summaries were sent to various people inside The Sentinels who would not join the journey. Then, just minutes before Sarah's team set out, a series of empty decoy vehicles left in secret from a different bay, following the northbound routes. The idea was that, if any one of those vehicles ran into trouble with Les Luminaires, the source of the leak might be narrowed down to those who had been told about that route. Meanwhile, all the equipment and people who needed protection would be hundreds of miles south. They would wait here for two days and then make use of alternate transportation to reach their destinations. Only those who were now in San Antonio knew they were coming here, and Samuel alone knew the entire plan.

Sarah was furious. She stomped away in search of Samuel and found him a few minutes later in the dining room talking with the three scientists. "Two days?!" she shouted, interrupting their discussion. "Who knows what they'll do to Grandpa between now and then? We are wasting time!"

"Miss Sarah," Samuel replied in a warm, gentle voice, "our agents are keeping a close watch on all known routes and strongholds of Les Luminaires. Until we gather some useful intelligence, any action we take would require us to blindly choose a target, further endangering you and your grandfather in the process. Please trust me, little one. This is our best strategy."

"Trust you? Why? I don't know you. The only people on Earth that I trust right now are Grandpa Kirk and Duke."

"Then you must ask yourself who it is that *they* trust."

Sarah gritted her teeth, but she couldn't argue. She knew he was right. "So what, then? I'm supposed to sit here and do nothing?"

Michael cleared his throat and gave Samuel a meaningful look.

Samuel glanced at Michael, then back at Sarah. He closed his eyes, furrowed his brow, and took a deep breath. At last he said, "There is one thing you can do that would be very helpful. Tonight, if you are willing, I will allow you to assist our efforts."

"Yes! Of course! Anything!"

ONCE AGAIN, SARAH HAD BEEN ASSIGNED TO BUNK WITH AUBREY AND Duke. Both were waiting for her in their room when she returned.

"You like hiking?" Aubrey asked.

Before Sarah knew what had happened, the three were walking together alongside the little river that flowed through the middle of the Alvarezes' land. Or rather, Sarah (having never seen one) called it a river. It was more like a good sized creek, and Aubrey (who had seen real rivers) did not argue. Sarah's shirt was soon damp with sweat, and though she was still worried about Grandpa Kirk, it felt good to be on her feet and outside in the hot Texas sunshine.

"See that spot over there?" Aubrey pointed to a limestone boulder a few yards ahead of them that jutted into the river. "Fred and I go fishing right there every summer—whenever he isn't running off with his girlfriend, anyway." She sighed and brushed the hair from her face. "Every year, we come here with other shifters for a sort of reunion and training thing. The Alvarezes feed us the most wonderful food, and we spend time together. The older shifters teach the younger ones, and we have classes on survival skills and surveillance and stuff. It's all taught by Taborians, so we can get into stuff that wouldn't work for other types of agents."

"Have you been an agent your whole life?" Sarah asked.

"Yeah, I guess. All training and research until now, though."

They walked to the boulder. Sarah took off her shoes and let her toes dangle into the water. It was cool and felt nice on her hot feet. Duke sniffed around the bank but never wandered far. Aubrey laid down on her back and looked at the sky.

"So hey," Aubrey began, "I've been wanting to ask you something."

"Yeah?" said Sarah.

"Did I do something that offended you at school?"

"What?"

Aubrey didn't answer. She seemed to be thinking out loud to herself now. "Or maybe it would have worked better for you if I had looked different. Maybe if I'd been blonde or had glasses or something."

"What are you talking about?" Sarah asked, a little offended.

Aubrey returned from her thoughts. "Nothing. I mean, well, my assignment was only to keep you safe, but I thought, and your Grandpa agreed, that it would be easier to do that if you and I were, you know, friends or whatever. I didn't have any trouble with the other kids—"

"Yeah, no joke," Sarah interrupted.

"Was that it then?" Aubrey sat up. "Was I too popular? Fred said I was being too likeable, and that I should try to make some enemies. Then again, he thought I was wasting my time trying to be friends with you at all."

"No!" Sarah said, annoyed by the question. "How shallow do you think I am?" Of course she been annoyed by Aubrey's popularity, but that was never the real issue. Sarah had disliked Aubrey before she made all those friends. "It was just…" she said after a moment, "I guess it was the way you looked at me on your first day. It rubbed me the wrong way."

"The way I looked at you?" Aubrey sounded surprised.

"Yeah, at lunch. I hadn't even met you, and you were sitting by yourself. I was pretty new too, so I probably should have said 'hi' or something, but then I saw you, day one, totally confident, and you shot me a look like you already had me all figured out. I don't know, I felt like you were targeting me. I guess it makes sense now that I know I was your assignment."

"But I didn't look at you," Aubrey protested.

"Sure you did. Not that I was watching you or anything, but I caught you staring at me out of the corner of my eye while we were eating. It was weird. The same sort of proud-of-yourself look you gave me the day they hauled Mr. Litchfield off, and I knew you had something to do with it."

"I didn't look at you then either!"

"I just know what I saw."

"No, really." Aubrey was adamant. "It's part of my training, something I'm good at." She was on her feet and pacing now. "I use my hearing, peripheral vision, and other shifter senses that are, well, kind of like human intuition, I guess, to get a read on everything that's going on in a room without actually looking at anybody. Both of those days, I was looking straight down at my hands so I wouldn't give anything away, not shooting you self-satisfied glances."

"Well, I guess I caught you slipping up, super spy," Sarah jeered.

Aubrey didn't reply, but Sarah could tell from the sound of her breathing that she was still bothered. Duke climbed onto the rock and curled against Sarah's back. Sarah scooted forward a bit and laid back on him. After another minute, she spoke up. "Okay, my turn. I have a question for you."

"Shoot." Aubrey's tone was softer now.

"What do you really look like."

"What do you mean, *really?*" Aubrey sat down next to Sarah and crossed her legs.

"Well, you can look like anything you want. Right? And you told me you're seventeen, so I assume this younger girl thing is just a costume you wear when you're undercover."

Aubrey laughed. "It is not! I mean, it's weird. I never really thought about it."

"For real?"

"For real. Asking me what I really look like is like someone asking you which of your clothes are your real clothes. It's not me, it's just how I look."

Sarah squinted at Aubrey. "So you don't have a real body?"

"Of course I do! This is real." Aubrey pinched her own arm.

"You know what I mean."

"Yeah. You want to know if I have a usual form—something I return to when I'm not shifting into some sort of disguise form. Right?"

"Yes!" Sarah sat up.

Aubrey giggled. "I bet you expect me to be blue with spikey skin." Then, when Sarah didn't respond, "No. I mean, lately, I've looked like this because it fit the assignment, and honestly, this is pretty much how I feel."

"You feel like a seventh-grader?"

"Sort of. I guess." Aubrey thought for a minute. "Okay, you know how dogs don't age the same way humans do?"

"Sure." Sarah didn't know what this had to do with anything, but she played along. "What is it, seven dog years for every human year?" She reached behind her and scratched Duke's back.

"Yeah, something like that. Have you ever seen a dog who had to learn how to bark? No way. They're sort of born knowing. They start out more advanced, and then they grow up really fast, and then they age slowly, depending on the breed. We—Taborians, I mean—we're kind of like that."

"You're like dogs?" asked Sarah.

"No. Don't be stupid. It's just an example. I mean, we don't age the same way humans do. That's all. We're born able to do lots of things you humans can't do yet because we can shift into a body that's able to do them. We can talk within a couple of months, and we mature faster. But then we slow down and stay kids for a long time. If I had to guess, I'd say that I'm pretty much in the same life stage at seventeen that you're in at thirteen."

Sarah grabbed a flat, round rock from the dirt beside the boulder and skipped it across the water. It bounced five times before it sank. She smiled. Grandpa would have been proud. "So will you live to be hundreds of years old?"

"Ha! Oh no. I'm no Aravatis like the Watcher. Most of us die off in our thirties or forties. We age really fast once we finally grow up. My mom died when she was thirty-two. I was still a baby. And my dad just passed away a couple of months ago. He was almost fifty."

A pang struck Sarah's heart as she remembered her own mother's death. "I'm so sorry, Aubrey. I didn't know."

"It's okay. Like I said, I don't even remember my mom, and my dad was old. Anyway, we weren't close like you and your parents. It's a thing with Taborians. Our parents die young and we don't stay little as long as humans, so we don't do families the same way. I've just been lucky to have Fred around most of the time. He gives me a hard time, but he watches out for me too. And I guess I'd say the Watcher's been kind of like a grandfather to me."

"But you still call him 'the Watcher.' You don't even use his real name."

"Yeah. Kind of weird, I guess."

Sarah slipped her socks and shoes back onto her feet, and they walked a little farther downstream. Then Sarah asked, "What was his name?"

"My dad? Gregory. He was a great guy. You've actually met him. You just didn't know it."

"When?"

Aubrey bit her lip. "Well, actually, I shouldn't tell you that. I shouldn't have said anything at all. Sorry."

"Why not?"

"It's just, well, it isn't my story to tell. Anyway, it's getting close to dinner time. We should head back."

Sarah's curiosity was driving her crazy, but she let it go. There were so many more important questions she should ask. She shook it off and changed the subject. "What was it you said Samuel, I mean the Watcher, was? Ara—"

"Aravatis."

"They live a long time?"

Aubrey gave Sarah a knowing smile. "You should ask him how old he is sometime."

14

TO CATCH A THIEF

The fajitas that night were the best Sarah had ever tasted, and she drank horchata for the first time in her life. She didn't know why anybody ever drank anything else when something this cinnamony and delicious existed.

When dinner was over, Sarah reminded Samuel that he had said she could help with something. Samuel nodded and said that a meeting had already been arranged for her to discuss it with Dr. Benjamin Allen.

A few minutes later, with Duke by her side, Sarah followed Samuel to the front porch. The scientist was seated on the top step, cutting an apple with what looked like a scalpel. He rose and bowed to Samuel who returned the gesture and then motioned for Sarah to join him. She sat down on the far side of the wide, wooden stair and gazed into the distant twilight as crickets and grasshoppers played their nightly songs. Duke sat next to her, and she scratched him behind his ears, grateful for something to do with her trembling hands. Samuel said that he had other business to tend to and left them to talk.

"Lovely evening," said the scientist. "It's a far stretch from the English countryside, but a bloke could learn to love a landscape like this."

Sarah nodded and waited for him to explain why she was there. When a few awkward seconds had passed in silence, she spoke up. "Dr. Allen?"

"Just Benjamin, please," he replied. "At least, whenever the Watcher isn't around." He smiled and held out a slice of apple. "Here, would you like a piece?"

"No, thanks. Samuel said you need my help with something," she said, trying to sound grown up. "What's the plan?"

"Well, Miss Sarah, we need to find out what Blackwood knows about you and your grandfather, what he was after, what they're planning." He sighed. "But he hasn't been willing to talk. Actually, he hasn't said anything at all. Not so much as his name, rank, and serial number. So Duncan suggested that we set up some of our equipment here and attempt, umm, a cognitive reading. With any luck, his brain will tell us where they're taking your granddad, whether his mouth cooperates or not. Maybe more, if we can manage it."

"So the plan is to steal his memories." Sarah crossed her arms. "That's what you want me to help you do?"

"Well, it's not stealing, exactly. It's—"

"Yeah, yeah, yeah. I've heard it already. You're *making a copy*. Doesn't make it any better."

Duke laid his head between his front paws and wagged his tail.

Benjamin pushed his fingers through his hair. He looked up at the stars. "You're right. Of course, you're right. I hate it."

Sarah cocked an eyebrow at him. "So why are you helping?"

"Well, it might get your granddad back, then, won't it? And besides, do you think Blackwood would be any more civil to you if you were his captive? It's not as if we have a better option at the moment."

Sarah looked away.

"Look. I know you don't know me," Benjamin continued. "I don't really know you either. But I do know your grandfather. He's a good man, Sarah. Did you know he gave us the land where the lab was? It had been in his family for years. He divided it up and gave a plot to The Sentinels. Wanted us to have a place where we could conduct our experiments quietly, away from prying eyes. I only met him myself a little over a year ago when I was assigned to this team. He welcomed us into his home. Cooked for us. He grills a fantastic sirloin, that Bo. And he went on and on about you and your mum and dad. He was so proud. He'd hoped you'd all move nearer for ages. I wish you could've seen him light up when he found out you were going to move in after your mum passed. It had been months since any of us had seen him smile. But when he gave us the news that you were coming, well…"

Sarah felt a tear trickle down her cheek.

"Oh, I am sorry. I'm babbling on like a nitwit."

"It's all right."

Benjamin took a deep breath and looked at Sarah. "Your granddad, he loves you. He deserves to see you again. And if pinching this hooligan's memory will get him back sooner, then I'll do it."

Sarah sniffed and dried her face on her sleeves. He was right. The plan was awful, but it was their best shot at finding Grandpa before anything terrible happened to him. "Okay. You win. What do I do?"

"Well," Benjamin sighed, "all *you* have to do is stand still for a bit."

Sarah stared at him, puzzled, through blurred eyes. "How is that going to help?"

"Blackwood just needs to…" Benjamin started. "No, back up. What we're going to do is…That is to say, well…" He dropped his hands and let out an exasperated sigh. "Perhaps I should give you a bit of context? I'm not sure it's allowed, come to think of it, but if you're going to help, you deserve to know what we're doing. It'll be an hour or more before they're ready for you, and you'll have an easier time understanding your part once you know how the technique works. All right?"

Sarah agreed.

Benjamin went on to explain that a scientist he had worked with at the University of Southampton, Dr. Absalom Drake, had invented the process for reading a person's memory several years before. All his initial work had been performed alone, after hours, in an office he rented near the University. He spent his life's savings on equipment and supplies. Drake's hypothesis had been that the only computer capable of communicating with a human brain was another human brain. So he developed a device which connected hundreds of electrical sensors attached to one person's brain—the subject—with another set of probes attached to matching points on another person's brain—the reader. Between the two, a finely tuned electrical amplifier boosted the output. The result was that anything the subject felt, thought, or remembered was instantly transferred to the reader as an electrical signal. The first prototype was rudimentary, and since the reader was busy sensing and thinking as well, the external thoughts became jumbled with the internal ones, and attempt after attempt failed. None of the early test readers kept their sanity, and all were horribly scarred by the holes drilled into their skulls.

Sarah asked where Drake had found human subjects for such horrific experiments, but Benjamin wouldn't tell her—he said it wasn't the sort of thing he liked to talk about—nor would he say what happened to the test subjects when Drake was finished with them. Sarah thought she could guess.

"Over time," Benjamin continued, "Drake refined his equipment and process. Sensors and probes were inserted into the brains of both subjects and readers so that two way communication was possible; a reader could request or suggest certain memories, and the subject could respond. Areas of the brain were added or eliminated until Drake had isolated the sectors responsible for verbal input and memory access. Then he added drugs."

"Drugs?" Sarah asked.

"Yes. The human memory, it turns out, is a fragile thing. Every time we remember something, it's as if we pull the memory out, change it a bit, stamp it with our current thoughts and feelings, and store it again. This becomes especially problematic when two people access the same memory. So, to keep subjects from fighting with readers or lying with their thoughts, Drake drugged them into unconscious submission. Readers were also drugged into a state of cooperative stupor to minimize the effects of their own subjectivity.

"Finally, after years of secret work, Drake achieved his first true success. He connected two heavily sedated people and had one retrieve a specific memory from the other. All that remained was to perfect the surgical process and work out a few remaining kinks related to biological and neurological rejection.

"Now, I'm a neuroscientist, and—not to brag—I was fairly respected in my field, so he approached me," Benjamin explained. "Drake tried to win me over with the promise of riches once he sold his invention. I refused, of course. I was horrified at the thought of it. But Drake couldn't let me walk away once I knew what he was up to, so he, umm, knocked me out. I suppose he must have slipped something in my drink, but I don't actually know for certain. I awoke a few days later in the care of Michael and Duncan—Dr. MacPherson and Dr. Connolly, that is. Saved my life, they did. Turns out, they'd been suspicious of Drake for a while. Apparently, they'd bugged my pocket calculator and overheard the whole conversation. But by the time they got me out, it was almost too late. Drake had already given me these."

Benjamin clutched his hair and pulled it loose from his head, revealing a bald scalp covered in tiny metallic dots.

Sarah gasped.

"It's a toupee," Benjamin explained, "and these are what Drake called 'reader ports.'" He replaced the wig. "Doesn't hurt or anything, but it does itch a bit." Benjamin half-smiled. "I still have nightmares filled with another man's memories. Awful stuff, that." Benjamin's eyes drifted. "No idea how much of it was him and how much I've embellished it since. Memory is a tricky thing."

He returned his gaze to Sarah. "Well anyway, Drake got away and found himself a sponsor. Les Luminaires. He's got all the funding he could want now, I expect. We know they've set up shop, and we know they're testing Drake's technique. Found a couple of his victims. We suspect they're after some of our secrets. Maybe more." He paused. "The Watcher can fill you in when he's ready."

Sarah sat stunned. This was too much to digest all at once. "So we're going to stick metal things into Blackwood's brain?" she asked, all the color drained from her face. Duke snorted and slapped his tail against the porch.

"Oh no! No, no, no. That's the beauty. We've got something Drake never dreamed of: a bit of technology we built ourselves, umm, with a bit of help from a, umm, friend, that will make this all relatively painless. Decades ahead of its time, I daresay. Maybe centuries." Benjamin leaned toward Sarah and lowered his voice. "We've built a device, you see—we call it the scanner. We'll pop Blackwood's head into it for a few seconds, and in a flash, it will take a three dimensional scan of his brain, layer by layer, making a digital blueprint, so to speak. Then, later, we'll print it out and read it."

Sarah was confused. "You'll print out the blueprint and read it?"

Benjamin laughed. "Ah, yes. Well, in a manner of speaking. We will use a different machine—another bit of Sentinel tech—that works something like a printer. But instead of putting little dots onto paper, it builds biological tissues, molecule by molecule. Absolutely fascinating. The process takes several hours, mind you, but given enough time, we can print an exact duplicate of a human brain exactly as it existed at the moment it was scanned."

"You can print a brain?" Sarah's eyes darted as the puzzle put itself together in her mind. "So that's why you had a brain in the lab!"

"Oh, you saw that, did you? Yeah, that's the printer. We were printing a test run of your granddad's brain, actually. His idea. As soon as he heard we were ready for trials, he volunteered. Him and a handful of others. We'll scan Blackwood's brain tonight, if you'll help us, and then print it. Tomorrow, when it's ready, I'll take some drugs —much milder than Drake's, thank Heaven—connect up, and have a go at reading it. Haven't had a chance to try reading a printed brain yet, but we're pretty confident it will work." Benjamin chewed on a fingernail for a moment, then said, thoughtfully, "We'll have to shock the brain to life for a moment and pray it's long enough to get what we need." He sighed. "Then again, if it doesn't work the first time, we can always print another."

Sarah felt sick. She shook her head and tried to focus. *This is for Grandpa*, she reminded herself, even if it did involve recreating the experiments of a bona-fide mad scientist.

Then a new thought struck her. She frowned. "Why are The Sentinels scanning and printing brains at all?" she asked. "I mean, we're doing this one for Grandpa, but what about the others? Why even build the machine in the first place? What are you trying to find?"

"Excellent question. Let me say for starters that we are not after anybody's memories as such. We are protectors, not spies. It is, however, helpful to have a way to find out how much an unfriendly person like Blackwood knows about us. More importantly, if Les Luminaires have the ability to read our minds when we are captured, then we must find ways to protect our secrets. This technology gives us a way to experiment and practice."

It wasn't a great answer, but it was something. She screwed up her mouth and looked at the scientist, trying to decide if he was being honest with her or not. Finally, she said, "So where do I fit into your plan?"

"Well, since we only have a moment to dig around in Blackwood's memories, it's crucial that we bring the important ones right up to the surface. If he sees you, he'll remember a number of things related to you whether he wants to or not—orders, information, plans. Then we'll scan him before he has a chance to think of much else."

Sarah wrinkled up her forehead. "How is he going to see me?" she asked. "I'm here, and he's back at Flatland Hall in the oubliette, right?"

"Ahh, no. The oubliette, well, that's another thing entirely. Physics. Quantum physics, really. Michael's and Duncan's realm. But suffice it to say, we can access Blackwood from anywhere. The oubliette isn't tied to a fixed position in space. So we'll just let him out for a bit so he sees you, and then, well, that's the easy part. Isn't it?"

IT WAS TIME. SARAH WIPED HER SWEATY PALMS ON HER PANTS AND focused on the machinery now scattered around the Alvarezes' library.

"If you don't want to go through with this, it'll be all right," Aubrey whispered. "Nobody will blame you. And I can do both parts, one at a time."

"No. I'm good," Sarah said. "Let's do this."

The lights went out. A makeshift spotlight hacked together from a truck's headlight and aluminum foil shone on the girls. Aubrey transformed to look like Grandpa Kirk, and Sarah's stomach turned over as she reminded herself that the person next her wasn't really Grandpa. She closed her eyes and tried to prepare for what she was about to do. She squeezed Aubrey's hand. It felt just like his.

"All right, now, ladies," Michael called from the other side of the room. "Are you ready?"

Sarah set her jaw and nodded her head. In a dark corner of the room, she caught the bright reflection of Duke's vigilant eyes. She felt a little better knowing he was nearby.

"Here we go then! Three. Two. One. Action!"

There was a popping sound and the room fell into darkness except where a solitary spotlight shone down on Sarah and Aubrey. Blackwood was outside of the spotlight's beam, but Sarah could just make out his face as he finished the terrified scream he had begun before he went into the oubliette. A look of confusion overtook his frightened expression and then transformed to rage as he recognized Sarah and Grandpa Kirk.

"What did you do to me?!" he bellowed and took a step toward them. The bandage on his neck glistened red.

Sarah stood her ground and tried to be brave. Everything inside her wanted to bolt, but she stood firm.

"I've got a better question." Aubrey said with Grandpa Kirk's voice. "What were you sent to do to us?"

Just then, an air gun fired, and a tranquilizer dart penetrated the uninjured side of Blackwood's neck. He slapped at the sting, but it was too late. Blackwood fell into an unconscious heap on the floor.

"Got him!" Michael shouted. "Outstanding performance, ladies!"

The lights came back on. Duke was by Sarah's side before she knew what had happened. Aubrey transformed into her familiar appearance. Benjamin and Duncan were already on the floor rolling Blackwood onto a stretcher.

"Quickly now," Michael called. "Into the scanner."

Samuel placed a hand on Sarah's shoulder. "You were very brave," he said, leading her out of the room. "You should be proud of yourself."

As they walked through the doorway and into the dining room, Sarah heard the hum of the scanner powering up behind her.

"That's all? It's over?" Sarah asked.

"Yes, little one. You were perfect."

Somehow, Sarah did not feel perfect.

15

DOUBTS & DECISIONS

Sarah lay in bed that night, unable to sleep. It had been two days—though it seemed much longer—since Grandpa Kirk had been kidnapped. The feeling that she was out of place among The Sentinels had grown from a nagging whisper in her mind, drowned out by loneliness and worry, to a roaring shout that refused to be ignored. At first, Sarah had told herself that her time with the Sentinels would be short; Grandpa would be rescued in no time, and life would go back to normal. But now she saw that, even if he returned tomorrow, "normal" as she had known it was a thing of the past. The Sentinels were part of her history and her future whether she liked it or not. What was worse: the more time passed, the less likely it was that Grandpa would ever be rescued.

Sarah forced her mind away from what might be happening to Grandpa Kirk. Instead, she thought about all that had happened in the past two days. She worried that The Sentinels were not as concerned with rescuing Grandpa as they should be. Samuel had already mentioned that they had other important missions to consider. Perhaps their other agendas were even more important to them. Benjamin had said they were stealing Blackwood's memories to find out what Les Luminaires had done with Grandpa Kirk, but what if he had lied? Blackwood knew other things The Sentinels would love to dig out of his brain. Sarah wondered if she had actually helped Grandpa or if she had simply become a pawn in these people's game. Even if they were not interested in saving Grandpa's life, what could she do about it? She was at their mercy.

Sarah rolled onto her back and stared at the dark ceiling for what felt like the hundredth time. A wave of guilt washed over her. If helping The Sentinels steal somebody's memory, even somebody as awful as Blackwood, didn't lead directly to Grandpa's rescue, she was sure she could never forgive herself.

Sarah pulled a spare pillow over her head and tried to block the noise of her own accusing thoughts. No good. She tossed the pillow aside and stared wide-eyed at nothing. Moonlight projected the shadows of breeze-blown branches through the window and played violent scenes on the walls. She closed her eyes and tried to remind herself how sleepy she felt. But she didn't feel sleepy; she felt uncomfortable. The scrapes on Sarah's knees and elbows stung. Her legs twitched. The air was too hot for a blanket and too cold to do without. She was thirsty. Aubrey's breathing was loud. She flipped over, stuck a leg off the edge of the bed, and covered her ear with an arm.

A collage of disturbing images floated uninvited through Sarah's imagination: the printed brain in the lab, Benjamin's metal-studded scalp, Grandpa Kirk falling in a heap after Mr. Litchfield hit him, Blackwood falling in much the same way after being tranquilized, the look of terror on his face when he'd emerged from the oubliette. She could still hear him screaming, "What have you done to me?!"

Ugh! she thought. *I can't take it anymore.* Careful to be as quiet as possible, Sarah pulled away the covers and tiptoed to the door. She turned the handle and pulled. The hinges creaked. Duke sat up with a jolt and looked at her. She put a finger to her lips and then waved at him to come along. He jumped up from his neon green bed and followed her into the hallway. All was dark and silent.

"I can't sleep" Sarah whispered as they crept toward the large spiral staircase that led down to the dining room. "Let's get a drink of water."

Duke nuzzled against Sarah's side, and she stopped to pet him at the top of the steps. Somewhere downstairs, a light switch flipped on.

Sarah could hear quiet voices. She put a hand on Duke's back and crouched behind the banister to listen.

"I know." It was Duncan's scratchy voice. "I thought that strange as well, but in our tests, everything has always completely stopped in there. Makes sense, really. Whatever goes in doesn't exist, so to speak, until it comes out again."

"But you are aware of Mr. Lewis's theory," Samuel's voice responded.

"More of a philosophy if you ask me. Spiritual nonsense. It can't be observed, so it can't be proven or disproven. Hardly scientific."

Duke scratched at Sarah's knee. She pushed his paw away and craned her neck further into the stairway.

"But if he is correct," Samuel continued, "then perhaps it is possible to perceive—"

"Yes, I see where you're going. Maybe. Though, it doesn't fit the mathematical model we've been using, and again, I can't imagine how we'd prove it."

"Perhaps when Dr. Allen has had a chance to perform the reading?"

"Perhaps. But I doubt it. Since there's no space, there's no matter and no movement. The neurons wouldn't fire, and—"

"Ahh, but if some level of perception exists beyond the physical bounds, then a memory could, in theory, be carried over long enough to be recorded afterward?"

"I suppose it's possible."

Duke grabbed the hem of Sarah's pajama shirt and tugged her toward the bedroom. She ignored him.

"Please have Dr. Allen report his findings regarding this question."

"Yes, sir. He's off getting some beauty sleep now, or at least, he ought to be, so I'll have a chat with him in the morning."

"Very well. When do you expect your team will be ready?"

"Dr. MacPherson is loading the data into the printer now. Process should be complete some time tomorrow afternoon. Then we'll have a bit of prep work to do, and, of course, Dr. Allen will need to be sedated. I'd say, barring any complications, we'll be ready to give it a go by eight o'clock tomorrow evening."

Duke rounded to the top of the stairs and pushed Sarah toward the bedroom with his head. She swatted at him and planted her feet into the carpet.

"I must tell you, this experiment makes me quite uncomfortable. Are you confident it will work?" Samuel asked.

"Well, to be honest," Duncan replied, "no. But Dr. Allen is convinced. Or at least, he's convinced it's worth the risk. I tell you, he's been a man on a mission since they took Bo—I mean Mr. Kirk—and I think meeting the young lass put him right over the top. I haven't seen him this riled up since we came to the States."

Duke jammed his head beneath Sarah's torso and pushed her to a stand, surprising her with his strength.

"Okay!" she whispered. "Just a sec!"

Duke froze, ears and tail at attention. Sarah realized she could no longer hear anybody speaking. She held her breath.

"Miss Sarah," Samuel's voice called. "If you are determined not to sleep, then please, join us." After a moment, he added, "Duke, we would be honored by your company as well."

Duke's head fell and he let out a snort before trotting down the stairs. Sarah followed a few paces behind.

"Trouble sleeping, lassie?" Duncan asked with a sly grin when she entered the dining room. He was seated at the far end of the long dining table near a set of windows that would face the sunrise in a few hours. Samuel leaned against a wall near the archway that led to the kitchen.

"Yes, sir," Sarah replied with the steadiest voice she could manage. "I was thirsty." She pulled up a chair at the closer end of the table and sat down. Duke curled up on the floor next to her.

Samuel smiled. "And I would imagine there is much on your mind. Milk?"

"Yes, please."

Samuel bowed and disappeared into the dark kitchen.

"Well," said Duncan, "I'd better be off to bed. It's been a long day, and tomorrow will be long again. Goodnight, Miss Sarah. Duke." He stood and left.

Samuel returned a moment later with a glass of milk and a plate of pastries. "Mrs. Alvarez baked these. I do not remember what she called them, but there is chocolate in the middle." He squatted into a chair that was too small for his towering frame and scooted near the table.

Sarah took a pastry and thanked him.

"Now, tell me, little one, what is bothering you?"

"It's nothing," Sarah replied, avoiding his eyes. "I just needed a drink."

"Nothing?" Samuel pressed. "You are not at all lonely? Sad? Worried about your grandfather? Perhaps a little afraid?"

Sarah said nothing.

"You were very brave tonight when you faced Mr. Blackwood, but perhaps it disturbs your peace now?"

"Maybe," Sarah admitted.

"Does he frighten you?"

"No! Well, a little, but that's not it."

"What is it, then?"

Sarah looked down at Duke. He wagged his tail and nosed her leg. She took a deep breath and forced herself to face Samuel. "It's just, well," she struggled to find the right words. "Two days ago, my entire world was just me, Grandpa, and Duke. Things were weird, yeah—I knew something was going on—but I didn't care. Not really. We were going to leave town, and it wasn't going to matter anymore. I'd never heard of The Sentinels or Les Luminaires. If someone had told me there were dwarves and talking animals and whatever Tellurak is," she almost smiled, "living all around me, I would have thought they were crazy. But now, here I am, with you and a bunch of strangers, hundreds of miles from home…" Sarah could feel tears welling up. "And Grandpa's who-knows-where. I don't even want to think what they might be doing to him.." Her voice faltered. "And I'm useless! I asked to help, and all I was allowed to do was stand there while you people stole his memories. And you didn't even need me for that, did you? Aubrey could have done it on her own. You just wanted me to feel like I was helping. I hate this! I just want my Grandpa back!" A sob escaped from Sarah's lungs, but as soon as it was out, she caught her breath and clenched her fists.

She sniffed. "And I don't want to sit around and wait while Grandpa's in danger. I can't!" She could no longer hide the panic in her voice. "What if I never see him again, and all I did to help was what I did tonight?! It's not enough! What if Blackwood doesn't know anything? What if Benjamin can't read anything in that printed brain? What if it takes too long, and by the time you find out where they took him, it's too late? Don't you understand? It's my fault he was alone in the house when they came, and it'll be my fault if he dies. My fault!" Sarah buried her face in her arms on the table and shook with sobs. "I have to get him back!" she squeaked when she caught her breath.

Duke put his head in Sarah's lap and whimpered.

Samuel was quiet for a time. Then he crossed the room and knelt next to her. He took both of Sarah's hands in one of his, and he stroked her hair with the other. In a gentle voice, he said, "Be at peace. Hush now. Hush. Breathe. Good. Now, look at me, little one."

Sarah sniffed and looked up.

"Miss Sarah," Samuel said. "Listen to me. Sometimes horrible things happen, and though it is painful, there is nothing we can do about it. Tragedy and suffering are part of life, especially for those of us who spend our lives protecting others, like your parents and your grandparents. You can neither escape this nor control it." He smiled at her. "Ah, Miss Sarah. You are so much like your father. You are not one to simply let life happen to you. And when you discover that circumstances are beyond your control, you feel helpless and small, just as your father did when your mother died. So you make it your fault, just as he did. You blame yourself, little one, because, like him, you cannot accept a scenario in which there was nothing you could have done to make things better. It almost destroyed him, and if you are not careful, it will destroy you. So I will tell you what I told him: you must accept what is and choose what you will do next. That is all you can do. Of course, you may choose to do nothing, and nothing will be the thing that you choose to do. But it is not in your character to do nothing. Is it?"

Sarah wiped her eyes and shook her head.

"Sometimes the best, the most helpful thing you can do is the very thing that makes you feel the most helpless: trust others to do what you cannot accomplish yourself. This is difficult, but it is true."

Sarah stifled a sob.

"At other times," Samuel continued, "you will need to act, to take risks, to be cunning, to make the right decision. But always you must trust others, and always you must work to gain trust through compassion, courage, and wisdom. Trust is necessary. It is only for you to decide whom you will trust." He pulled Sarah's hands close and looked into her eyes. "But blaming yourself will help no one. None of this is your fault."

Sarah pulled her hands away from Samuel and wiped her eyes. She sat up straight and took a deep breath. "Okay," she said, "but there has to be something else I can do to help. Please. If you're really trying to find him, let me help. I am a pretty good spy, you know. I mean, I managed to get into your lab, didn't I?" She managed a half-smile. When she saw that Samuel did not return her smile, she sighed and laid her head on her arms, folded on the table.

"Please understand," he said. "I do not begrudge you the opportunity to help. But I am under certain obligations to protect you. I promised your parents that, until you were old enough to…" He did not finish the sentence.

"To what?" Sarah asked.

Samuel looked at her thoughtfully but did not answer.

"There has to be *something* I can do," she repeated. "Please!"

Samuel paused for a long moment. Then he stood and began to pace. Finally, he faced her and spoke. "Very well, Miss Sarah. You wish to do more, do you? To be more involved? To risk your own safety to protect another?"

Sarah looked up at him and nodded, her eyes full of hope.

"Then I set before you a choice: You may either continue as you have and I will do all I can keep you safe, or," he took a breath, "you may join The Sentinels. Now. As a junior agent, of course, but with all the responsibilities and privileges that position entails."

Duke sat up, his ears perked.

Samuel gave Duke a meaningful glance and then sat down in the chair next to Sarah. "As your godfather, little one, my primary responsibility is to your safety. However, if you became an agent of The Sentinels, our relationship would change. I could allow you to be a bit more involved." Then, as if speaking to himself, he looked at the ceiling and said, "Your parents expected you to join someday, and nobody placed a restriction on when that could happen." He took a long, deep breath. Then he looked back into Sarah's eyes and continued. "I would still be your godfather, and I would still protect you. Always. But you would have to take orders. You would not be obligated to approve of every decision that is made, of course, but you would no longer have the freedom to complain and argue."

Sarah blinked at him.

"If you choose to join, your training will begin immediately following an oath ceremony in which you must promise to trust and obey your superiors without question, take our secrets to your grave, and dedicate your life to our mission and to those whom we are sworn to protect. Do you understand?"

Sarah nodded, but her mind was dizzy with questions.

"Good. I will give you tonight to consider, but I must have an answer in the morning. If we are to accomplish any training before our next move, we must begin right away. Now, off to bed."

Sarah stood and followed Duke to the stairs, half in a daze.

Samuel collected the dishes from the table and then called to her before she started up the steps. "Join us or do not. Trust me or do not. You—and only you—must choose your next step. But whatever you choose, do not give in to fear or guilt, little one. Do not let this beat you. You may not be strong enough or influential enough to change things outside yourself, but you are absolutely human enough to take your eyes off of yourself, rise above your pride and your fear, and do whatever good is within your reach."

16

A NEW DAY

THE FIRST RAYS OF SUNSHINE CREPT OVER THE EASTERN HORIZON, illuminating the bedroom window. Sarah sat up and stretched. Aubrey (hidden beneath her sheets) and Duke (whose tail stretched around the foot of the bed) were still asleep. But Sarah was wide awake. There was no way she had slept enough, but she was too excited and too nervous now to feel it.

Careful not to wake Aubrey and Duke, Sarah pulled her backpack from the floor and extracted her mother's diary. One day, she would read it all, page by page, savoring the sweet sound of her mother's voice in her mind, but right now, she only had a few minutes. Sarah had a decision to make, and she hoped to find some direction between the covers of this book—words of advice from the person she had loved and trusted most in the world.

She skimmed the first few pages. School stuff. Boys. Drama with a girl from class. Lots of silly little pictures drawn in the margins. She skipped ahead to an entry near the end of the diary. This one was from 1974—a year before Sarah was born. Her parents were still newly married when Sarah's mom wrote these rambling, sappy paragraphs about being young and in love, and scribbled all these hearts and flowers. Sarah pretended to gag and flipped to the diary's middle.

The page she landed on next mentioned Samuel. July 13, 1971. Her mother would have been eighteen. In the top right corner she had drawn a little eagle. Sarah stopped and read it.

Dad and I met Samuel at the Eagle and Child pub in Oxford today. I wish Mom could have been with us. She would have loved every minute.

It was strange seeing Samuel again. Dad's stories make him sound larger than life, like a warrior giant out of some medieval legend. But to me, Samuel is still the polite, gentle giant who stayed with us once when I was a little girl and told me "true" fairy tales at bedtime. He looks exactly the same. Now that I'm grown and officially an agent, I suppose I should call him the Watcher like the rest of The Sentinels do, but he's always been Samuel to me, and it wouldn't feel right to call him anything else.

Of course, the conversation turned to work. So much for being on vacation. Apparently, there's some trouble with a group of aenimos halfies that live in a wood near Guildford who've been seen by some of the locals. It sounds like the concealment team here has got their work cut out for them.

Tomorrow, Dad and I will be visiting a few spots around London. We're going to some place called Guildhall to see some statues. Dad has a story he wants to tell me about them. Something to do with Samuel, I think. I am not looking forward to it, but as long as Dad doesn't try to make me taste blood pudding or spotted dick again, I'll put on a smile and try to enjoy myself.

All in all, it's been a nice trip. I wish we could stay longer, but it will be good to get back to work. I hope Susan hasn't finished the Pukwudgie report without me.

This was not the helpful advice Sarah had hoped for. She sighed and turned to the previous entry. It had been written more than a year before, and there was no mention of the Sentinels. She thumbed through a few more pages, moving back in time. All were bordered by doodles and filled with nothings about high school life. There was no entry from the day Sarah's mom had joined the Sentinels. Sarah skimmed several entries in the second half of the diary. While most of these mentioned The Sentinels, none contained the sorts of details she needed. There were no professions of adoration or hints of suspicion that would help Sarah make her decision.

She closed the book and slipped it into her backpack. This was not going to be as easy as she had hoped. She stared at the ceiling for a moment and then dug in her bag for a pen and her new empty diary. She opened it to the first page, wrote the date in the corner, and tried to list all of the questions she wanted answered before she could pledge herself to The Sentinels. It didn't take long to see that the list would be surprisingly short, and she realized that, as strange as it was, there was a part of her that really wanted to join.

Sarah scolded herself for being silly. Of course she wanted to be a "secret agent," even if all that meant was that she was a junior level nobody in a secret organization. It was the sort of thing she'd daydreamed about and pretended for years. She told herself that real agent work would be hard and way less exciting than her fantasies. Then again, it was the only way she could make a difference in the search for Grandpa Kirk. She wondered what he would think. Surely, he wouldn't approve. Or would he? Grandpa had believed strongly enough in these people and their mission to commit his own life to The Sentinels, after all. But would he want her to do the same?

A few minutes later, Sarah finished her list and closed the diary. She thought about waking Aubrey to ask her a couple of questions, but then she decided that waking a shape-shifting spy was a bad idea. Besides, Sarah thought, Aubrey would be biased. She was thrilled to be on her first assignment, and she adored Samuel. Sarah sighed and laughed at her own hypocrisy when she realized that she considered Aubrey, who was several years older than herself, to be too young and naive to ask.

Duke sat up, yawned, and stretched. Sarah scooted toward the wall, and he hopped up onto the bed beside her.

"If you could talk, you would tell me what to do, wouldn't you, boy?"

Duke gave her a funny look and then turned a circle and curled up with his head in her lap.

"No. I'm sure you wouldn't. That would be too easy." Sarah brushed her fingers through his thick white fur and moaned. "How am I supposed to decide with nobody to talk to?"

Duke lifted his head and thrust his nose into Sarah's sternum.

Sarah blinked at him, puzzled.

Duke's mouth opened into something like a smile. Then he poked her with his snout again.

"Wait. You understand me, don't you, boy? I guess I could run some of these questions past you. Would you mind?"

His tongue fell out to one side, and his tail wagged and thumped against the mattress.

"Oh gosh, that would be great! I don't know how we're going to do this, but I could sure use the help." She thought for a second. "Maybe you could bark or something."

Duke looked at Aubrey and whimpered.

"Oh, you're right," Sarah said, careful to keep her voice low. "Better not." She closed her eyes and tapped her forehead. "How about scratching? Can you do that?"

Duke pawed at the blanket in response.

"Great! One scratch for 'yes,' two for 'no'?"

Scratch.

Sarah picked up her diary and scanned the list of questions. "Ugh. Most of these are not yes or no questions. Hmm."

Aubrey rolled over. She was still asleep, but her head came out from beneath the covers, and Sarah saw her for the first time that morning. Her hair was a tangled red mess, her skin was pale and freckled, and she was drooling.

Sarah gasped. "Why does she look like me?"

Duke did not reply.

After a moment's thought, Sarah decided maybe she didn't want to know after all, so she changed the subject. "That isn't really what I look like when I'm sleeping, is it?"

Scratch.

Sarah shuddered. "Except I don't drool, right?"

Duke cocked his head to one side and scratched once.

"Was that a 'yes,' you agree that I don't drool, or a 'yes,' I do drool?"

Duke scratched one more time and then covered his face with his paws, snuffling in a way that sounded a lot like laughing. Sarah hit him with a pillow. Duke sat up and licked her face.

"Stop it!" Sarah giggled. "That tickles. You're going to make me wake Aubrey."

Duke nuzzled Sarah's shoulder and then sat and pawed at the notebook.

"Right," Sarah said and picked it up. "Back to business," She twisted up her mouth and stared at the page for another minute. "All right," she said at last. "Let's start with Aubrey. What do you think? I mean, *this* is creepy," she gestured toward her drooling doppelgänger, "but she has been pretty nice to me the past couple of days. And I guess she was only trying to protect me before that. Can I really trust her? Do you?"

Scratch.

"I guess that's good enough for me, then." She wrote a D (for Duke) next to Aubrey's name in the diary. "And Samuel. Is he telling me everything?"

Scratch, scratch.

"No. Of course he isn't. Then again, I don't think Samuel tells *anybody* the whole story." She considered this for a few seconds. "But I guess I don't have to know everything to trust him. So? Do you?"

Duke scratched once, an emphatic look in his eyes.

"All right. Got it." She wrote another D in the diary. "Here's a better question: If I join, am I going to wish I hadn't?"

Nothing.

"I mean, do you think they'll ask me to do things I won't want to do?"

Scratch.

Sarah frowned. "Are they doing bad things?"

Scratch, scratch.

Sarah looked back at the window. All was bright now. Through a gap in the curtain, she could make out the truck she had ridden in yesterday. She remembered how cramped and dark the smuggler's compartment had been, but she also remembered the pillows and the brisket sandwiches she had been given to make the ride more comfortable. She remembered being greeted by friendly faces and delicious smells when they arrived in San Antonio, but she also remembered with frustration that she hadn't even known they were going to San Antonio until they arrived. Something twisted in Sarah's chest.

"So should I join or not?" she blurted and rubbed her temples. "Just tell me what to do! Please."

Duke didn't move. He only stared at her with big, comforting eyes.

"Come on, Duke. You've got to give me something. I have to make a decision this morning, and I don't have anybody else I trust besides you."

Duke pushed his nose into Sarah's chest again, and this time she understood. He was telling her to trust herself.

Samuel sat at the small desk in Mr. Alvarez's study. His legs did not fit beneath it, so he sat sideways in the high backed, leather, swiveling chair, his knees visible above the top.

"Have you considered my offer?" he asked.

"Yes sir, but if it's all right, I have a few questions before I decide."

"Certainly. If you had made your decision without first asking questions, I would be concerned." He grinned.

Sarah opened her diary and started with the first question. "What is the point of The Sentinels? I mean, what do you do?"

"Excellent question, little one. You have seen already that there are more sorts of intelligent creatures on this planet than you had ever imagined. Their wellbeing is our mission. The word "sentinel" refers to a guard or a watcher. And that is what we do—we guard and watch out for those who live on this Earth but have otherworldly ancestors. We ensure peace and safety as best as we are able."

"By keeping them secret from people like me?" Sarah asked with a hint of sarcasm.

"Yes. Indeed, that has been a vital part of our strategy from the beginning."

"Why?"

Samuel sighed. "The answer to that question is long and complicated. I will summarize. Do you remember when I told you at Flatland Hall that there was a time when otherworlders traveled freely between this realm and their home worlds?"

"Yeah. And when I asked what happened, you just said 'humans.'"

"Correct. Things became hostile. There were wars and death on all sides. In the end, it was the humans who, with some aid, forced out their enemies. They locked the doors between realms and allowed only a remnant of peaceful otherworlders to remain. But even after many years had passed, there was still unrest between humans and non-humans. Battles were still fought. Many died. And it was humans—your ancestors, Miss Sarah—who made the decision to keep my people and Aubrey's and all the others hidden from humanity for the sake of peace. We have worked to honor that decision ever since."

"But why were they fighting?"

"Many reasons. Control. Power. Fear, mostly."

Sarah nodded.

"What else?"

Sarah looked back at her list of questions and considered which to ask next. Finally, she asked in a serious tone, "Why are The Sentinels stealing memories."

Samuel furrowed his brow. After a moment, he said, "It is not our objective to steal memories at all. We have been in the business of obscuring memories for as long as we have existed, for the protection of our secrecy, but we have never sought to obtain the thoughts or memories of others. We did not seek this technology. It came to us through a message from Desjardins to Dr. Allen. He, of course, has been opposed to its use except as a means of discovering ways to defend our own memories from others. I wholeheartedly agree with him. There are, I admit, some in our organization who would use it aggressively, albeit with the best of intentions. So far, however, the technology and its use have been contained within our scientific special task group, and it has only ever been used for research purposes. That is, until today. Dr. Allen will read Mr. Blackwood's memory in hope that we might locate and rescue your grandfather with information he will obtain. I was reluctant to allow it. However, since this is a rescue mission, and since Mr. Blackwood will not be harmed, I have allowed it. I am hopeful that it will, indeed, help us find your grandfather."

The answer was as good as Sarah could have hoped for. Samuel seemed to be sincere and honest. His story lined up with Benjamin's, and if it was true, it meant that The Sentinels were not the memory thieves Sarah had imagined them to be.

"Okay," she said, "last question." She took a deep breath and gathered her courage. "Did you send my dad away last year?"

Compassion filled Samuel's eyes. He reached across the desk and took Sarah's hands. Then, looking straight at her, he said, "No. That was all your father's plan. I advised against it, but he thought this was the best way to protect you and the secrets he holds. I did not have the authority to restrain him. I did, however, agree to look after you in his absence, and I helped to coordinate his escape."

Escape? What was he running from? And why didn't Samuel have authority to stop him? What did it mean? Was her father in danger? A thousand questions flooded Sarah's mind, and panic rose in her chest.

Samuel must have sensed her thoughts. "Your father is neither dead nor in captivity," he said. "More than that I cannot tell you. It is a matter of security. If you take the oaths and join, I will be able to tell you more about what has happened until now, but even then, I will not be at liberty to share his whereabouts or future plans."

Sarah did not hesitate. "I'm in. When is this ceremony?"

"Miss Sarah, are you certain that—"

"Yes." Sarah took a deep breath. "Look. Yeah, I'm curious about my dad. And no, I still don't know if I really trust The Sentinels. But I know my family did. Does. And I know Duke does. So I'll try. And anyway, this is the only way I'm going to get to help at all. So yeah. I'm in. What do I do?"

17

SECRET AGENT

"The sacred duty of The Sentinels of God is," Samuel began.

All those in attendance—Aubrey, the three scientists, Boarsmash, Bonk, Tellurak, two dwarves Sarah recognized from Flatland hall but had not met, and Mr. and Mrs. Alvarez—chanted the next words back to him, "to watch over the peoples of the seven realms, to discover and preserve our mutual history, and to ensure lasting peace." Duke, who sat beside Aubrey, wore an expression of dignity and barked his agreement.

"The pillars upon which this peace stands are," Samuel continued.

"Secrecy, serenity, and trust," the small crowd replied.

"A true Sentinel is marked by," said Samuel.

"Courage, compassion, valor, and wisdom," they replied.

"Today, I present Miss Sarah Ann Lewis. I nominate her for acceptance into our society as a junior agent. If anyone among you knows of anything that would disqualify or discredit Miss Sarah, please speak it now."

There was a long, uncomfortable silence as every eye in the room stared at her. Sarah, who stood near the fireplace next to Samuel, felt her cheeks redden. The cutoff shorts and *Punky Brewster* tee shirt she wore now seemed embarrassing and inappropriate. She glanced at Aubrey and Duke, hoping for a reassuring smile, but their faces were solemn and silent like the others. Even Boarsmash did not break his stern expression when she met his eyes. Sarah looked down at her shoes and tried to ignore the tightening sensation in her stomach. She wanted to run. But no; she had made up her mind. She clamped her teeth together and stared back into the faces of the crowd.

Finally, Samuel broke the silence. Turning to Sarah, he said, "Since there are no objections, I ask you to consider these oaths. They are sacred, and you must not take them lightly. If you wish to change your mind, this is your opportunity." He paused dramatically and then began the oaths. "Do you vow, Miss Sarah Ann Lewis, to join The Sentinels in our solemn duty to watch over the peoples of the seven realms, to discover and preserve our mutual history, and to ensure lasting peace?"

Sarah nodded, then, seeing the look on Samuel's face, cleared her throat and said, "Yes, sir."

Samuel smiled. "And do you promise to join us in upholding the pillars of peace for those we protect, to fight with us for their secrecy, serenity, and trust?"

"Yes, sir."

"Finally, do you swear to strive to exemplify the characteristics that define a true Sentinel: courage, compassion, valor, and wisdom?"

"Yes, sir," Sarah repeated.

"Hold up your right hand. Good. Place your ring finger to your thumb, like this. Yes. This is the sign of The Sentinels. It means peace and respect for all. It is the sign of the number seven, representing the seven realms. It is a symbol of blessing passed down through the ages upon those who strive to uphold peace. Place it over your heart and repeat after me: I pledge my life…"

"I pledge my life…" Sarah repeated.

"To the good and noble cause of The Sentinels of God."

Sarah repeated every line Samuel spoke.

"From this day forth…I will honor our traditions…and protect our secrets…so help me God…I promise to obey my superiors without objection…to respect my fellows without condition…and to keep our secrets for as long as I shall live."

"Upon that pledge of good faith, Miss Sarah, it is my great honor to welcome you into the company of The Sentinels. Please kneel."

Sarah lowered herself onto one knee. She had never knelt before, and it felt awkward. She wondered if someone would touch her shoulder with a sword like she had seen on TV.

"Sentinels," Samuel said, "please welcome our newest agent."

As one, they stood, threw their right hands into the air, ring fingers touched to thumbs, swept their hands across their chests to cover their hearts, and bowed.

Sarah's heart leapt, though she did not understand why. She started to stand, but Samuel touched her shoulder, and she stayed put.

"You may now bestow your blessings," Samuel said to the guests.

One by one, starting with Mr. and Mrs. Alvarez, they each crossed the room, stopped in front of Sarah, put a hand on her head for a few seconds, and then left. A few of them laid objects at her feet. Aubrey left an old wooden handled pocket knife which, Sarah discovered later, had belonged to Aubrey's grandfather. Aubrey's father had inherited it from him and blessed her with it when she took the oaths. Now she was passing it on to Sarah, saying that she knew Sarah had lost the pocket knife Grandpa Kirk had given her. Benjamin left a shard of charred, sparkling, metallic rock with a tag tied to it that read "L-421: Luxephorean Alloy." Boarsmash left a large shale arrowhead. When she asked him about it later, he told her he had found it while excavating new tunnels near Grandpa Kirk's house and he hoped it would remind her of home. Samuel left his enormous hand on her head for what seemed like a very long time. Then he bowed before her, laid down a simple wooden box, and whispered that she should open it when she was alone. Finally, when everyone else was gone, Duke approached, put a paw on her head, and dropped a slobbery golden key from his mouth onto the floor. Unlike the others, Duke did not leave. Instead, he sat patiently while Sarah examined her gifts. The key, she noticed, was familiar. She was sure she had seen it before.

"This looks like the key Mr. Smith gave me for the trunk," she said. "Did you take it from my suitcase?"

Duke scratched once on the floor, turned toward the door, and barked.

"All right, I'm coming."

Sarah put her other gifts into her suitcase before she unlocked and opened the old trunk. Its contents were toppled and disarrayed from the journey. Duke poked his head inside, removed the cedar jewelry box, and laid it gently on the floor. E.A.L. was engraved into a silver placard on the top in a flowing script. The silver ring Sarah wore on her index finger—set with a strange color-changing pearl that was now a dark shade of blue—had come from within this box, and she remembered that a set of earrings remained inside. She looked at Duke with a puzzled expression.

"It's just some old earrings," she said. "They were my mom's."

Duke barked.

Sarah didn't usually wear jewelry, and she certainly wasn't likely to wear keepsakes like these except, perhaps, on special occasions.

Duke nudged her and made a whimpering noise.

Sarah opened the box. The blue jewels seemed luminescent in the silver stud settings. She looked at Duke. "You know," she said, "if you wanted me to wear these, you should have told me *before* the ceremony. I could have put on something nice too, made myself presentable."

Duke barked again and wagged his tail.

Sarah pulled the earrings from the black fabric folds that held them. Something hung and then came loose. The backs were heavier and bulkier than she expected. A thin, clear, curved piece of something like flexible glass was attached to each. She turned them over, examined them for a moment, and wondered what they were. She pulled a stud from its back, and the blue jewel seemed to darken a bit. She reconnected it. The jewel brightened. "Look Duke," she said, "I think they're electric or something."

In response, Duke shook his head so that his collar jingled. Among the usual tags, a silver ornament hung with a blue stone at its center. It looked very much like the jewels set into the earrings Sarah now held in her hands. She had spent some time looking at the ornament on Duke's collar the day Grandpa brought him home, but she had not thought about it much since then. Now she saw that it seemed to glow as well.

Sarah pulled both earrings apart and put one into the hole in her right earlobe. She pushed the backing onto the post and adjusted it until the curved piece rested against the back of her ear. A faint humming noise filled her mind from somewhere on her right. Duke jumped and shook his back end like an excited puppy. Sarah clasped the other earring onto her left earlobe, pressed the clear piece to the back of her ear, and noticed that the humming sound now surrounded her. "Okay Duke, what is this about?" she asked.

Duke sat still with his eyes closed and wiggled his jaw as if chewing a piece of rubber. Suddenly, Sarah heard a robotic, monotone voice that seemed to come from within her own head. "HELLO, SARAH."

"No way!" Sarah exclaimed.

Duke continued the chewing motion. "YES WAY." There was a brief pause. "SECRET."

Sarah smiled so widely that her cheeks hurt. "This is rad! Though, it would have been nice if you'd shown me this before our barking and scratching session this morning."

"SECRET," Duke repeated.

"What do you mean, secret?" she asked.

"TOO LONG." Pause. "ASK WATCHER." Another minute of silence passed while Duke moved his mouth. "DO NOT TELL OTHERS."

Sarah descended the stairs, followed by Duke. In the kitchen, Samuel, Mr. and Mrs. Alvarez, Aubrey, and Michael were having a hushed discussion. They stopped talking as soon as Sarah entered. Michael looked away awkwardly.

Mrs. Alvarez crossed the room with a beaming smile stretched across her round face. "Ahh, chiquita," she said, "we are so happy for you!" She pulled Sarah into a tight hug. "Now, let me get you some food. You haven't had breakfast yet, and you're going to miss lunch. Samuel was just telling us what a long day of training you have ahead of you."

Samuel. Apparently, Mrs. Alvarez didn't call him "the Watcher" either.

"Do you like migas?" Mrs. Alvarez asked.

Sarah was not sure what migas were, but she was too preoccupied to care. "Uhh, sure. I mean, yes, ma'am. Thank you."

Mr. Alvarez sat with his elbows propped on the table, massaging his forehead with one hand. Michael conspicuously flipped through the pages of a notepad. Aubrey glared at him, her arms folded. Only Samuel seemed to be relaxed. He wore a contented smile and leaned back in a chair that was much too small for him.

"Aubrey, querida, you should eat too," said Mrs. Alvarez, "Migas?"

"Yes, please," Aubrey replied. Her tone was flat, and she did not take her eyes off of Michael.

"Come, little one," Samuel said to Sarah, still smiling. "Sit with us."

Sarah found a chair and sat down. Duke followed and sat on the floor next to her, his eyes fixed on Samuel. Sarah petted the dog's neck and glanced around the room.

A strange look of understanding crossed Samuel's face, and his eyes shifted between Sarah and Duke. "Yes, very good," he said to himself.

"Could we go talk now for a few minutes?" Sarah asked Samuel. "About Grandpa, I mean. And my dad."

"Perhaps there will be a little time after you have eaten. But as Mrs. Alvarez mentioned, you have a busy day ahead of you. Under normal circumstances, a new recruit would work through a much longer and more formal training process. However, since we are on assignment, we must improvise." He glanced toward Michael who stuffed the notepad into his pocket, sighed, and forced a smile at Sarah. Aubrey relaxed a little.

"We do not yet know what tomorrow will bring, so we have planned only for today. Here." He slid a piece of paper across the table to Sarah. "Your first lesson will be self defense with Miss Aubrey. She is very skilled. Learn all you can from her. At three o'clock, you will meet Mr. Boarsmash in the basement. He is quite fond of you, and I have given him permission to share some of his historical knowledge of The Sentinels. I believe he is preparing his lesson now."

Sarah saw a smile force its way onto Aubrey's face.

"At four-thirty," Samuel continued, "Dr. MacPherson will give you an introductory science lesson in the library. I warn you that this will not be the sort of textbook lesson you may have received in public school. Dinner will be ready at six thirty. Afterward, I have set aside the remainder of my evening to spend with you. There is much that I must explain, and—"

Samuel stopped and cocked his head to one side. Quick footsteps approached from the hallway. All heads turned to see who was coming. A moment later, Duncan entered. As soon as Michael saw the look on Duncan's face, he hurried off.

"Sir," Duncan said to Samuel with urgency in his gruff voice, "there's something you'll be wanting to see right away."

"Thank you, Dr. Connolly." Samuel lowered his head in a quick bow and then stood and walked toward the hallway. Before he left, though, he turned back to Sarah and said, "I am sorry, little one. Work hard. I will see you at dinner, and then we will talk."

18

THE MAKING OF AN ESCAPE ARTIST

"What was all that about?" Sarah asked as she followed Aubrey across the lawn. She was hauling a huge duffle bag Aubrey had given her and having a hard time keeping up. Duke trotted beside her, tail wagging and tongue out.

"What was what?" Aubrey asked as if nothing had happened.

"You know, when Duncan—"

"Dr. Connolly."

"Huh?"

"It's *Dr. Connolly* now that you're an agent, Miss Sarah."

"Oh," said Sarah, taken aback by the sudden formality. "Right. So. Dr. Connolly seemed upset about something. What happened?"

"No idea," Aubrey answered and shrugged.

"Do you think, I mean, everybody's all right, aren't they?"

Aubrey brushed the hair from in front of her eyes. "I really don't know. Could be anything."

"Do you think it's about Grandpa?"

Aubrey shrugged.

"Are you mad at me?" Sarah asked after they had walked a bit farther.

"Huh? Oh. Nah. I'm fine. I'm certainly not upset with *you*."

"Oh. Good." Sarah heaved the bag higher onto her shoulder. She had fallen a few steps behind Aubrey and jogged to catch up. "You didn't seem very happy with Michael—" she caught herself, "I mean, Dr. MacPherson earlier."

Aubrey grunted a contemptuous little laugh and walked even faster.

"Well? What happened?"

"We had a disagreement, but it doesn't matter." Aubrey sighed. "You should ask him about it when you get to your science lesson this afternoon." Then, in a sarcastic tone, she added, "I wouldn't want to put words in his mouth."

Duke barked and ran ahead, bounded over a fallen limb, and disappeared into a thicket of stubby trees.

Aubrey stopped, inhaled a lungful of fresh air through her nose, and exhaled a sigh that sounded much happier. "Ahh. We're almost there," she said. "Come on."

Sarah followed Aubrey through the trees where Duke had gone. They descended a winding stairway of pitted rocks that opened into a flat bottomed basin. The place was walled in by rocky slopes overgrown with unkempt oak trees and brush. Several boulders were strewn around the dirt floor. To one side, two thick stumps stood near a felled tree trunk. It had been stripped bare and laid between the stumps so that the arrangement reminded Sarah of a couch with a pair of end tables.

"All right. Sit down over there. Let's get you fitted out," Aubrey said and motioned toward the couch-log. They crossed the clearing, and Sarah sat, dropping the duffle bag at her feet. Aubrey unzipped the bag and pulled out a padded helmet. "Here's your headgear. It goes on like this," she said, "and buckles here." She handed it over and watched as Sarah lifted it onto her head. "Oh wait. You'll want to take those earrings out first. And lose the ring. No jewelry. Wouldn't want it to get caught on anything. You could tear an earlobe."

Sarah glanced at Duke who nodded at her from the end of the log. She turned her head to one side and then the other so that Aubrey could not see the earrings as she removed them and dropped them into a pocket on the side of the duffle bag along with the color-changing pearl ring, now scarlet with a midnight blue streak along one side. "Can I ask you a question?" she asked.

"Sure."

"What's up with all the *Dr. This* and *Miss That* stuff?"

"It's the Watcher's thing," Aubrey replied. "He says that we all tend to think more highly of people who are like ourselves and less of people who are different, especially when they're *really* different, even if we don't mean to. So the Watcher likes for us to be extra respectful to everybody, especially other Sentinels. The titles are just part of it, but he's pretty insistent about it. Best to get into the habit. Fred thinks it's stupid and old fashioned, but he's not about to argue with the Watcher. I don't mind so much. I think it's kind of nice."

"But what about Duke?" Sarah asked in a strained voice as she squeezed her head into the padded headgear. "Why is he just *Duke* and not *Mr. Duke*?"

"Apparently, Duke won't allow it, and even the Watcher won't overrule Duke the Ancient. I suspect it's because he's, well, he's a dog. If outsiders heard us treating him with too much awe and respect, they'd have a hard time forgetting it, and sometimes we need people to forget things. But that's just my theory."

Duke barked.

Aubrey giggled. "Does that mean I'm right?" she asked.

Duke wagged his tail in response. Then he bounced around in the leaves, digging and playing before he finally laid down.

Sarah worked to tighten the chin strap. "And why do you say *the Watcher* instead of *Mr. Bin-Per-whatever-his-name-is*?"

"Ha! Because that's what he *is*."

"What do you mean?"

"He's...well..." Aubrey began. "No. You know what? You can ask him yourself tonight. Right now, we have work to do."

Aubrey removed a few more items from the bag and shoved them into Sarah's lap. "Gloves. Shin guards. Elbow pads. Rib guard. We might need to adjust these a little. And here." She handed Sarah a thick, black foam pad with a leather belt threaded through roughly cut holes near the top. Two smaller belts hung from similar holes at the bottom. "When I was learning, this saved my butt more than once. Literally. Here, let me help you." They both stood. Aubrey buckled the larger belt around Sarah's waist, leaving the foam pad to hang over her rear end, and then strapped a smaller belt around each of Sarah's thighs.

"Okay, so now that I'm dressed like a punching bag, what are you going to do to me?" Sarah asked, laughing.

Aubrey laughed and attached a shin guard to Sarah's left leg. "We'll start with the basics. You need to know just enough so that, if we run into danger, you'll have a fighting chance at getting away. No real combat, just ways to get out of bad situations. Most of it comes down to quick thinking and running away, really, but there are also some moves and techniques we can work on."

Once all of Sarah's protective gear was strapped into place, Aubrey told her to jog in place a little. One leg strap and both elbow pads were too tight, so Aubrey helped her adjust them. Then they did some jumping jacks and stretches (which Sarah thought would have been more effective before she was padded from head to toe) to warm up.

"All right," Aubrey said, "let's get started." She paced and eyed Sarah with a mischievous grin. "You aren't likely to be in danger from anybody your own size, so—" In a flash, Aubrey transformed into the lumbering shape of Mr. Litchfield. Her smile widened behind a stubbly black beard, and she shouted with a familiar nasally voice, "let's see how you do with someone a little bigger."

For the next four hours, Sarah worked as hard as she had worked at anything in her life. Aubrey shifted between various adult bodies—mostly teachers they both knew from school—and walked Sarah through a dozen different escape and defense scenarios. Sarah's first priority, Aubrey repeated over and over, was to get away. If she was caught, Sarah was to use any means she could to escape. If she could avoid being caught in the first place, that was even better. Aubrey coached Sarah to use her small size, her speed, and her surroundings to her advantage. If she could fit into or climb onto something her attacker could not, that might be her best hope for safety. On the other hand, a poorly chosen refuge could turn into a trap, so she had to think fast and always have a plan B.

Aubrey had Sarah scream as if she was being kidnapped and needed to attract the attention of an adult. She taught Sarah how to roll out of a fall, how to throw a proper punch, how to kick with her heels, and three different ways to leverage her (admittedly light) weight to topple even a very large adult. Sarah learned about the best places to hit an attacker: the groin, the throat, and the eyes. Aubrey showed her how to break away from common holds by hitting with her palms, fists, elbows, and head if needed. Sarah learned a technique that involved falling to the ground and kicking the assailant repeatedly just below the knee. When trapped, Aubrey instructed Sarah to flail, scream, hit, kick, punch, pinch, scratch, and even bite to get away.

Aubrey made Sarah run through every scenario and practice each new skill over and over. If Sarah could not escape and run all the way to the far end of the clearing before she was recaptured by whichever adult form Aubrey had assumed, she had to repeat the exercise, no questions asked, no complaints allowed.

And Sarah did not complain. Every time something seemed too difficult, she thought of Grandpa Kirk. Whenever she wanted to stop, lungs burning and muscles aching, she imagined her Grandpa with a shaved scalp dotted with metal ports like Benjamin's, and all thoughts of quitting faded. There was no rest. They took no breaks. By the time they finished, both girls were exhausted, sore, and thirsty.

Sarah wiped sweat from her eyes and examined herself. Her side ached. She had several new bruises and felt as if she might vomit. The cut she received the night Grandpa was taken had opened up again. She sat down on one of the stumps and glanced at Aubrey, who was already seated on the log near the duffle bag—a black eye and a bite mark on her hand to show for their hard work. Sarah laughed, though she wasn't sure why, and the two sat panting and smiling at each other as Sarah removed her headgear.

Aubrey produced a bottle of Gatorade from the bag and tossed it to Sarah. "Here," she said between gasping breaths, "you've earned it."

Sarah caught the bottle, removed the cap, and poured it down her throat. It wasn't cold, but she didn't care. "Thanks," she said when the bottle was empty.

"Man, kiddo, you don't quit. Do you?" said Aubrey.

"*Miss* kiddo," Sarah quipped, still trying to catch her breath.

Aubrey laughed. "Seriously, Miss Sarah, that was amazing. I didn't think you'd be able to keep going."

"Me neither," Sarah said, now aware of the throbbing in her ribs. Behind it, though, a sense of accomplishment swelled.

"I mean, you need more practice for sure," said Aubrey. "We didn't spend enough time on anything for you to build muscle memory, but wow! You are a machine. Maybe, if we don't leave tomorrow, we can…" She noticed Sarah wincing. "Are you all right?"

"Yeah. I'll be fine." Sarah said.

"We might have overdone it."

"No," Sarah insisted. "If Dr. Allen gets anything useful out of Blackwood's brain tonight, we could be leaving to go after Grandpa tomorrow. And I won't do anybody any good if I get caught in the process."

"Smartest thing I've heard you say yet."

Aubrey helped Sarah pack the sparring gear into the duffle bag. When they finished, Sarah replaced her jewelry and downed a second bottle of gatorade and a bag of cashews. Then Duke led them back up the trail and toward the Alvarezes' mansion.

"How come you still have that bite mark?" Sarah asked.

Aubrey gave her a puzzled look and the obvious answer: "You bit me." She rubbed her hand.

"Well, yeah, but you weren't *you* when I bit you."

"Sure I was," said Aubrey.

Sarah rolled her eyes. "You know what I mean. I didn't bite this hand. I bit Mr. Litchfield's hand. It was rough and hairy. If his skin and his hair are gone, why do you still have the bite mark?"

Aubrey smiled. "I can't heal myself. If I get injured, I'm injured."

"Could you, I don't know, hide it?"

"Well, I could make it so you don't *see* it," Aubrey replied. The marks disappeared from her upheld hand in demonstration and then faded back into existence a moment later. "But they'd still be there. It would still hurt. And honestly, I'm pretty proud of these marks. They prove that you made more progress than anybody expected. I must be a pretty good teacher!" She chuckled. "Here, let me carry that bag for you."

19

THE SEVEN REALMS

Introduction to The Sentinels promised to be entertaining and informative, if not as exciting as self defense. That was fine with Sarah. Her body ached, and she supposed she had put it through enough excitement for one day. Duke curled up next to her on an old loveseat in the cool, damp basement. Sarah tried to relax, but everything hurt, and her thoughts kept wandering into anxious territory. She worried about Grandpa and what Benjamin might find in Blackwood's memories later that night. It was difficult to think of anything else, but she did her best to clear her mind and learn all she could.

Boarsmash said he had convinced Tellurak to stick around and help him teach, though Tellurak didn't look like he intended to do anything of the sort. He was lying on a dusty old couch with his horned head propped up at one end while his hairy feet hung over the other. He sighed and flipped through a copy of *Time* magazine that had Superman on the cover and did not show even the tiniest interest in anything else that was happening. Boarsmash, on the other hand, was set to lecture. His plan was, apparently, to mimic teachers he had seen on television sitcoms. He cleared his throat, instructed Sarah to raise her hand and refer to him as "Professor Boarsmash" if she had a question, and stood proudly on top of an old milk crate in front of a chalkboard-on-wheels that had been stowed in a corner of the basement. Despite her worries, Sarah had to bite her lip to keep from laughing when he wrote his name on the board. Even atop his perch, he could only reach the bottom half.

"Today you swore to help us watch over the peoples of the seven realms," Boarsmash began, "so you will need to know a few things about those realms and the people who come from them. I'm here to give you an overview." Sarah flipped open her diary to take notes, and the dwarf beamed with pride. He dove right in.

"The first of the Seven Realms is…" Boarsmash said and paused to write on the board, "Cosmos. That is the realm we are in now. It contains Earth, humanity, and everything you know. Cosmos is represented by a diagram of the solar system, or sometimes a simple circle."

Tellurak flipped a page in the magazine and sighed loudly. Sarah massaged a throbbing muscle under her right arm that she hadn't known existed before.

"Second," Boarsmash scribbled a number two onto the board, "is the realm of Aureulis."

"Oh, you're promoting it to second, are you?" Tellurak mumbled from the couch.

"Well, it is a lot like Cosmos, so I thought it made sense," Boarsmash said in a matter-of-fact tone.

"It's not all that similar."

"Well, it's not the most similar, but it's my favorite. We can change the order if you want. I don't mind."

"Oh no. Go on, *Professor*."

Boarsmash smiled at Sarah. "Don't mind him. He's bored and annoyed at being stuck here."

Tellurak flipped another page without response.

Boarsmash turned back to the chalkboard and continued his lesson. "Aureulis contains the dwarves' home world of Fodinara. Do you remember the brown banner from Flatland Hall? That's ours. Our symbol is a circle with little points on the inside, like this." He drew a rough illustration on the board. "Fodinara, you see, is somewhat like Earth, but outside-in. That is to say, the dwarves there live on the inside of a giant planet. It has mountains, but instead of pointing out toward space, they point inward, toward the middle." He tapped the symbol he had drawn. "When my ancestors stood on the ground of Fodinara and looked up," Boarsmash said with increasing excitement in his voice, "they didn't see the sky; they saw the other side of the world, faint in the darkness, thousands of miles away! There was no horizon, no sun—not one that they could see anyway—and no night or day. The whole planet, if that's what you want to call it, was lit by millions of brilliant stones that my ancestors dug up from deep in the ground." He took a deep breath and let out a mournful sigh. "Of course, none of us alive have ever been there. It's all stories now. But if there was a way to get there, I'd give anything to visit my kinsfolk and see the land of my ancestors with my own eyes."

There was a moment of silence before Boarsmash regained himself. "Enough of that. Let's move along. The third realm is the most famous, thanks to a certain British author who shares your last name. It is called Narinaelia—"

"Narinaelia?" Sarah interrupted. "You mean, like *Narnia?*"

"Precisely," said Boarsmash. "It is the home of the planet Aenimor and the aenimos people, it is symbolized by the golden lion, and, as you have no doubt guessed, it seems to have loosely inspired—whether he knew it or not—C.S. Lewis's magical land of *Narnia*. Mr. Tellurak, would you like to cover this one?"

"Not if you're going to use *those* names for it," Tellurak said. "There are better names, you know. Older names."

Boarsmash turned to Sarah and smiled. "The names I'm teaching you for the Seven Realms and their people," he explained, "are European names—Sentinel names. They're mostly Latin or occasionally Greek renderings of words from otherworld languages. But there are many cultures that have other words for the same things that are more common outside of The Sentinels."

"You mean there are otherworlders who aren't part of The Sentinels?" Sarah asked.

"Oh, yes," said Boarsmash. "Thousands. The Sentinels organization has only been around for a little more than three-hundred years, after all. We were founded in Normandy—that's in France—by a missionary named Father Pierre Daniau. He felt his mission extended beyond caring for other humans to caring for all of God's creatures, great and small. That included what he called the 'secretive creatures of myth' he had met while traveling. It's a very interesting story. In the end, he was burned alive for his defense of otherworlders. But I'm rambling now. The point is that most of the founding human members of The Sentinels were clergy, which means they spoke Latin, so they created Latin-based names for most everything. The Sentinels' headquarters have been in London for more than a hundred years now, and we haven't been a Catholic organization since the council of 1737, but the Latin roots have stuck. And some of our members, especially those with non-European heritages like Mr. Tellurak here, resent our use of these names and wish we'd respect other traditions and cultures by teaching the regional names for things. So far, though, none of their efforts to change things have worked, so the council—the ones in charge—use only the Latin-based names." He paused and aimed a raised eyebrow toward the couch. "But, since this isn't official training, Mr. Tellurak, you're more than welcome—"

"My great-grandparents called it Kunlun," Tellurak interrupted from behind his magazine. "There was no difference between the realm and the world in their minds. It was all Kunlun. They couldn't picture another universe, so they described it as a mountain. You can take it from there." He tossed the magazine aside and closed his eyes.

"All right," Boarsmash said. "Kunlun—or the world of Aenimor in the realm of Narinaelia—was the homeland of people you have probably identified as talking animals."

"Like Ms. Nita?" Sarah asked, forgetting to raise her hand.

"*Doctor* Nita," Tellurak chimed, eyes still shut.

"Exactly!" said Boarsmash. "Narinaelia is the closest thing Cosmos has, as far as we know, to a twin universe. The key difference is that there were never any humans on Aenimor. Instead, there were *many* species of intelligent creatures. Brilliant people, really. Not all of them looked like Earth animals, but many did and do."

Sarah raised her hand again. Boarsmash nodded for her to speak. "And Mr. Tellurak is..." she started, then turned to face the couch. "Mr. Tellurak, you're from there. Right? From Kunlun?"

"Me?" Tellurak asked. "No. I'm from California, just outside of San Francisco."

Boarsmash laughed.

"I mean, weren't your ancestors from there?" asked Sarah.

"I am sorry, Miss Sarah," Tellurak said and sat up. "I am not being very helpful or polite. Mr. Boarsmash is right. I've been bored and frustrated, and now I've taken it out on you. I apologize. I hate being cooped up in this house while people are in danger. I want to be out there, making a difference."

"I know that feeling," said Sarah.

"To answer your question: yes, some of them were from Kunlun. Some were human. The slang term for people like me is *halfies*, but we prefer to be called by our unique species names. I am an almast—probably the only one you'll ever meet. The Sentinels helped my family move from the jungles of Vietnam to the Redwood forests of northern California when I was young. I was my parents' only child, and they both died years ago. As far as I know, there are no others of my species in America."

"Are there other sorts of—" Sarah started.

"Halfies?" Tellurak finished.

"Yeah."

"Certainly. There were once many more Kunlun hybrids than there are now. Many have been hunted down and killed, but many still live in seclusion. I assume you are familiar with stories of centaurs, minotaurs, sphinxes, satyrs, fauns, mermaids, and the like? These and many other mythical creatures are based on Kunlun hybrids," he snorted and sighed before continuing, "more or less."

"More or less? What do you mean?"

"Only that many details have been changed in popular stories—sometimes to protect our people, sometimes for money, sometimes to make humans look better."

Sarah was quiet for a moment. "Were the people who wrote them Sentinels?"

Tellurak and Boarsmash exchanged meaningful glances.

Sarah looked from one to the other for an answer. Finally, Boarsmash continued. "This isn't our department; it's your Grandpa's.

Some researcher somewhere within the Sentinels knows the answer to that question for every popular story, poem, painting, sculpture, book, play, movie, or television program that has been released within the past three-hundred years."

"We know that The Sentinels have directly or indirectly influenced a good many of them," Tellurak noted.

"Yes," said Boarsmash. "Though, it's certainly not public knowledge which are which. I suspect a lot of them were created by people who knew exactly what they were doing, and others were created by people who had seen us and were made to think they dreamed or imagined what they'd seen—it's a trick we've been pulling on humans to protect ourselves for far longer than The Sentinels have been around. Of course, lots were created by people who had simply heard stories and made up new ones of their own."

"Wait," Sarah interrupted, again without raising her hand. "Back up. You can make people think they imagined things?"

"Yep!" Boarsmash answered. "Works pretty well, especially when there's a good base of fiction around what they saw so we can convince them it was something they read somewhere."

"Though, I daresay, it works better for pureblood Kunlun than for hybrids like me," said Tellurak.

"How do you do it? And why does it work better for purebloods?" asked Sarah.

"Wouldn't you like to know?" Tellurak laughed. "There are things we can do, and there are things you humans can do, and we don't reveal our secrets. Though, your father was famously opposed to this arrangement, and the Watcher knows more than most about both sides, so I will leave it to him to decide what he will share with his goddaughter."

"But—" Sarah began.

"As to the *why*," Tellurak continued, ignoring Sarah's protest, "if a man sees a horse chatting with a sheep, he will simply assume his mind has played a trick on him. On the other hand, if a man sees an almast like me, he will know that he has seen a fellow human, only one with fur and horns, and that is harder to ignore. If he is frightened, he might try to kill me. If he is curious, he might try to dissect me. If he is greedy, he might try to capture me and sell me to the highest bidder. All these things and worse have happened to people I have loved. Humans think us the monsters, but reality is quite the reverse."

Sarah looked at Duke for comfort, for disagreement, for something. She wanted to hear the robotic voice in her head telling her that Tellurak was biased and that humans were basically good and trustworthy. Instead, Duke only glanced up at her with sadness in his eyes and said nothing.

After a moment, Boarsmash spoke up. "Right then. We've gotten a little sidetracked. Where did we leave off?"

Neither Tellurak nor Sarah spoke for the rest of the lesson. Boarsmash continued his lecture with explanations of the remaining four realms and the people who came from each.

Next up was Malemorphos, the realm which included Aubrey's home world of Tabor. It's banner had been the one with the red swirled emblem. She'd heard a little about it from Samuel during the meeting at Flatland Hall. Malemorphos, she now learned, was like Cosmos in many ways except that it had an extra dimension of space. Boarsmash could not explain what that meant except to say that it gave Taborians their ability to shapeshift on Earth

Next they covered Lumovitae, the realm of living light whose emblem was a silver star. It was from there that Duke's people had come, and it was the most unlike Cosmos of all the realms. It had no planets or even matter in any form humans could understand. Time existed there, but it was "more fluid and malleable than Earth time," whatever that meant. The pentrafax, the creatures from Lumovitae, existed within Cosmos as immortal, telepathic, wisps of light, often perceived as muses, phantoms, and the like. While most only ever interacted with earthlings in fleeting moments, leaving their mark when they did but generally preferring to keep to themselves, the class of pentrafax known as the psuchamora preferred to inhabit the minds of earthling animals and carry on symbiotically within their hosts for as long as the animals lived. Duke, Boarsmash explained, was a *high* psuchamora, which meant that he was exceptionally powerful and wise, revered as a leader by other pentrafax.

Sarah gazed at Duke with fresh awe. "You mean, he's like a parasite?"

Tellurak laughed, and Duke huffed through his nostrils.

"No, no, no," said Boarsmash. "It's not like that at all! It's more like they become one thing. Now, I'm no expert on the pentrafax, of course, but my understanding is that Duke the dog remains every bit a dog while Duke the psuchamora makes him…well, better. He's still loyal; he still wags his tail; he still likes to have his ears scratched. But he's bigger, stronger, and smarter than any German Shepherd you've ever seen. He'll live longer than a normal German Shepherd too. And when the dog is old and ready to move on, Duke the psuchamora will leave this body and enter another one."

Finally, Boarsmash introduced Sarah to the realms of the purple and black banners: Vaelhala and Obsinder. He explained that Vaelhala was the real universe from which the ancient Norse derived their mythology of Valhalla, and Obsinder was the real universe from which most legends of hellish places were descended. Little was known about either realm because, Boarsmash said, there were no remaining pureblood descendents of either realm on Earth. He admitted, though, that there were always rumors that one had been sighted somewhere and that many cults had sprung up throughout history to worship these legendary beings. So far, however, their actual existence on Earth had never been confirmed.

Many legends of dragons, sea monsters, and fire-dwelling demons had their roots in early accounts of the Obsinders from before The Cataclysm. Most of the classical Norse, Roman, and Greek gods were based on ancient legends of the Vaelhalar or their half-human descendants, the Aravatis. Only a few Aravatis, blessed with large, strong bodies and long lives, remained on Earth. The Watcher was the most famous of them all.

As far as The Sentinels were aware, Boarsmash continued, no Obsinder halfies had ever been created. According to legend, the mingling of Obsinder blood with other races would have been seen as an abomination to their kind. Obsinders, more than any other species, reviled humans and halfies, and had been banished for their violence against earthlings in The Cataclysm.

Sarah asked about The Cataclysm. Both Boarsmash and Tellurak had mentioned it, but neither had explained what it was.

"Ahh," said Boarsmash. "Yes. That is a very important subject. It is the reason you are here and the Obsinders are not. But our time today has run out, so we will have to cover it tomorrow. You don't want to be late for your first science lesson!"

20

ANTISOCIAL SCIENCE

The Alvarezes' library, which now served as a temporary laboratory, was alive with the hum of half a dozen machines and the commotion of hurried work. Three men and two dwarves rushed from makeshift station to makeshift station, scribbled notes on paper pads, and fumbled for equipment in cardboard boxes that sat in a haphazard line against one wall. Nobody noticed Sarah and Duke.

Sarah cleared her throat and glanced at her watch. The longer the day wore on, the more impatient she felt. Soon she would have time alone with Samuel, and then she would get to ask the questions she most wanted to ask.

"Oh, there you are," said a honey-smooth voice with a Scottish accent. "All right, Miss Sarah, let's get on with it then. I haven't got all day. Have a seat."

Sarah sat in an uncomfortable wooden chair near a bookshelf and opened her diary (which was becoming less and less the thing it was intended to be with each note she took). Duke stood by her side like a guard at attention. She was sure he sensed her anxiety in this room where, hours before, Blackwood had appeared out of thin air and screamed at her.

Dr. Michael MacPherson lifted his goggles onto his forehead, dabbed the hot tip of a soldering iron onto a wet sponge, and set it back into its cradle. "Dr. Allen," he shouted, "you'll have to finish this bit. I've an appointment just now." Then he pulled up a matching chair, turned it backward, and sat facing Sarah with his legs straddling the chair back and his arms folded across its top. "Well then," he said through a toothy smile, "the Watcher, good man that he is, didn't give me much to go on. So. What do you want to learn?"

Sarah didn't know what to say. She had expected a science lesson, not a question and answer session. She massaged a sore muscle in her arm and asked, "What do you mean? Aren't you supposed to teach me some science stuff?"

"Perhaps so," Michael replied, "but let's face it, I'm no teacher, lassie, and even if I were, I've hardly had time to prepare a lesson. But since I can't very well disobey a direct order from the Watcher himself, here I am. I'm an open book. Ask away, dearie, and I'll answer you from my vast stores of scientific knowledge." He grinned.

Sarah was not amused. "Well, I haven't got any questions," she said and crossed her arms, "so you'll just have to figure out something to teach."

"What's that?" Michael asked. His smile grew even wider. "You haven't prepared any questions? Tisk tisk. Very well, then. Another time, perhaps." He unfolded his arms and stood.

"Why don't you ask him how to calculate transmutational beta state mass," Duncan said from across the room. He was wearing dark goggles and heating a green liquid in a glass beaker with something that looked like a welding torch. "If he hasn't still got his knickers in a twist about being called out in front of Dr. Nita."

Michael turned and glared at Duncan. Over his shoulder, Sarah saw Benjamin grin and laugh to himself as he picked up the soldering iron Michael had abandoned. It was good to see Benjamin smile. Sarah knew the job ahead of him would not be pleasant.

"Very funny," Michael shot back. "Maybe you would like to put that wit of yours to better use and give Miss Sarah a lesson yourself?"

"Well, I'm certain I could come up with something a bit better than, 'what do you want to know,'" said Duncan, "but unfortunately, Dr. MacPherson, the Watcher didn't ask me; he asked you. So I suggest you try a bit harder, yeah? Like you did when you boiled shapeshifting down to ballpoints and soda water. Wouldn't want the Watcher to find out you turned his goddaughter away without so much as the periodic matrix to show for it."

"Seriously, Dr. Connolly?" said Michael. "You're threatening to tattle if I let Miss Sarah go play with her little friends so I can get back to the real work we're doing here?"

Duncan laughed and put out the torch. "Don't have to, then, do I? Her faithful companion there is quite capable of making himself understood when he wants, and I'm sure he'd have something to say about it."

Duke barked in response.

"See what I mean?"

"All right, then," Michael said. "Fine." He sat down and faced Sarah again.

Sarah glared at him. "I see why Aubrey, I mean *Miss* Aubrey was so mad at you this morning. You didn't want to do this," she said.

"Aye. That was part of it, yeah," Michael admitted. "And I might have said I thought you were too young to enlist. And then she may have had the nerve to accuse me of leaking information to Les Luminaires, saying that I never wanted you around in the first place! Of all the—" Michael caught himself. "Please understand, Miss Sarah, it's nothing like that. I've nothing against you. You seem a right delightful young lady, even if you did spy on us. It's just that we're incredibly busy just now, and it seems a dreadful waste of time to be jabbering with you when there are so many preparations to be made for tonight."

"Don't worry about the preparations, Dr. MacPherson," said Benjamin. "Dr. Connolly and I can handle the last of them. You go on."

"Oh, I bet you can," said Michael. "Just don't you forget anything. I didn't make that checklist without reason. If I find that one box has been left unchecked—"

"We can handle it," said Benjamin. Then, to Duncan, "Honestly, you'd think we were children the way he goes on."

Duncan laughed.

"Well maybe if—" Michael began.

Sarah cut him off. "Actually, Dr. MacPherson" she said, "if it's still okay, I do have one question."

Michael eyed her suspiciously. Behind him, Benjamin and Duncan both raised their eyebrows at her and then went back to their tasks.

"All right then, go ahead." said Michael.

"Dr. Allen gave me this at the ceremony today." Sarah pulled the strange metallic rock from her back pocket—she had retrieved it from the suitcase after her lesson with Boarsmash—and handed it to Michael. "What is it?"

Michael examined it and then shouted over his shoulder, "Hey Benjie, is this the same bit of—"

"That's Dr. Benjie to you, sir," Benjamin replied before Michael could finish his sentence. "Better remember your manners in front of our new recruit." He winked at Sarah. "As for the specimen, yes, that's it. It's a bit charred now—too damaged to be any good to us. It was headed for the scrap bin before I took it. But if I've put my facts together correctly, the explosion that damaged it is the same one that first alerted Miss Sarah to our existence. I'd say we owe that rock a debt of gratitude."

Michael grunted and turned back to Sarah, his eyes still rolling. "Very well then. This, my dear, is a fragment of an artifact from another universe. How much do you know about the multiverse?"

"We can't call it that anymore," said Duncan.

"It was our word first!" argued Michael.

"I know that as well as you, but it'll be too confusing for—"

"All right. Fine," Michael huffed. "When physicists outside of The Sentinels talk about the multiverse, they mean a theoretical, infinite set of alternative versions of this universe. Cosmos, that is. What we mean is—"

Sarah finished his sentence. "The seven realms?"

"Aye. What do you know about them?"

"I just had a crash course with Mr. Boarsmash." She flipped back a couple of pages in her notes and looked at what she had written.

"Not much, then," Michael replied with a sigh. "Well, he told you about Vaelhala at least, didn't he? Good. This is a shard of an ancient Vaelhalar shield. At least, we think it was a shield. It's hard to tell for sure, but that's what we call it. It was, supposedly, created on the Luxephorean plane of Vaelhala and brought to Earth thousands of years ago. It's what we call an alloy. Do you know what that is?"

"Yeah," Sarah said. "I looked it up after…after I listened to the recording I had made of your conversation in the lab. It's a metal that's made by combining other metals. Right?"

Michael's forehead was knotted. "Yes," he said, drawing the word out. "Yes, that's correct." He took a long, slow breath and looked as if he were about to scold her, but then he shook his head, exhaled, and went on. "Well, that's a sufficient definition in general Earth-science terms anyway, and it's the best word we have to describe this. It is made of a combination of materials that somewhat resemble our own metals but are unlike anything that comes from this world. And it has certain properties that exist on a plane that we cannot directly observe with eyes and instruments that were created for this three-dimensional universe."

"Do you mean that Vaelhala has more than three dimensions? I thought only Malemor…whatever-it's-called had an extra dimension."

"Rubbish. Every universe has more than three dimensions. There's more to everything than meets the eye."

Duncan interrupted from across the lab. "A little demonstration might be in order, don't you think, Dr. MacPherson?" He tossed a gray cloth bag across the room.

Michael caught it. "Here. Hold this a moment, would you?" He handed Sarah's fragment of L-421 back to her and opened the bag. Then he reached inside and removed a glowing, green, translucent gem the size of Sarah's fist. "This is one of the light-emitting stones from the dwarves' home world of Fodinara. Aureulis and Vaelhala both have similarities to Cosmos, but they have many differences as well. These otherworld elements exist, in a form, here on Earth, but they're both a far cry from the magnificence they would have displayed in their native worlds, no doubt about it. Both have attributes—very real, physical parts—that simply cannot be observed here. But that doesn't mean those bits no longer exist. They just exist outside of the three cosmic dimensions. And sometimes they intersect in a way that is hard to explain, so I'll show you instead." He held out the gemstone. "Why don't you knock that bit of Luxephorean shield against the blessed arkenstone here?"

Benjamin snickered at that.

Sarah took the gem in her left hand and the bit of L-421 in her right. She pushed them toward each other cautiously, half expecting them to repel one another like magnets turned the wrong way. But instead of the springy resistance of magnetism, they hit a solid but invisible barrier, like a force-field, and slid past one another less than an inch apart. She turned the metallic rock over and tried again. They slid away from each other again, at a different angle this time, and without getting nearly as close. She spun both pieces and tried to bang them together; they bounced away from each other when they were still a foot apart, but there was no sound of impact. She turned the specimens once more, put her fingers between them, and squeezed them together. They stopped before her fingers touched, but still she felt nothing between them.

"Amazing, isn't it?" said Michael. "Try this: Place one piece flat on your hand and move it with the other."

Sarah attempted the experiment, but to her surprise, neither would move the other. She stood, set the metal shard on her chair, and tried to push it aside with the gem. When she pushed with all her strength, the gem wiggled a little, but it never moved from its place. "What on Earth?!" she exclaimed.

"Well, that's the point, isn't it?" said Michael as he snatched up the gemstone and tossed it from hand to hand, light as a baseball. "It's *not* on Earth. Not all of it, anyway. You've demonstrated what we refer to as *interdimensional friction,* and it reveals a number of odd anomalies about the interplay of matter from different universes. It's as if they are out of phase with one another—like two notes right next to one another on the piano. They'll each harmonize well enough with another note further down the keyboard, but play the two together, and you'll get a nasty dissonance. Likewise, these two artifacts play nicely with our Earth elements, but put the two together, and you get friction that has the potential to yield unpleasant results. Now, you didn't apply enough pressure to be in any danger, of course, but if you were to force the two together to within a few microns, and if you weren't very careful to go slowly—"

"Or if you miscalculated the—" Duncan interjected.

"Yes, yes," Michael admitted. "Or if you miscalculated the transmutational beta state mass—I'll explain that another time—that *friction* might very well escalate and cause a large enough explosion to attract the attention of a nosy young know-it-all."

"Though," Duncan added as he removed his black goggles and walked toward them, "if you get the angles just right and apply pressure just so, and if the conditions are favorable, you could theoretically open up a gateway to another universe."

"More likely, though," said Michael, "you'd just re-invent the oubliette."

The door flew open behind Sarah, and Samuel entered the room. "I apologize, Dr. MacPherson, but I am afraid I require your pupil."

Sarah's stomach sank. Something was wrong. She could feel it.

Michael stood and bowed with an air of unspoken understanding. "Yes, sir. Of course."

"Please continue the experiment, and then proceed with plan beta zed fifty-seven. Understood?"

"Understood," Michael replied.

Duke ran to the door and waited there.

"And when you have your findings," Samuel started.

"You'll have them right away."

"Thank you, Dr. MacPherson. Gentlemen." He bowed, and everyone in the room bowed in return. Then he opened the door and gestured for Sarah to follow. "Come, Miss Sarah. Your next adventure awaits."

21

OVER THE RIVER

"This way," Samuel urged. They hurried down a long hallway toward a part of the Alvarez mansion that Sarah had not yet explored.

Something was wrong, but Sarah could not put her finger on it. She stopped. "Wait a minute. What's going on?"

"I am afraid there is no time." said Samuel. "I will explain in a moment."

Sarah took a few quick steps and then stopped again. She had looked down at the piece of L-421 she was still holding, and as she did, she had caught a glimpse of *something*—something about Samuel that was not Samuel. A feeling of suspicion overtook her, and she wondered if she would be too sore or too slow to outrun him. Samuel turned to face her, and again, there was something about him that did not look like him. Sarah stayed planted, ready to bolt at the first sign of danger. "Who are you?"

Samuel stared back at her, silent, an expression of surprise on his face.

"I don't know who you are," said Sarah, "but you are not Samuel, and I'm not taking another step until I know what's going on."

The giant's face twisted into a wry smile. He stepped closer and lifted a hand revealing a set of scabbed-over teeth marks. "You're quick kiddo," the accented voice whispered. "Apparently there's no fooling you. Now come on. Watcher's orders." He turned and continued on his way.

Before Sarah could make sense of what was happening, a robotic voice spoke in her ears. "COME." Duke was already jogging alongside Samuel's doppelganger as they rounded a corner and disappeared from sight.

She ran to catch up. "Hang on! Where are we going?"

"In here."

The three ducked into a small bedroom at the end of the hallway. Aubrey closed the door behind them and transformed once again into the form of a young girl.

"All right, listen," said Aubrey, "the Watcher got a tip-off—several, I think—that Les Luminaires are on their way here. Right now. We don't know how they found out where we are, so we're being extra cautious. The four of us are leaving now, and—"

Sarah interrupted. *"Four of us?"*

"I'm coming too!" said a voice from the other side of the room.

Sarah turned and saw a familiar face. "Oh! Boarsmash!" she said. "I didn't see you before."

"*Mr.* Boarsmash," said Aubrey.

"Sorry," Sarah apologized. "I keep forgetting."

Boarsmash smiled.

Aubrey pressed on. "There is a strong possibility that someone inside the Sentinels leaked info to Les Luminaires. Maybe someone back at Flatland Hall who put two and two together, or maybe somebody here sold us out. I have my suspicions, but it could have been anyone. And since we don't know who to trust, we're keeping everyone in the dark. Only the Watcher knows the full plan moving forward. I know a little, but there's not enough time to go into it now, so I'll summarize: we're gonna jet. The Watcher will meet us later. By the time Les Luminaires make it here, only Mr. Tellurak and Dr. MacPherson will be left to meet them. I think they're going to offer Blackwood as a trade for your grandpa, but I doubt Les Luminaires will take that deal, so there might be trouble. We have to be long gone before that happens."

"No!" said Sarah. Not only did this mean another delay before they could go after Grandpa, but now more people were putting themselves in danger to keep her out of it. "We can't just leave—"

"Yes we can. And we will. This is not up for discussion," Aubrey replied. "You are a brand new junior agent, Miss Sarah, and you will follow orders."

Sarah gritted her teeth and nodded. Taking orders was going to be harder than she thought.

"Besides," Aubrey said, softening her tone, "it'll be fine. Dr. MacPherson probably won't be much help if it comes to a fight, but trust me, Mr. Tellurak is not somebody you want to mess with, and I bet we will have backup hiding somewhere."

"But—"

"Seriously, Miss Sarah. We don't have time for this. Just trust us."

"All right, all right! Where are we going?" Sarah asked.

"It's a hideout Mr. Alvarez told us about. You'll see," Aubrey replied. "But first, travel arrangements. Duke, if it's all right with you, I think you should carry Mr. Boarsmash and stay under tree cover as much as possible. Miss Sarah, you'll ride with me on the motorcycle."

"But…You mean we have to split up?" Sarah asked, glancing at Duke.

"Well, no. We don't have to," said Aubrey. "We could all walk together and hold hands and sing *Kumbaya* and get there sometime tomorrow afternoon. But the motorcycle is our fastest option, so I think we should use it. And since only two of us can fit on the bike—"

Duke whined.

"I'm just not sure…" Sarah started. Nothing about this felt right, and separating from Duke made it worse. She started to say that she didn't feel safe without Duke by her side, but she didn't want to sound afraid or like she didn't think she and Aubrey could defend themselves. Cowards, she was sure, would not be allowed on a rescue mission. "I mean…Do you think Mr. Boarsmash and Duke will be okay on their own?"

"Are you for real?" Aubrey laughed. "Mr. Boarsmash is a dwarf, not some tender-skinned human. And you've seen Duke in action. I don't think they're the ones we need to worry about."

"She's right," Boarsmash added. "Duke and I can take care of ourselves. I'm more concerned about you.

Sarah scowled.

"Not that you aren't tough too!" said Boarsmash, "It's just—"

"No, no. It's fine. I get it. Sure. We'll do your plan, Aubrey."

"Are you sure?" asked Boarsmash. "We can all go together if—"

"I said it's fine! Let's just split up. It'll be faster this way."

"Great!" said Aubrey. Then, turning, "Duke, come look at this map so I can show you where we're going." She produced a folded map from her back pocket. Sarah wanted to ask where that map had been while Aubrey was impersonating Samuel, but she didn't get the chance.

"Miss Sarah," Aubrey called as she spread the map on the floor, "all your things are over there." She pointed, and Sarah saw that her suitcase and chest were stacked in the corner next to her backpack. "You've got two minutes. Fit whatever essentials you can into your bag. The Watcher will bring the rest later."

Sarah hurried across the room, opened the trunk and the suitcase, and dumped out her backpack. She strapped the dagger onto her belt, tucked the pocket knife Aubrey had given her into her front pocket next to the piece of L-421 she still carried, and threw her flashlight, the water bottle, and what remained of her beef jerky into the backpack first. Then she added a couple of pairs of underwear and socks, a pair of blue jeans, and a sweatshirt. This filled the main compartment of the bag, and she zipped it shut with some effort. The puzzle cube went back into the trunk, but she found room for both her own diary and her mother's in a large pocket of the backpack. She also found pocket space for the arrowhead from Boarsmash and the wooden box from Samuel. There might, she thought, be time to look at them later.

"All right," Aubrey called. "Is everyone ready?"

Seconds later, they piled out of the window and left a dark, tidy bedroom behind.

DUKE RAN LIKE A WARHORSE. THE DWARF WHO PERCHED ON HIS BACK

and clutched his collar seemed no burden at all as they disappeared into a clump of trees.

Aubrey only had one helmet, and she insisted Sarah wear it. "Hop on," she said. "We'll be off-road for most of this trip, so you'll want to hold on tight. And remember to lean with me when we're turning, all right?"

Sarah clasped the helmet's chinstrap and hiked her right leg over the back of the motorcycle behind Aubrey.

"Ouch! What is that?" said Aubrey.

"What?"

"You're poking me in the back! Ouch! Get off!" Aubrey swatted at nothing near her tailbone.

Sarah scrambled away from the bike with an incredulous look on her face. Nothing had touched Aubrey's back. She hadn't even made it all the way onto the seat yet.

"What did you do that for?" Aubrey asked.

"Stop spazzing! I didn't do anything!" Sarah insisted.

"Well *something* hit me!" Aubrey rubbed her lower back. "All right. Try again. And be more careful this time."

Sarah once again lifted her leg to mount the bike, slower than before, and as she shifted her weight onto the seat she saw Aubrey wince.

"There it is!" Aubrey scooted forward and wriggled, trying to escape the pain. She swatted again, hard, and made contact with something invisible. "That! What is that?"

Sarah felt something shift ever so slightly inside her pocket. "Wait!" she said. She dug in her pocket, took out the piece of Luxephorean alloy, dropped it into a side pocket of her backpack, and then sat down behind Aubrey. "Better?" she asked.

"Yeah! What was it?"

"It was..." Sarah's voice trailed away.

"Well?"

"Nothing. I'll explain later," Sarah said. "Let's just go."

"Roger that. Hold on tight, kiddo!"

The engine growled and the seat shook beneath them. Sarah wrapped her arms around Aubrey's torso, gripping her own forearms on the other side. With a jerk, they flew forward. The mingled sounds of the speeding motorcycle and rushing air filled their ears. Sarah's tee shirt flapped like a wind-torn sail as they shot over the rocky trail toward the creek.

"Lean right!" Aubrey yelled as they approached a curve in the trail. Sarah squeezed her eyes shut and leaned. The bike tilted to the right as they turned. Sarah felt herself being pressed firmly into the seat as if the force of gravity had been turned up a notch. Then the path straightened, the bike righted itself, and the Earth resumed its usual gravitational pull. "Left!" Aubrey shouted. They leaned to the left and the sensation repeated itself.

Sarah opened her eyes and looked over her shoulder. The house was already a small silhouette on the distant horizon. Below, she watched the overgrown straw grass, gravel, and dirt blur into a streak of browns and grays.

"Hold on tight!" she heard Aubrey yell. Sarah lifted her head so that she could see over Aubrey's shoulder. The creek was directly in front of them, and the throttle was open wide. They were going too fast. There was no chance of stopping or turning in time. Sarah closed her eyes.

"Here we go!" cried Aubrey. "WOOOOOHOOOOOO!"

The motorcycle rose suddenly, pushing the girls skyward. Though she could see nothing, Sarah knew they were airborne. The rumble of rough ground beneath the tires was gone, and the seat seemed to be slipping out from underneath her. Sarah's stomach turned upside down. They were falling. Time seemed to slow almost to a stop. At any moment they would hit water—or worse, slam into the embankment on the far side. Sarah braced herself for the worst.

But the worst did not come. With a jolt, they were back on solid ground, accelerating again. Sarah loosened her grip and looked back. A huge rock, now shrinking into the distance, jutted skyward on the far bank. They had jumped the creek like Evel Knievil, and that rock must have been their ramp.

"Left!" Aubrey shouted.

Sarah, who was still turned backward, leaned the direction that seemed like her left, but felt Aubrey lean the other way.

"Your *other* left!"

Sarah corrected just as the bike made a sharp left turn. The tires spun beneath them, and they drifted dangerously close to a patch of prickly pear cactus before the motorcycle regained traction and jerked away.

On they rode across rocky trails, over hills, and through groups of trees Sarah might have called forests. From time to time they stopped, cut a barbed-wire fence or pushed aside an old fence post and walked the motorcycle through to the other side. Twice they crossed paved roads. Both times, Aubrey shifted to look like an old farmer and walked out to the road so she could be sure nobody was coming before they crossed.

Finally, just as the sun touched the western horizon, they stopped. Aubrey killed the engine and motioned for Sarah to be silent. They pushed the motorcycle a hundred yards or so, and then hid it in a thicket of mesquite trees. Aubrey removed a pair of saddlebags that hung from the bike and slung them over her shoulder. They marked the spot with a large rock and hiked on without speaking for what felt to Sarah like several miles, watching their surroundings darken and turn gray. They pushed through a line of cactus and brush and then into a grove of cedars and oaks. Sarah pulled her flashlight out of her backpack, and with its help, they walked through the darkness until they found the place they were looking for: a decrepit wooden shack at the edge of a clearing on the far side of the woods they had just crossed.

"In here," Aubrey whispered.

The door creaked on its hinges, and—remembering what Grandpa Kirk had taught her about such places—Sarah searched the ground for snakes before stepping inside.

22

THROUGH THE WOODS

That night was one of the longest Sarah had ever experienced. The air grew cooler and cooler, but they had no sleeping bags or blankets to keep themselves warm. Aubrey would not allow a fire—not that they had any matches—nor would she allow Sarah to use her flashlight or to speak above a whisper. Slivers of light from the crescent moon shone through the gaps in the wood slat walls, so that once her eyes had adjusted to the darkness, Sarah was able to see a little. But the shifting shadows of trees and clouds became alive in her imagination, feeding Sarah's fear that at any moment something might slither or crawl up her leg.

Whispering, Aubrey told Sarah that the shack where they were hiding was an old deer blind on property that belonged to Mr. Alvarez's elderly father. She said that he did not hunt anymore, and that only wandering cattle were likely to visit it these days.

Sarah asked about what was going on back at the mansion, and Aubrey filled her in on the little she knew. She said that Samuel had sent the Alvarezes away for a few days. Benjamin and Duncan were supposed to leave with their lab assistants as soon as the reading of Blackwood's memory was completed. Nobody knew where Aubrey and Sarah were hiding now except for Duke, Boarsmash, and Samuel.

Sarah shared some beef jerky and water with Aubrey and tried to pry more information from her. But after a handful of I-don't-knows and I-can't-tell-you-thats, Aubrey folded her arms and turned to peer through a gap in the wall. Sarah put everything back into her bag and leaned against it, watching Aubrey.

The minutes crept. Sarah's body ached worse with every chilly gust that blew through the drafty old shed, but she refused to complain. Worried questions filled her mind. What was happening back at the mansion? Did Benjamin find anything helpful when he read Blackwood's memory? Would Les Luminaires want Blackwood back badly enough to make an exchange? If not, would there be a fight? Where would Samuel take her next? How long would it be before before she would see Grandpa Kirk again. *Would* she ever see Grandpa Kirk again?

After a while, Aubrey began pacing.

"What's wrong?" asked Sarah.

"Duke and Boarsmash should have been here an hour ago. They had to go slower and take a longer path, sure, but it shouldn't have taken them *this* long. The Watcher will be here any minute, and then we'll have to go find them." Aubrey lifted a wooden shutter that covered a small, square window and looked out. "Any minute," she repeated.

Another hour of pacing, checking her watch, and shivering passed before Aubrey finally slumped down into a corner of the shed. Sarah, chilled to her bones, slipped her extra jeans and sweatshirt on over her clothes, curled up next to Aubrey, and fell into a restless sleep.

Minutes or hours passed—Sarah could not tell which—when she was shaken from her sleep. She opened her eyes and almost screamed when she saw her own face staring back at her. Aubrey covered Sarah's mouth with a strangely familiar hand and held a pale, slender finger to copycat lips. "Shhh! Somebody's out there. Listen."

For a moment, they were silent. Then Sarah heard it: twigs snapping beneath heavy feet, strange voices talking in loud whispers.

"I'm going out," Aubrey whispered, "but you stay put. You got that?"

Sarah glanced toward the door and did not answer.

"I mean it. Whatever happens, do not leave this deer blind. That's an order."

Sarah nodded.

Aubrey reached into the saddlebags and pulled out something that was shaped like a miniature baseball bat. It was shiny and black and covered in little silver squares that gleamed in the pale moonlight. She stuffed the thing into the back of her jeans, crossed to the door, and waited. At the sound of the next gust of wind, she pushed the squeaky door ajar and slipped out. Several long, quiet minutes passed. Sarah tried not to breathe.

Thump! Crack.

"What was that," a voice said. "Did you hear that?"

"Yeah. Sounded like it came from over there."

Quick footsteps grew louder and then faded away.

"See anything?" The voice was distant now.

"No. Nothing. Where's—"

Whack!

Sarah heard a yelp and then the sound of something falling hard onto a bed of leaves and twigs.

"Lipstein! Lipstein?!"

Sarah heard several sets of feet running, and through a gap in the shed's wall, she glimpsed flashlight beams bobbing in the distance.

"Everything all right?" a voice asked.

"We're not alone. Look."

All was quiet. A cold breeze rustled the leaves of nearby trees. An owl hooted. Then Sarah heard someone shout, "Over there! It's the girl!"

Sarah's heart froze in her chest, certain that someone had seen her. But she watched as the flashlights disappeared over a hill. She breathed a sigh of momentary relief before the truth hit her. "Oh no!" she gasped. They hadn't seen her; they had seen Aubrey.

Sarah did not think twice. Orders or no, she would not leave Aubrey to fight alone. She hurried to the door but stopped before she opened it. Leaving the blind at all was dangerous, but leaving it empty-handed would be worse. So she dove for her backpack and stuffed anything she might be able to use into her sweatshirt pockets:

the arrowhead, the flashlight, the fragment of an ancient Vaelhalar shield. She emptied the backpack before she remembered that she already had the dagger on her hip and the pocketknife from Aubrey in the pocket of her jeans. Then she flung the door open and sprinted after Aubrey's unknown pursuers, leaving the bags behind.

Before she reached the top of the hill, Sarah stopped, caught her breath, and listened. Somebody might be nearby, and she wouldn't be any help to Aubrey if she was captured before Aubrey could get away. But she heard nothing. As quietly as she could, Sarah tiptoed from tree to tree, keeping to the shadows as much as possible, until she reached the hilltop where she crouched and hid between the trunk of a tree and a prickly bush. The other side of the hill, she saw, fell onto a rough, unkempt field that might once have grown corn or cotton. Sarah counted four figures combing the treeline that ran along the left side of the plain, pointing their flashlights into the brush as they walked into the distance.

She had no real plan, but she thought maybe she could give Aubrey a chance if she could create a diversion. She just needed to come up with something to draw these people away from Aubrey without giving away her own location. *Think,* Sarah told herself. She set the things she had been carrying in her pockets onto the ground. The flashlight might be good, but only if she could somehow turn it on from a distance. And it would be great if she could make the attackers think someone was holding it. She racked her brain until a plan took shape in her mind. It wasn't a great idea, but it was an idea.

Quickly, she removed the shoelaces from her sneakers and tied them together. She looped them over a low tree limb and tied the free ends to the flashlight so that it hung nearly level. Next, she spit on the ground until her mouth was dry and stirred the saliva into the dirt. It wasn't much, but she managed to make a mud ball a little smaller than a ping pong ball, and that was all she needed. She pressed the mud into the rough bark of the tree trunk, level with the dangling flashlight, and then pressed the bulb-end of the flashlight into the mud. Cupping a hand around it like a shade, she flipped the switch. No light was visible through the mud. She turned the flashlight off again and pulled it free. Then she removed her sweatshirt, draped it over the prickly bush beside her, and tied one sleeve to the flashlight before she shoved it back into the mud. It didn't look much like a person, but maybe it would be close enough to buy some time. She looked around for something that could be used to free the flashlight when the time came. A fallen limb as big around as her arm and twice as long lay on the ground nearby. She picked it up and leaned it against the tree at a precarious angle so that, if it slipped, it would fall onto the flashlight. Carefully, she clicked the flashlight back on and backed away from her invention, praying that it would work. Sarah tiptoed down the hill and hid behind an oak tree near the bottom where she could watch and wait for a gust of wind to topple the limb and reveal her flashlight-wielding decoy.

Several minutes crawled by, but nothing happened. Finally, Sarah decided to sneak back up the hill and throw something at it. She kicked off her shoes, which kept slipping from her feet now that the laces were missing, and turned to climb. As soon as she had stepped out from around the tree, though, she saw something that made her heart stop. Something was moving in the trees half way up the hill.

Sarah froze and held her breath. The thing slipped through the shadows, graceful and silent. Whatever it was seemed to blend into the trees in a way that made it impossible for her to pick out its features. Only movement revealed its presence, and only for an instant before it disappeared again. But each time it reappeared, it was closer than before. For a moment, Sarah lost track of the thing altogether. Then, suddenly, a voice whispered in Sarah's ear.

"I told you to stay put, Miss Sarah!"

Sarah jumped. "Aubrey?" she whispered, a little louder than she intended.

"Yeah. And you're lucky I saw you before they did. Now come on. I've got to get you out of here before they figure out I gave them the slip."

Sarah turned and gasped at what she saw: a tall, thin, body, covered from head to toe in an intricate camouflage pattern. Even Aubrey's eyes were dark, and she had no hair at all.

"How did you get away?" Sarah whispered as they crept back toward the deer blind.

"I snuck up on two of them and knocked them out before they knew what hit them. When I realized there were five more, I changed my tactic and led them away before I doubled back to get you."

"Wait," said Sarah, "*five* more? I only counted four."

"Five," said a woman's voice. A flashlight clicked on directly in front of them and shone into their faces. "Hello, Aubrey. Nice to see you again. And you must be Sarah. I've been looking forward to meeting you."

There was a snap followed by the electrostatic sound of a walkie-talkie. "I've got 'em, boys," the woman's voice said.

23

FIGHT AND FLIGHT

For a moment, Sarah could not move, stunned by the woman's sudden appearance and blinded by the bright beam shining in her eyes. Then the light was gone, blocked by Aubrey's body as it flew at the woman. But the woman was ready for her. She spun counterclockwise and jumped aside. Aubrey twisted in midair to meet her. The swinging flashlight caught Aubrey's shoulder hard, but not before her fist made contact with the woman's cheek. Aubrey rolled backward onto the ground and sprang to her feet, producing her black and silver baton from nowhere. With an inhuman roar, she shapeshifted into a much larger, more muscular and menacing version of the same dark, camouflaged body.

The woman had turned her back on Sarah to face Aubrey. "Feeling feisty, are you?" She dragged her sleeve across her mouth and dropped the walkie-talkie to the ground. "All right then."

This was Sarah's moment. A scenario from her self defense training that afternoon flashed into her mind, and she knew exactly what to do. She would run and plant her heels into the backs of the woman's knees while she wasn't looking, and then she and Aubrey would run for it. But before she could take a step, Sarah saw the woman, silhouetted by the light of her flashlight, pull a gun from behind her back and point it at Aubrey. Sarah's entire body froze.

Cold dread filled her from hair to toenails. Aubrey was mouthing at her to run away. She wanted to shout that she couldn't, but her mouth and lungs would not obey. She couldn't even breathe.

"Still feel like fighting now?" the woman sneered, her pistol in one hand, flashlight in the other—both trained on Aubrey.

"How did you find us?" Aubrey asked through clenched teeth as she dropped the baton and raised her hands over her head.

"Oh, now you want to talk. That's good. Much easier than fighting." The woman crept to her right and turned slowly. Soon she would be able to keep an eye on Sarah without losing sight of Aubrey. "My associates will be here in a moment. No need to die before then."

Move! Sarah told herself. But she did not budge.

"How did you find us?!" Aubrey demanded, shouting now.

"The thing you must remember about humans is that, while they might not be able to pull off such impressive stunts as shapeshifting, they do have a certain talent for technology. I'll bet you didn't even think to check your motorcycle before you rode off into the sunset." She laughed. "What lies did you tell your little friends when you got back, I wonder? Did you brag that you and the big bad bear scared us all away?" The woman glanced toward Sarah and then back at Aubrey. "We only wanted the girl. And you led us straight to her. So thank you."

A glint of light reflected in the woman's eyes just then, and it caught Sarah's attention. In that moment, this grown woman did not look like a terrifying adult with a gun; she looked like a young girl, maybe a year or two older than Sarah, and she looked frightened. The vision caught Sarah off guard. Why would she be scared when she was the one holding the gun? Sarah gazed in wonder at the woman who did, indeed, appear to be grown up and confident again. She turned her attention to Aubrey, trying to read her expression. Had she seen it too?

"My bike," Aubrey mumbled, her eyes fixed on their captor. "So you tracked us."

"Very good," the woman said, still taking slow steps backward and glancing between the two. "You're not as stupid as I thought. Too bad you won't be able to pass that information along to your precious Sentinels."

Distant shouting reached Sarah's ears.

The woman with the gun turned her head toward the sound and shouted, "Over he—!"

But before she finished, Aubrey was on top of her, knocking her to the ground. The flashlight shot out of the woman's hand and landed several feet away, throwing a spotlight onto the two figures as they struggled for control of the gun.

Aubrey looked more terrifying than ever. She had pinned the woman's gun arm to the ground and raised a fist—which grew to twice its previous size and sprouted grotesque, bony protrusions on the knuckles—to strike. Then she slammed the hideous appendage into the dirt with a loud thud, missing the squirming woman's face by an inch.

Sarah, whose feet still refused to move, forced her head to turn so she could see if the others had topped the hill yet. They hadn't. She noticed, also, that there was no sign that her flashlight had broken free from the mud to provide any sort of distraction. *Brilliant idea, Genius,* she thought to herself.

She turned back to the fight and caught sight of that strange *something* again. Only this time there was more, and it pulled at her. In an instant, Aubrey was the girl she knew from school, fists flying and teeth bared as she wrestled another girl, young and frightened and furious. This time Sarah did not shake it off. She didn't focus her eyes to confirm what her mind had seen. Instead, she gave in to the vision. Time slowed to a crawl. Sarah's eyesight blurred, replaced in her consciousness by this new, ever-sharpening image. The world fell silent, but the fear and the fury of the two girls frozen mid-fight became so tangible that she could feel both their hearts beating inside her own chest. The tension of their straining muscles reflected in her own limbs. She could taste salty sweat on the tip of her tongue, and the familiar scents of dirt and cedar flooded her mind. Her heart raced, and the world spun around her. Then the scene changed as in a dream. Aubrey and the woman were gone, and Sarah was transported back to the mountain. It was Friday night again, and she was running as fast as she could toward the house, panicked and screaming for Grandpa. Images of Duke attacking Blackwood and Mr. Litchfield knocking Grandpa unconscious flashed before her.

Bang!

Reality snapped back into place. The pistol had launched a stray bullet into the black sky before Aubrey sent the gun sailing from the woman's hand. Before she knew what was happening, Sarah found herself racing into the fight. Fear was lost in the moment. These people had hurt Grandpa, had taken him away, and she would not let them hurt Aubrey too. She dove at the struggling woman, fists raised, with all the force she could muster. But at the last instant, the woman rolled and thrust Aubrey between herself and Sarah. Sarah slammed head-first into Aubrey's ribs, knocking her aside.

Sarah's feet flew over her head, and she landed flat on her back on top of a gnarled tree root that punched the breath from her lungs. The stars seemed to spin in the sky above her. A blurred mass darkened Sarah's view and lifted her by her hair until she was standing. Sarah felt a hand brush against her hip, and a moment later something cold and sharp was pressing into her throat.

"Show yourself, Aubrey" the woman screamed, "or I swear to God, I'll kill the brat with her own knife!"

Sarah patted her hip. The dagger her father had given her was not in its sheath.

There was a moment of silence. Then a girl who looked exactly like Sarah stepped into the light of the abandoned flashlight. "Let her go," Aubrey said with Sarah's trembling voice. "I'm the one you want. Not her." She was shivering, and her lip quivered. Sarah thought she saw tears welling up in the other Sarah's eyes.

"Very clever!" the woman hissed and spat.

"No!" the real Sarah cried. "Just leave me! Run!" She tried to bite the woman's arm and missed.

"Shut up and hold still!" spat the woman. She yanked Sarah's hair for emphasis.

"Go!" Sarah yelled. "Get out of here before—"

"No. It's okay," her clone said and sniffed. "You don't have to pretend anymore, Aubrey. I'll go with them." Then, to the woman, "Let her go! Please!" Her voice quivered with convincing desperation.

"I said *shut up!*" yelled the woman. "Both of you!"

There was a moment of tense silence. Then Aubrey spoke, her words cracking as if fighting frightened tears. "My name," sniff, "is Sarah Ann Lewis," she said. "My father is Jacob Alexander Lewis, the Weaver, direct descendant of Esau Midyan, founder of Les Luminaires. I'm the one you want, I swear! Ask me anything! I'll prove it."

"Nice try," the woman said, though she did not sound confident anymore.

"Please believe me!" Aubrey persisted. "Too many people have been hurt already! You don't need her. You've already got Grandpa, and now—"

"Yes we do, thanks to you. That old codger wasn't the mark, you know. They were only supposed to take the girl. But then you fools interfered, and—"

"Stop it! Please! *I'm* the girl. *I'm* Sarah, not her. If you'll just let her go, I'll come right now, without a fight, I promise." Aubrey stifled an incredibly realistic sob. "I know what you're after! I can't do it for you, but I know who can. I can help you find him. He'll come for me, and then you can—" The words ended in a choking sound. Aubrey's expression changed from one of desperation to one of anger. She huffed. Then in a tone of exasperation, she shouted, "Or don't! Whatever! Have it your way. Go back to your bosses without the *one little girl* you were sent to kidnap. I'm sure they'll love that!" Aubrey turned and stomped into the shadows.

"Stop!" the woman shouted. For a moment, her grasp loosened on Sarah's hair, and the blade of the ancient dagger faltered. A vision of the frightened girl's face flashed in Sarah's mind once again, and something clicked. *No way*, Sarah thought. *She can't be a shifter. Aubrey said Les Luminaires agents were all human.* But she had to be a shifter. Sarah knew it. She couldn't identify what it was, exactly, but something wasn't right—something she could only catch when she wasn't really looking. This is what had made her mistrust Aubrey at school. She had seen it happen with Fred during the meeting at Flatland Hall.

And it had happened earlier that night, before Sarah agreed to ride with Aubrey on the motorcycle.

A new plan began to form in Sarah's mind.

The woman was shouting at Aubrey again. "All right then, if you're the girl, then maybe I'll let this knife *accidentally* slip." The pressure of the blade against Sarah's throat made it hard for her to breathe.

"No!" Sarah heard her own voice shout from somebody else's mouth.

Sarah took advantage of the moment and shoved her hand into her pocket.

Aubrey stepped back into the light. "I mean, please don't! You won't, will you?" She was inching closer now. "You still don't know which of us is which. That's why you've been stalling, isn't it? You need one of us alive."

The woman took a step backward, causing Sarah to stumble. "Do I?" Her voice shook. "I don't think I do. Oh, they would *prefer* to have the girl alive. Some of them even think she might have the gift too, the fools! But I know better. Just like I know that you're a shifter, and a pathetic one at that." She took another step backward, but this time Sarah was ready and stepped with her, leaving one foot forward. "Your stupid persistence and her pitiful trembling gave you away. You're no human, and she's no weaver. She doesn't even have his DNA, does she? She's only a red-headed stray who was adopted by a couple of pathetic bleeding-heart Sentinels who couldn't have a kid of their own. She'll do just as well dead as—"

But the woman never finished her sentence. Filled with anger, Sarah simultaneously pushed herself backward as hard as she could and threw her fist upward, clutching the fragment of Luxephorean alloy she had finally freed from her pocket. The woman shrieked as her knife hand collided with the invisible remnant of a Vaelhalar shield. The dagger cut a line into Sarah's forehead as it flew from the woman's hand. But Sarah did not hesitate or flinch. She spun as fast as she could and drove the L-421 into her assailant's ribs. Then, when the woman doubled over in pain, Sarah thrust it up into her face as hard as she could.

It was easy. The artifact was so light. Sarah never felt the impact of the shield against the woman's skull, but she heard the crunching sound it made.

The woman fell backward into the shadows and did not move.

For a moment, all was quiet. Then Aubrey whispered, "Whoa. How did you—"

Sarah did not reply. She stood, mouth ajar, barely breathing, staring at the motionless body, and said nothing.

"There they are," a far off man's voice said.

"Sarah, you've got to go." said Aubrey.

But Sarah did not budge. She looked from the woman's feet to the thing in her hand and then up at Aubrey.

"Sarah! Wake up! They're coming!"

Bang! A bullet struck the ground between the two girls, sending a small explosion of dirt and leaves flying. The shouts and footsteps were growing louder.

Aubrey shoved Sarah behind a tree. "Sarah!" she whispered, slapping Sarah's cheeks. "Listen to me. You've got to run. Now! I can hold them for a few minutes, but you've got to get out of here before they—"

Bang! This time splinters flew from a small tree behind Sarah's back.

Sarah shook her head. Tears filled her eyes.

"Don't be stupid," Aubrey said. "If they catch you, The Watcher will have us all looking for *you*, and nobody will be left to rescue your Grandpa. So you have to get out of here! Now!"

Sarah ran. She ran until she could no longer hear the shouts and gunshots of her pursuers. Though her vision was blurred with tears and blood streamed down her face, she ran. Between trees and over fences, across wide expanses of rocky dirt and brush she ran, ignoring her stinging lungs and her aching, shoeless feet. And when she could run no more, she stumbled forward until, finally, her legs would no longer carry her, weakened by weariness and blood loss. When at last she fell, Sarah dragged herself into the cover of a thicket, hidden from anyone who might come looking for her. Only then did she close her eyes and surrender to utter exhaustion.

24

THE THICK OF IT

Sarah woke to the odd sensation of something cold and slimy on her face. For a moment, she thought she was at home in her own bed and wondered what was going on. But as she regained her senses, she realized that she was lying on hard ground. The air was hot. She could hear the sounds of birds and insects and whatever was squishing against her forehead. It stung.

"Ouch!" she squeaked. Then she sat up and bumped the top of her head on a low hanging branch. "OUCH!" Sarah rubbed her head and groaned. Her whole body hurt.

"Careful, now," said a raspy voice. "You're in a bad way already. No need to go making it worse." Sarah pried her eyes open. Before her was a grayish, cat-like creature with black and white stripes on his face and back. He stood on his hind feet and held a lump of green moss that dripped into a clay bowl on the ground beside him.

Sarah froze. "Are…" she started. "Are you a, umm—"

"A badger? Sure seems that way, don't it?"

"I was going to say a Sentinel." Sarah put her thumb to her ring finger, mimicking the gesture she had seen at the oath ceremony. She was sure she should feel frightened or at least startled, but she wasn't. There was a dull sensation of impatience mixed with something like sorrow, but mostly she felt hollow, drained.

The badger harrumphed and said in a mildly sarcastic tone, "Naw. Just one of the hidden." He sighed. "Now, hold still and let me clean that cut."

Sarah was not sure that letting a strange badger wipe her face with moss was a good idea. She flinched away.

"Don't worry. It's got iodine in it. It'll keep you from getting infected."

Sarah hesitated a moment before she decided that this was hardly the strangest or most dangerous thing she had done in the past couple of days. So she nodded and leaned forward, squeezing her eyes shut.

"I'm Ced, by the way," said the badger. "Well, Cedric, but everybody just calls me Ced." He paused. "And you're Jacob Lewis's girl, huh? That true?"

"Mmhmm," Sarah hummed, trying not to wince as Ced dabbed the wet moss against the cut on her forehead. She opened her mouth to ask how he knew, but he spoke again before she had the chance.

"Ain't that something? He's practically royalty! A king among men. I guess that makes you—"

"Don't say it," Sarah groaned.

"...a princess." Ced finished. "Good as one, anyway; that's what I say. Though, it's funny, you don't resemble him much. But I guess there's no accounting for humans."

"Yeah," Sarah muttered. "Guess not." Then she thought to herself, *Or maybe there's a very good reason I don't look like my parents.* But no. Surely not. The woman must have been lying. Sarah's parents wouldn't have kept something so important from her. Would they?

"Well then, young Miss Lewis, I'm right proud to be at your service." The badger stepped back, gave a little bow, and then went back to cleaning Sarah's face. "Things still ain't what they ought to be, of course, but they're a sight better than they were before your dad came along. Next time you see him, you tell him the folks at Rancho Alvarez said 'thanks,' would you? We haven't forgotten."

"Yeah, sure," Sarah replied, eager to change the subject away from her dad. "How do you know who I am? And how did you find me?"

"Well," Ced replied as he reached into the clay bowl for a bit of fresh moss. "I wouldn't know who you are if I hadn't been in the right place at the right time last night. Overheard a bit of the talk before you went running, and I recognized your dad's name. And as to how I found you, well, I tracked you same as any wounded animal: I followed the blood. You left a pretty good trail all the way from Buzzard Hill where you took out that no-good, filthy bag of," he paused and cleared his throat, "I mean that awful woman." He had moved on from her forehead and was now dabbing at the days-old cut on her chin.

"Yeah.." A picture of the woman's motionless body flashed into Sarah's mind.

"Yes, ma'am. I've got to say, that was some bit of fighting you pulled off. Course, I wouldn't have expected any less from the Weaver's kid. I bet he taught you all kinds of—"

"*He* didn't teach me anything," Sarah muttered.

Ced cocked his head to one side. "I see." He sighed and resumed his work. "Well, Miss Lewis, it was a good thing you got out of there when you did. We—I mean, some of the other folks who live around here—helped fight those bullies off, but your shifter friend didn't make out so well. She's—"

"Aubrey's hurt?"

"I'd say so. She's in better shape than the woman who gave you that cut, but I won't lie, it's bad. My cousin Lucy's seeing to her now. Treating shifters is tricky business, but Lucy's the best medic we've got. She'll be all right."

"Where is she?" Sarah asked and moved toward the edge of the thicket.

"Whoa, now. I'm afraid you're not going anywhere. It ain't safe."

"I don't care," Sarah said in a matter-of-fact tone. "I have to find Aubrey and get her back to The Sentinels."

"That's very noble of you. But just you stop and think first. Whoever was after you will be back. Might even be out there now. We've got some scouts watching the perimeter, and we sent a couple of flyers to look for your Sentinels already, but until we find them, you'd best stay here."

Sarah slumped against a wall of tangled branches. "Fine. But if we don't know something by—"

"Let's just give it some time before we go making plans. All right? Now, I think I've got some things that belong to you." From beneath a bush behind him, Ced produced Sarah's shoes and backpack. "Here you go."

Sarah gasped. "How did you find them?"

"I didn't. I was here with you. A friend of mine brought them by while you were sleeping."

Sarah took the bag and unzipped it. Her dagger, which had been stuffed into the top of the main compartment, fell onto the ground at her feet.

"They found your knife in the brush near that woman," Ced explained. "That is your knife isn't it?"

"Yeah," said Sarah as she placed the dagger back into its sheath on her hip. Then she reached into the backpack and pulled out her sweatshirt. She slipped it on over her dirty tee shirt, grateful for the warmth.

"They found that and your shoestrings—I believe they're in the front pocket—at the top of Buzzard Hill. Said you had it tied to a flashlight that went swinging just as the bad guys were closing in. It surprised them all pretty good, apparently, and it gave your shifter friend—Aubrey, did you say?—a fighting chance. She knocked one of 'em clean out before he knew what hit him. You done good, cub. Rigging up everything like that was pretty clever. Well, for a human anyway." He paused. "No offense, of course, but you aren't exactly the brightest species on the planet."

Actually, until that moment, Sarah had been certain that humans were the brightest species on the planet. She remembered Boarsmash saying that the aenimos were brilliant, but she had only thought of them as smarter-than-normal animals. Maybe she had been wrong. Maybe to them, she was a smarter-than-normal animal.

"Whatever," she said. "It was stupid. Maybe if the thing had actually worked the way it was supposed to, Aubrey wouldn't be hurt at all."

Cedric squinted at her. "Seems to me, you aren't giving yourself enough credit."

"Credit for what? Making sure everybody who spends time around me gets hurt? Sure. I should take more credit for that."

"Now, that's not what I—" Ced began.

"Forget it," Sarah said. "I didn't mean it." Only, she did. Her mom had died. Grandpa had been kidnapped. Now Aubrey had been hurt. And she had no idea what had happened to Samuel and Duke and Boarshmash. A tear dripped down her cheek.

For a while, Ced said nothing. Then, slowly, he approached and sat on the ground next to Sarah. The two sat in silence for several minutes while Sarah replaced her torn and filthy socks with a clean pair from the backpack and then slipped her shoes back on and started lacing them up.

"Listen, cub," he said at last. "I've been around for a good long time. I've seen a lot of life. And let me tell you something: people—human or aenimos or whatever—they don't put themselves in harm's way without a good reason. It ain't some sense of duty or stupid courage that keeps a shifter impersonating a red-headed little girl while grown men beat the ever-loving tar out of her. Oh no. Make no mistake about it. Your friend chose that beating because she thought something was worth it. She thought *you* were worth it."

Sarah huffed. "She's an agent, and I'm her assignment. She was just doing what she was told."

"I doubt it. Obedience only goes so far. In my experience there are only two things that'll motivate a person to do a thing like that: fear and love. In the end, it's usually some of both, but one always comes out on top."

"It was a stupid thing to do either way. Aubrey just met me. She should have left me there. She should have run away."

"Well, I'm sure your dad will be grateful she didn't."

Sarah finished tying her shoes. She almost said something sarcastic about how her dad might be grateful if he was still around to find out she was safe, but she couldn't bring herself to say it. Instead, she said, "I don't want to talk about it, okay?" and laid back down on the dirt. She closed her eyes and tried not to think. It didn't work.

She found herself missing her dad terribly and remembering the first time her dad had ever called her "Sprinkles." That had been a great day. She had been four or five years old. He stood next to her, holding her hand as they waited in line. Sarah peeked around a pair of grown-up legs at the glass counter to see the endless selection of glazed and frosted confections. The legs walked away, and he pulled her forward.

"I'll have a dozen plain glazed and whatever this little munchkin wants." He scooped Sarah up and held her high so the cashier could hear her.

She had been wearing a pair of pink polka-dotted cotton pajamas that day, worn and pilled from many washings. "I want chocolate...with sprinkles!"

"Sprinkles?!" her father laughed. "Yes! Give this girl some sprinkles. In fact, give her *two* chocolate donuts with *extra* sprinkles, please." He squeezed her tight, and Sarah giggled as he rubbed his nose against hers. "That's the most important part, after all, isn't it?"

"I love you, Daddy," she remembered saying.

"I love you too, Sprinkles." He smiled.

"More than donuts?" she asked.

"More than all the donuts in the whole world."

The memory was interrupted by a flurry of wings. A great barn owl descended into the thicket.

"Hey there, Barnabas. What's the news?" Ced asked.

"We have to get you two out of here," said the owl, "and quick. There's a fire at the southern border, and it's spreading fast."

25

INTO THE FIRE

"What about Aubrey?" Sarah shouted between panting breaths.

Several yards ahead of her, Ced called over his shoulder, "Don't know. Lucy will take care of her." Then he darted around a large tree and out of sight.

The badger was surprisingly fast. Even on her best day, Sarah could not have outrun him. Now, between her bruised feet, aching muscles, and the backpack bouncing on her shoulders, it was all she could do to keep up.

Barnabas the owl surveyed their path from above and hooted signals that Ced seemed to understand. At a sound, he would shift to the left or to the right, always staying under the cover of trees, always finding the quickest path northward. More than once, Sarah lost sight of her guide, but always he reappeared, leading her ever onward.

The smell of smoke on the hot southern wind kept Sarah moving despite the pain. She would not stop until they reached safety.

When she rounded the next bend in the trail, however, she found Ced stopped in the middle of the path, one paw held out toward her, motioning for her to stop too.

Sarah skidded and froze. They were not alone. Barnabas was perched on a low branch next to a hawk. And beside the trail, in the shadow of a tree, sat an enormous cougar. Sarah's heart pounded, and she inched backward.

"It's all right Miss Lewis," said Ced. "Frankie won't hurt you."

"Francesca, if you please, Cedric," said a rumbling voice that made Sarah's insides jiggle.

Ced rolled his eyes and continued. "*Frankie* was one of the bunch who fought off your attackers last night, and she's been stalking them ever since, keeping an eye out for more trouble."

"Enough talk," said Barnabas, motioning toward the hawk, "Thomas has news for us."

"And keep your voices down," whispered the cougar. "There are hounds not far from here sniffing out the human's scent."

Sarah gasped.

"That's right," said Thomas. "We must be swift." He turned his head from side to side and then made a bowing motion to Sarah. "I have spoken with the one called the Watcher. He will meet us at the large rock near Raccoon Ridge."

"But that's on the southern border! Clear on the other side of the fire!" argued Ced.

"Yes," replied Thomas, "The humans set the fire near that place and then drove around to the road south of Rancho Alvarez. Between the fire and their dogs, it would seem they mean to flush out our young friend."

"I hope she is worth it," said Frankie. "Our homes are burning."

"I'm so sorry," whispered Sarah.

"Nonsense," said Ced. "We wouldn't even have these homes if it weren't for the kindness of your dad and other good humans like him." Then to Thomas, "I'll stay close to her. What's the plan?"

"Follow the old creek bed. It won't be easy or safe, but it's mostly rocks, so it's your best shot. I've asked the Rattans to gather all the help they can and clear brush out of the way. Barnabas, you and I had better fly ahead and keep an eye on things. Frankie—"

"I'll bring up the rear."

"Perfect," said Thomas. "Let's move."

Sarah's feet still ached, and the wind blew wisps of smoke into her stinging eyes, but somehow running toward the fire seemed right, and that made it easier than running away. The longer Sarah ran, the more speed she found. Her lungs burned from hard breathing and coughing, but there was something else too: with every breath, a stronger sense of courage, determination, and excitement swelled in her chest. She spit the stickiness from her mouth, tightened the straps of her backpack, took a deep breath, and pushed herself to a faster pace.

They broke from the tree cover and sprinted across a wide grassy field dotted with cactus and brush. Overhead, Barnabas drifted left and right across the smoky sky, hooting directions to Ced. Higher still, Thomas circled and cawed. Sarah looked over her shoulder and realized that she could no longer see Frankie. She wondered where the great cat had gone, but this was no time to ask questions.

The ground became gradually rockier. Once, Sarah tripped and fell, but she was back on her feet and running again in an instant. A line of trees on her right grew steadily closer. Ced turned and disappeared over a little ridge between two of the trees. Sarah pivoted on her heels, slid on the dirt, and ran after him.

Just beyond the trees was a steep embankment that led down into the dry creek bed Thomas had described. The rocks on its floor were smooth, round, and gray. Most were as big as baseballs, and some were bigger than softballs. They slipped beneath Sarah's feet as she ran, and she was forced to slow down to keep from spraining an ankle. That was just as well. The smoke was thicker now, and it was harder to breathe. Ced stopped and waited for Sarah to catch up before going on.

The heat grew, and Sarah could hear the crackling of green wood burning not far away. The helpers Thomas had enlisted were busy at work. Armadillos, large rats, and other animals Sarah could not identify were scurrying to and fro, working together to push brush and dead wood to the edges of the creek bed. Further on, they came upon a group of rats, rabbits, and turtles trying in vain to force a fallen tree out of the way.

Other animals they passed, however, were running the opposite direction in the middle of their path, seeking shelter from the flames. "Out of the way!" Ced shouted at them. None of them replied, and none of them made any great effort to move aside.

Ced stopped and grabbed Sarah's hand. "Almost there, cub. We'd best catch our breath while there's still some air to breathe. It's cleaner down here." He pointed to the ground.

Sarah sat on the rocks and put her head between her knees.

"The fire will be here in a few minutes," said Ced. "Whatever happens, don't stop. You hear? Just keep moving. The creek bed gets narrower up yonder, and then you'll run into the dam. You'll have to climb it and make your way to the left if you can. There's a dirt road there, and just on the other side, you'll see a boulder, tall as a cedar bush up on top of a little ridge. That's the place."

Sarah sat up. "Aren't you coming with me?"

"If I can." Ced's nose twitched and he looked from side to side. "But you get there either way. Understand?"

Sarah did not reply. She looked at the sky and looked for Barnabas through the smoke. But what she saw was Thomas the hawk diving straight toward them from above the fire, falling so fast that Sarah thought he would crash into the ground. At the last moment, Thomas stretched out his great wings and beat the air, extending his sharp talons in front of him. "Dogs!" he screeched as he soared over their heads.

Sarah turned and watched Thomas collide feet first with the snarling face of a muscular brown dog who had appeared from around a bend in the creek a couple hundred yards away. The dog yelped in pain as again and again the bird attacked with beak and claw. Then three more appeared, running fast and bellowing.

"Run!" shouted Ced.

Sarah was on her feet and sprinting toward the fire before he finished the word. But the dogs were fast. Their barking grew louder with every second.

"Go on!" cried Ced. "Get to the boulder! I'll hold them off!"

"No!" Sarah screamed and slid to a halt. Time seemed to slow as she watched.

The first dog was still busy fending off Thomas, and Sarah saw that Barnabas had now joined the fight. The two birds were drawing it out of the creek bed. But the other three hounds were approaching fast. One of the dogs had outpaced the other two and was almost on top of Ced already. The badger hissed and bowed his back. Every hair on his body stood on end. The dog leapt, but Ced sidestepped and sank his claws into the beast's ribs. The dog yelped and rolled, revealing a dark line of standing hair that ran down the center of its back. It righted itself and then turned on Ced, snarling.

The other two hounds caught up and slowed to a crouching walk. But before they had a chance to join the fight, they were blindsided by Frankie who leapt onto them from out of the brush on the eastern side of the creek bed. Before Sarah knew what had happened, one of the dogs lay motionless while the other circled the cougar, growling.

The brave badger stared down the first dog, moving back and forth, hissing warnings.

He'll be okay, Sarah told herself. *Just run!* She took a few hesitant steps toward the fire again, but she stopped when she heard the bellowing howls of more hounds. Her heart sank. Looking behind, she saw three more dogs. It sounded like more were on the way. "Ced!" she shouted.

Ced, who had already spotted the danger, turned to her with panic on his face. "Run! Run, cub!" he called. Then he turned once again to face his foes.

But Sarah did not run. Something inside her hardened then, and she was not afraid. She would not allow one more person to be hurt protecting her. She was the one who had taken vows to protect others, after all. Who was this silly badger to be giving orders? "No," she said bluntly. "Not this time."

Sarah picked up a heavy dead branch, let loose a scream, and ran into the fight. She swung the branch like a baseball bat and hit the closest hound in the neck. The dog yelped and tumbled over the loose rocks. When it gained its feet, it turned to attack Sarah. Ced jumped onto the dog's hind end and tried to bite, but it shook him loose. Sarah swung the branch again, but this time the dog was ready. It ducked beneath the blow, and while Sarah was off balance, it knocked her to the ground. The branch flew from her hands. She heard Ced hissing and shouting, but the snarling beast would not turn away. She flailed and scrambled away and tried to stand before she was knocked again to her back. All the world was a blur of barking and growling, muscled jaws, sharp white teeth, and drool. She struggled and kicked, guarding her face and neck with her arms. Pain shot through her left forearm as the dog's teeth clamped down around the sleeve of her sweatshirt, just above her wrist. She punched with her free hand, but the beast would not relent. Desperately, Sarah reached around for another branch or a rock or anything she could use to defend herself, but she found nothing. Suddenly, she remembered the dagger in its sheath on her hip. She rolled onto one side, grabbed it, and swung blindly.

The blade connected with firm flesh and only slowed a little before it stopped against something hard. The fight was over. Her arm was free. She scurried backward and found her feet. When she finally took in the scene, she saw her dagger buried hilt deep into the hound's neck. The beast lay on the ground, making a horrible gurgling noise and twitching. She stood blinking for a moment before the sounds of barks and hisses called her back to reality. With some effort, she yanked the knife from the dog's body and turned toward the others.

Ced stood frozen, staring stupidly at Sarah, his mouth ajar. Beyond him, Frankie ripped into the second hound's face with a swipe from her massive paw. The dog fell to the ground, limp and lifeless.

The next three dogs arrived a moment later, snarling as they approached.

"Well, if you're not going to run—" Ced began.

"Not a chance."

"Then let's do this smart. All right? These dogs are pack hunters. They're stronger together. We've got to break them up. You take the left. I'll take the right."

Ced scurried up the bank on the right side of the creek. Sarah stepped to her left and walked steadily forward. The fire was hot on her back now, but she did not turn. She kept her eyes on the snarling teeth ahead of her.

Frankie crouched, waited, and then pounced on the advancing hounds. She landed with her full weight on the dog in the center, and the other two jumped out of the way. But before Sarah could join the attack, all three were barking and circling Frankie, baring their teeth, jumping forward to snap at Frankie's haunches, and then ducking away before the snarling cat could land a blow or a bite.

With a raspy screech, Ced leapt onto one of the dogs and bit its tail. The dog yelped and spun, flinging the badger to the ground. Ced found his feet and ran toward the burning woods. The dog ignored him and turned back toward Frankie. "Come on, you stupid mutt," yelled Ced. He threw a stick and hit the dog's backside. No response. He jumped onto its back again, and again he was flung to the ground.

Frankie hissed and rolled and batted and snapped her teeth at the dogs, but she could not connect.

"Hey mutts!" Sarah shouted, following Ced's lead. "Over here!" She picked up a tennis ball-sized rock, threw it at one of the dogs, and missed. She tried again. This time, she hit the largest of the hounds square in the jaw. The dog yelped and turned to bark at her.

"Come on, then!" Sarah shouted and walked toward it, scooping up another rock as she went. The dog growled and faced her, barking ferociously. It jumped. She held up her dagger, but the dog was too quick, and she was knocked to the ground before her blade found its mark. Sarah's head slammed into the rocks, and for a moment the world was dark and quiet. When she came back to her senses, she saw that the two great birds, Thomas and Barnabas, had returned and were taking turns dive-bombing the hound, clawing at it with each pass.

Sarah searched the ground and found her dagger nearby. She snatched it up and stood. But the birds had been too much for the dog, and it was limping away as quickly as it could. Frankie, too, stood over her third victim. But Ced and the last dog were nowhere to be found.

"Ced!" Sarah cried. "Ced! Where are you?!"

"He's there, in the fire," called Thomas. He motioned toward the edge of the creek bed. There, beneath an arch of flaming trees, Sarah watched in horror as a dog shook Ced's limp form in its jowls like a rag doll. Sarah ran, but Frankie outran her. By the time she reached the spot, another dog lay motionless beneath Frankie's enormous forepaws, no longer holding the brave badger.

"Where's Ced?" asked Sarah.

Frankie did not speak. She stepped aside, and Sarah saw a dark shape stretched on the rocks behind her.

All the world faded away for a long moment. Sarah had failed.

She felt herself being nudged forward into the creek bed by Frankie. "Go on," Sarah heard her say as if from a long way off, "they're calling for you. Go to them. If there were hunting dogs, there will be hunters not far behind. Go to your Sentinels before it's too late."

Then another sound caught her attention. "Miss Sarah!" Samuel's deep voice was calling her from beyond the flames. "Miss Sarah!"

Sarah did not reply. She scooped up the bloody, singed body of Cedric the badger and walked silently onward under a canopy of flame and smoke.

26

THE WEAVER'S KEY

"Was I adopted?"

Samuel hesitated. "Yes."

"Does everybody know?"

Aubrey looked away. Duke laid his head on the tile floor and whimpered. Boarsmash, who lay with his head wrapped in bandages on a nearby table, illuminated in reds and blues by warm sunlight through a stained glass window, did not respond. He had probably fallen asleep again, Sarah thought. Fred leaned against the wall, silent. The Sentinels had rushed him to San Antonio by helicopter as soon as they heard Aubrey was injured. He had arrived at the old church minutes after the others, and he had not said a word since.

Father Stephen had welcomed Samuel as an old friend and given them an unused room for as long as they needed it while other arrangements were made. Samuel had been on the phone most of the afternoon. This was the first chance they'd had to talk.

"Not everyone," said Samuel. "But yes. We have known."

"Then why didn't you tell me?"

"It was not our story to tell."

"Yeah, I've heard that before. Aubrey said something like that after she mentioned that I'd met her dad."

Samuel exchanged a look with Aubrey, then said, "Indeed."

"Well, if you weren't going to tell me, then who was? This is kind of big news for me."

"It was for your father to decide. However—" Samuel's voice trailed off.

"What?"

"He has," Samuel paused a moment, as if he were searching for the right words, "stopped communicating with The Sentinels. And with me. I do not know where he has gone or what he plans to do."

"What do you mean?"

"Your father is the reason Les Luminaires have been so interested in you and your grandfather. They have been trying to locate him, to force his hand. They believed, I am sure, that if they had you, he would come for you, no matter what."

Sarah glanced around the old church classroom. She thought about what Aubrey and the mysterious woman had said the night before. She looked at Aubrey, lying on a makeshift bed atop a folding table, and tried to remember every word. Aubrey was still covered in bruises and cuts, but she already looked better than she had when they arrived. It was strange to watch her heal. Broken bones and swelling healed so quickly that Sarah could see the change if she watched intently enough, like the moving of the minute hand on a clock, while some of Aubrey's scratches and cuts seemed not to heal at all.

"I fear," Samuel continued, "that they have somehow communicated to your father that they have captured you or that they will kill you if he does not present himself, and now…" He paused. "I do not know what he might do."

"But why? What do they want with him?"

Samuel sighed. "That is a long story."

"I'm not going anywhere."

He stood and began to walk around the room. "Long ago, when the people of all seven realms walked this Earth, there was a disagreement between the otherworlders about what should be done about humans. Some wished to welcome them as equals. Some—led by the Obsinders—wished to be less kind."

"Why?" asked Sarah.

"Humanity was the only native intelligent species on this planet. They were the rightful heirs of the Earth. But the Obsinders wanted to control this crossroads between realms. By eliminating humanity, they would eliminate the biggest threat to that control.

"Many of the Vaelhalar had already intermarried with humans, and the Narinaelians had used science to create half-human descendants for themselves, so they were natural allies and stood against the Obsinders. Most of the Fodinaran and Taborian tribes had made alliances with humans as well, but I don't believe any of them thought it would actually come to war.

"The Obsinders prepared their armies in secret and offered their protection to any frightened otherworlders who would ally with them. They spread lies to gain support. They said that the humans were disease-ridden savages who were violent and dangerous.

"According to most versions of the story, the fighting began when a group of twenty human men attacked and killed a high-ranking Obsinder who had kidnapped a young woman from their village. All but two of the men died in the fight. The young woman was never seen again. News of the attack spread. Both sides called it an act of war by the other side. Both sides saw it as proof that they were right and good while their enemies were evil murderers.

"Then the fighting began. The Obsinders attacked while the humans and their allies were just beginning to organize. The onslaught was swift and violent. The earthling armies were terribly outmatched. No doubt, you and I would not be here today if it had not been for one thing."

"The Weaver's Key," Aubrey whispered in a tone of solemnity.

"Yes. The Weaver's Key," Samuel confirmed.

"What's that?" Sarah asked.

"There are many tales of powerful and mysterious weapons from that time. Most of them are probably myths. But the Key, at least, is real. It was—and remains to this day—our surest protection against those who would invade and conquer this world. It is a device, created by a council of otherworlders, made of precious and—if you believe the stories—mystic materials from each of the Seven Realms. When it was completed, one worthy human was chosen to be the Weaver. He was blessed by the elders of each allied race—the blessings you received at the end of the oath ceremony were symbolic of that first blessing. The Vaelhalar's blessing for the Weaver was the gift of 'sight beyond sight' which enabled him to use the Key to open or close the gate between this universe and the others. Or at least, that is the legend."

"So what? He shut the door before the Obsinders could bring their armies through?"

"Oh no. Remember, their armies had already arrived and were slaughtering humans. But as soon as the Weaver used the Key, they surrendered and returned to their own world.

Sarah looked puzzled.

"You see, little one, to shut the gateway is to forcefully separate our universe from all others. No living thing caught on the wrong side of a closed gate can survive, this much is certain. An integral part of every otherworlder, a part you cannot see from this reality, extends into dimensions that can only exist in their own universe. Where the realities overlap, we observe them in part, but there is more to each of us.

"When the Weaver began to narrow the gate and the portal contracted, the otherworlders who were here on Earth—both enemies and allies—found themselves stretched and strangled in ways that no living thing should ever have to endure. The bravery and sacrifice of humanity's allies in those days is an everlasting testament to compassion and loyalty. The enemy armies were forced to surrender, and the Weaver demanded that they take their weapons and leave. The Vaelhalar all went home too. My people, however, like all the half-human species, considered Earth their home and remained. Many of the friendly otherworlders chose to stay as well, though it is said that most left. Then the Weaver used the Key to close the gate—tightly enough to make passage between realms impossible but not so tightly that the remaining otherworlders could not live comfortably on Earth—and the Key was hidden.

"For thousands of years now, the title of the Weaver and the secret of the Key's location has been passed from father to son. And since the beginning, it has been the duty of an Aravatis bearing the title of the Watcher to keep an eye on the Weaver and the Key."

"And my father is the Weaver now."

Samuel looked surprised.

"That woman, the one I—" Sarah couldn't bring herself to say what she had done. "She said something about it when she was threatening to…" Again, Sarah could not bring herself to finish the sentence. She shrugged and looked away. In reality, it had been Aubrey who referred to Sarah's father as "the Weaver," but something told Sarah that revealing this bit of information might get Aubrey into trouble.

"That woman was Arabella Minot. She, like Aubrey, was a Taborian earthling, but she was not a member of The Sentinels. We do not know why, but it seems she was working for Les Luminaires, and somehow she led them to you."

"I know how she knew," said Fred.

Everyone turned, surprised by his voice. Sarah had opened her mouth to say that she already knew the woman was a shifter, but that no longer seemed important.

"She was…" he choked and cleared his throat. "Arabella was my friend. I met her here in San Antonio a couple of summers ago. I snuck out with some friends and went downtown. Caught her shifting to sneak into a bar. We snuck in too. I made a joke or something, and we hit it off. So we stayed in touch. Phone calls and letters here and there. Turned out she hated humans. Thought the Sentinels were a bunch of puppets that promoted the oppression of otherworlders. I told her I wasn't a huge fan of most humans either but some weren't so bad. I guess she didn't like that because I didn't hear from her for a while. Then, last fall, she started offering to meet up. I could name the time and place. So we met a few times when I was off duty. I didn't say anything about it because I knew you'd get involved," he nodded toward Samuel, "and I didn't want you to scare her off. Besides, she told me that she had taken what I'd said to heart, and now she was working with some humans who were really nice and smart. She said they were trying to help her get to Tabor so she wouldn't have to hide anymore. I knew that was impossible, but I liked her, so I didn't make a big deal out of it. I just laughed and talked. And talked. Too much. I didn't know she was working for…for *them*."

Nobody moved. Finally, Samuel spoke. "What did you tell her?"

"I don't know," whispered Fred, a tear trickling down his cheek. "I mean, I don't remember. Lots of things. Lots of things I shouldn't have said. And I think it's my fault they knew who you were when you chased them down, Sis. I'd talked about you a lot, and I know I said something about how obnoxious you were on that white and gold motorcycle. I told her all about you. It's my fault you're hurt. I'm so sorry." He sniffed and wiped his nose on his sleeve. Then he walked out of the room before anybody could respond.

Aubrey closed her eyes and groaned. "And then they put a tracking device on my bike." She slammed her fist down onto the table. "Ugh! Between the two of us, we led Les Luminaires straight to you, Miss Sarah. Some protectors we turned out to be!"

Sarah shuffled her feet and stared at the floor. She wanted to tell Aubrey that it was okay, that it wasn't their fault, that she was the one with two dead bodies on her conscience, not them. But she knew it wouldn't help.

Samuel seemed to sense her thoughts and spoke up. "None of you are to blame for the actions of Les Luminaires. They set the fire. They ambushed me. They attacked Mr. Boarsmash and Duke—though it seems they were not prepared for that battle. They murdered Mr. Cedric and, I fear, many more of the peaceful aenimos people who live at Rancho Alvarez. Those who have survived have, at best, lost homes because of their actions. Les Luminaires are to blame for all of this. Not you. You all fought well, and I am proud to call you agents and friends. When Mr. Fred is ready, I will speak with him as well. He is a good agent who made a mistake, and he will learn from it. None of us must burden our consciences with the evil deeds of others."

"I still don't understand what Les Luminaires wants with my dad, though," said Sarah after a moment. "Are they trying to steal the Weaver's Key?"

"No, little one. They want your father to use it."

27

FAMILY SKELETONS

"They want him to use the Weaver's Key? To do what?!" Sarah demanded.

"We do not know," said Samuel. "Perhaps they wish him to close the gate completely."

"But wouldn't that—"

"Yes. That would be the end of all otherworlders in Cosmos. Probably, it would mean my death as well, though it is less clear what would become of half-humans like me."

"He would never...I mean, he wouldn't do that. Would he?"

"No. I do not believe that he would. He has spent his life fighting for the freedom and rights of otherworlders and half-humans. But a father whose child is in danger may do many things he would not normally—"

"Then there's nothing to worry about."

Samuel looked at her with a puzzled expression.

Sarah huffed. "It's not like I'm his real daughter. I'm adopted. Remember? You're safe."

"Do you believe that being adopted makes you something less than his real child?"

Sarah shrugged.

Samuel crossed the room and knelt before her. He placed one of his enormous hands on her shoulder and lifted her chin with the other. Even kneeling, he was so tall that she had to look up at his face.

"Ahh, Miss Sarah. I am sorry that you have been caught in the middle of this mess with Les Luminaires. I warned your father that if he left you behind without an explanation, you would feel he did not truly love you. It is his leaving, however, that proves—"

Sarah cut him off. "I really don't want to talk about it. Not yet."

Samuel sighed, took both of her hands in his, squeezed them, and then stood. "All right, little one." He walked to the other side of the room and said no more.

Sarah fidgeted and tried not to think about her parents, but there were so many questions boiling in her mind. Finally, she changed the subject. "How are you feeling, Aubrey?"

"Not great," said Aubrey, "but better than Mr. Boarsmash." Then to Samuel, "What happened to him?"

Samuel glanced at Duke and then turned his gaze to Boarsmash. "He fought bravely, but he was taken by surprise. We were, all of us, ambushed."

"What did they do to him?"

Again Samuel looked at Duke before he answered. "I am not certain. Duke has chosen not to share the details of the encounter with me. I only know that, when we found them, a dozen Les Luminaires comrades lay dead. Mr. Boarsmash was badly injured, and his arms, legs, and mouth show signs of having been bound. Duke, however, seems to have been unharmed."

Duke wagged his tail and made no sound.

"Do you think he called on the pentrafax?" asked Aubrey with wonder in her voice. "That would be—"

"Let us not speculate on what we do not know," said Samuel. But Sarah saw him wink at Aubrey.

"What about you?" asked Sarah. "You said you were ambushed too. What happened?"

"Let us say that it was unwise for those men to refuse my hospitality. Perhaps next time they will think better of it," said Samuel in a tone of finality.

"And the others?" said Aubrey. "The Alvarezes? Dr. Connolly and Dr. Allen? Dr. MacPherson and Mr. Tellurak?"

"Mr. and Mrs. Alvarez are safe and under guard. The scientists have all arrived safely in Austin with their equipment—yes, Dr. MacPherson is with them now. They are awaiting further instruction."

"What happened when Les Luminaires showed up at the mansion?" asked Sarah. "Did they take Blackwood?"

"They never arrived at the mansion. It is possible that was never their plan and the information I was given was incorrect, or it is possible that they changed their plans. I suspect we may have been seen leaving."

"I guess they didn't want Blackwood after all."

Samuel nodded.

"How did you find out they were coming to San Antonio anyway?" asked Sarah.

"There are, I am afraid, some details that I cannot share with a junior agent." He smiled. "I can say, however, that there were multiple sources. And I will tell you that the first warning came via a dot-matrix printer. It contained details helpful to our search for your grandfather. Unfortunately, however, it seems the printer malfunctioned before printing was completed, so we only received the first half page. Had we received the entire message, perhaps the past twenty-four hours would have gone differently, and perhaps…" He trailed off.

"To Miss Aubrey's original question, though," Samuel continued after a moment, "Mr. Tellurak is safe as well. He is working with some of the locals to coordinate security for the rescue and rebuild effort at Rancho Alvarez. Miss Sarah and I will see him tonight when we return Mr. Cedric's body to his family."

The sunset lit the sky in brilliant oranges and pinks above the western skyline. Sarah licked half-heartedly at the chocolate dipped ice cream cone Father Stephen had brought for her. She had not touched the take-out hamburgers and french fries. Aubrey and Boarsmash were both sleeping, and Samuel had taken Sarah and Duke for a walk around the church grounds.

"Miss Sarah," said Samuel, "I understand that you have much on your mind. This is not the right time for what I must say, and I apologize. But I am afraid I may not have another opportunity to speak to you alone for some time, and there are some things you must know. Have you opened the box?"

"What box?"

"The box that I gave you at your oath ceremony."

"Oh. No. I haven't really had a chance."

"I understand. When you do, please know that the gift inside that box was entrusted to me by your mother, and it is more than it appears. It will help you identify messages that your parents may have left you, and I suspect they have left many. It will be a help to you, just as your earrings help you communicate with Duke and the ring you wear helps you identify otherworlders—"

"It does?" Sarah held up her hand and gazed at the ring. The pearl was now a creamy purple along the left edge, nearest Samuel, and a deep blue on the right, nearest Duke.

"Yes. Its color can change to match the banner for each realm when a person from that realm is near." Samuel grinned. "Your father wore that ring with the stone facing his palm for many years before he gave it to your mother. It is one of several ancient items that," Samuel pointed to the gem on the front of his turban, "have been handed down through the generations among the families of the Weaver and the Watcher. These items must be kept secret."

"How old can they be? It sounds like I have a Speak & Spell in my head when he talks to me."

Samuel laughed. "The gems in your earrings and in Duke's collar are very old. They have facilitated communication by vibration for thousands of years. Your father did not feel he needed them, so he gave them to your mother. Now, your mother was quite a skilled engineer, and before you came along, she crafted the gems into earrings that would vibrate against the backs of her ears. Then she taught Duke morse code, and for a long time, that is how they communicated. Then, shortly before she died, she integrated some micro circuitry—"

"Wait. My mom knew Duke?"

"Yes. Duke has been, in many different bodies, the faithful companion of the Watcher and the Weaver for longer than I know. Your mother was quite fond of Duke, and he of her."

"But I don't remember seeing him."

"Indeed. Your parents saw him when they were at work. But they would not allow any of The Sentinels into your home. They would not even mention the name in your presence."

"Yeah, I figured that out." Sarah kicked at the grass and crossed her arms. "But why, Samuel? Why wouldn't they just tell me?"

"For your protection."

Sarah rolled her eyes. "Seriously? Again?! I wish people would stop trying to protect me and just tell me things."

Samuel swept the hair from in front of Sarah's face and sighed. "Ahh, little one. It is hard, I know. But if you are ready to talk about your family now, I can tell you some things that will help you understand."

Sarah stopped walking and looked away, biting her lip. Anger and curiosity were fighting in her brain. "All right," she said at last.

"Good. Listen to me, little one. This is important, and our time is short.

"Your great-grandfather, seven generations removed on your father's side, was a man named Esau Midyan—a cruel, proud, self-centered man. He was the Weaver in his day, and he was the last whom my father served as the Watcher before me. He lived in France, and when he was an old man, the French Revolution began. There is more to this story than I have time to tell, but for now, know that The Sentinels became involved—as they do in all wars—to protect other-worlders. Monsieur Midyan, however, was more concerned with human governments and politics. He believed that the interference of The Sentinels swayed the outcome of the war, and when it ended, he and his sons fled to Germany, renounced The Sentinels, and—with the financial support of other displaced aristocrats—he formed Les Luminaires. He told them our secrets and pledged to lead them into a new age in which they would rule the world together by creating an army of otherworld slaves—otherworlders forced into submission by a Weaver who would use his power against them. Obviously, to accomplish this goal, he needed to retrieve the Weaver's Key. But my father moved it to a new hiding place before Monsieur Midyan could reach it. When he found that his plan had been thwarted, he had my father assassinated."

Sarah stared up at Samuel. Her grandfather's grandfather's great-grandfather had murdered Samuel's dad. She didn't know what to think or feel, and she couldn't imagine how it must have affected Samuel.

He continued. "For several years, Monsieur Midyan continued to lead Les Luminaires and search for the Key. But when he died, his sons were not treated with the same respect. New leaders with new agendas were appointed. By the time your grandfather was a young man, Les Luminaires had shunned the Midyan family and begun to form sects—the Thule society and others—who sought power through mysticism and the occult as well as through science. When I found him wandering the streets of Berlin, your father's father, Abram Midyan, was a broken and disillusioned man who wanted nothing to do with Les Luminaires. We smuggled him into the United States. He changed his last name to Lewis and, when your father was born, he named him Jacob. When I asked your grandfather why he chose that name, he quoted the Bible to me: 'Jacob have I loved; Esau have I hated.'

"He was a good man, your grandfather, and he spent the rest of his life trying to make up for the damage done to The Sentinels by five generations without a Weaver. He and I hid the Key again, and he died protecting some of Mr. Tellurak's relatives in Vietnam during a conflict between Vietnamese natives and the French.

"Your father was a little boy when his father died, but when he was old enough, he became the most zealous Weaver we've ever had. He proposed more than once that the council should not only abolish the tradition of hiding otherworlders from humanity but that they should allow him to reopen the gateway between realms and establish inter-universal commerce. He believed that, having made it through two world wars, the moon landing, the American civil rights era, and similar movements around the world, humanity had progressed to a point where they could participate in peaceful community among the realms. This gained him many enemies both inside and outside The Sentinels, and the council rejected his requests. One thing he did accomplish, though. In 1973, he received the blessing of the council to open the portals a little wider so that we could attempt communication with the other realms. It was unprecedented. The Key had not been used in hundreds of years, and never had it been used to relax the gateways.

"Now, it is my belief that when this happened, it sparked something within Les Luminaires. They had been mostly harmless since the end of World War II, but after your father widened the gateway they became active again. I will not take time to tell all of the stories of homes that were raided, Sentinels that were murdered, and artifacts that were stolen. All that matters right now is that, in 1975, a book describing how the Weaver's Key was made and could be used was stolen.

"We were all devastated. Many believed that Les Luminaires would find a way to create a new Key to our demise. Your father assured them that this was impossible, that only the Weaver could use the Key thanks to the blessings handed down through the generations. But the council did not believe him. So he suggested the creation of a scientific special task group to explore the possibility of opening new paths between realms using science and technology. If such a thing were possible, we would discover it first and find a way to block Les Luminaires from closing the gateway and killing all earthling otherworlders if possible. The council approved the plan and recruited two highly respected Scottish physicists, Dr. Connolly and Dr. MacPherson, to begin working with teams of Sentinels and other scientists at the University of Southampton. Then they sent your parents into hiding in Fort Worth.

"Your parents did not simply hide, though. Your father researched the legends surrounding the Weaver's key more than anybody else had done in hundreds of years, and he managed to slip away and recover a handful of lost artifacts. Your mother worked tirelessly on her own experiments with interdimensional elements and reported all her findings to the Southampton team. It is likely that her cancer was caused by radiation exposure from these experiments. That may also be why she was unable to bear children."

Sarah looked away. She could feel tears building behind her eyelids again.

Samuel grabbed her hand. "So in 1977, your parents adopted a beautiful little red haired girl named Sarah who had been in the Texas foster system for more than a year. When the council found out, they were furious. They demanded that your father leave you and your mother and marry another woman who could produce a male, genetically-linked heir to the Weaver's Key. Your father, of course, refused. He pointed out the hypocrisy of simultaneously believing that the blessings could be replicated scientifically and that they required a male descendant. He told them you were his heir, and that birthrights were not limited by gender and genes. Then he refused to speak to the council again. He slowed his research and focused his energy on you. He and your mother raised you as best as they could to be a normal child and to know nothing of The Sentinels until you were ready."

Sarah was stunned. For a moment, she didn't know what to say. Then she realized, "I still don't understand why they kept The Sentinels a secret from me. Why not just tell me what they did and who they were?"

"Because, Miss Sarah, of what happened to Dr. Allen."

"What?"

"I am sure he told you that his old colleague, Dr. Absalom Drake, discovered a way to invade minds and read memories and that he now works for Les Luminaires. If either of your parents or anybody close to them were captured and their memories were stolen, the fact that you were not only adopted but also knew nothing about The Sentinels would make you uninteresting."

Sarah rubbed her temples and stared at the floor.

"When your mother died, little one, everything changed for your father. He no longer spoke of his dreams of opening the gateway or the injustice of keeping dwarves and the aenimos people on what amount to reservations. He only cared about your safety.

"Then, last December, he called me. I had been in London at headquarters. He told me he had caught two thugs trying to break into your apartment. They both wore rings bearing the insignia of Les Luminaires. He called in favors with every shifter he knew. On the morning you left, twelve identical cars bearing people who looked like you and your father left that parking garage and went in different directions. Your father went to the airport, and you were taken by Miss Aubrey's and Mr. Fred's father, Mr. Gregory Dvorak, to live with your grandfather. He had shifted to look like your father, of course, and did not speak to you during that drive because he feared you would be able to detect the difference in his voice. Mr. Gregory died the next week, and his children took over his watch."

Sarah felt herself tearing up. She sniffed, dried her eyes, and watched an airplane cross the darkening sky. "Why are you here with me, then? Aren't you supposed to keep an eye on the Weaver?"

"If your father and I are correct, then I am keeping an eye on the Weaver right now as well as if I were with him."

A jolt of energy shot through Sarah's chest. "What do you mean?"

"The council and most of The Sentinels believe the Weaver's gifts —sight beyond sight and the others that make wielding the Key possible—are passed from generation to generation through DNA. Your father, however, believes it is something else—a birthright that is passed from soul to soul. He believed that, just as otherworlders have parts of themselves that extend into their home realms, every human has a part of their consciousness—a soul, you might call it—that extends beyond the physical bounds of Cosmos. It is there that the blessings reside, and it is there that they are passed."

"And you believe him?"

"I did not at first, but I do now. He has proved it to me."

"How?"

"He split the birthright. When Les Luminaires became more aggressive and your parents went into hiding, your father passed part of his blessing to your mother. That is why he gave her the stones in your earrings and why she began to work with Duke."

"But—"

"It was a safeguard. Neither of them could use the Key alone. He had an old artifact, a black cube made of many smaller cubes with—"

"With weird symbols all over them?"

"Yes. You've seen it?"

"I have it. He left it for me in the trunk. It's in my backpack."

A strange expression of amusement and worry overtook Samuel's face. "I see. It is a training tool for the Weaver. Once he passed his half of the birthright to your mother, he could no longer use the cube alone. They could only do it together."

"But my mom—"

Samuel held up a hand and interrupted her. "She passed her share of the blessings to you before she died. This is the second reason your father left you here. As long as the two of you do not work together, the Key cannot be used."

"No way. It's not true. It can't be. I'm not—"

Samuel interrupted again. "Tell me, Miss Sarah—have you seen things that you should not? Have you, perhaps, been able to sense Duke's thoughts without the earrings or detect the presence of—"

"Shifters. I can tell when shifters are, I don't know, pretending to be or do something they're not. Just a glimpse, like something out of the corner of my eye. At least, until—"

"Until what, little one?"

The vision of Aubrey fighting the frightened young Arabella Minot played in Sarah's mind. "It's nothing," she said after a moment.

Samuel looked at her questioningly, but Sarah changed the subject.

"You said you found out more details about Grandpa Kirk. Can you tell me?"

"Yes. Between what Dr. Allen learned from Mr. Blackwood's mind and what we saw on the partial message from Desjardins, we believe they are taking him to Berlin in the next two days."

"Germany?!"

"Yes. East Germany. They had hoped to capture you and lure your father into a trap. Since they have, so far, only captured your grandfather, we believe they are planning to take him to Dr. Drake's memory laboratory, which we now know is in Berlin. I suspect they hope to discover something of your father's whereabouts from—"

"We have to go! We can't let them—"

"We are working on plans now. You will come with me so that I can keep an eye on you, but I will not allow you to be part of the rescue mission."

"But—"

"No. Absolutely not. It is too dangerous. Have you heard nothing that I have told you today? If they capture you, your father will come for you. He gave up the world for you, and I fear he would let it burn to protect you. If they read his memories or yours, they will learn that they need you both to use the Key even if they find it. If they have you both, they could force you to cooperate—you are both prone to act irresponsibly to protect someone you love—and that cannot happen."

28

RESCUE & REBUILD

Ced's body had been taken from Sarah when they arrived at the church, and she had not seen it since. That night, however, when Tellurak appeared to escort them to Rancho Alvarez, Samuel retrieved the corpse, enclosed in a cooler of ice. It felt disrespectful, and Sarah was indignant, but she could not bring herself to speak.

Tellurak led Sarah, Duke, and Samuel to a black van with the words ALAMO CITY FENCE AND WELDING painted on the side. A man Sarah had never seen before sat in the driver's seat and nodded to Samuel as they passed. Sarah squeezed into a space in the van's cargo area across from Samuel and the cooler. Duke hopped in and found a place to sit near Sarah's feet. Tellurak shut the door behind them.

The drive was long and somber. When at last they arrived, the driver pulled the van onto the shoulder of the road near a barbed wire fence, let Sarah, Samuel, Duke, and Tellurak out with the cooler, and then drove on.

The four Sentinels crossed the fence and hiked through the dark night across a long stretch of rolling grassy hills. After a while, they crossed a second fence and climbed down a rocky incline. The odor of burned grass and trees made it impossible for Sarah to stop replaying Ced's death in her mind.

On they walked in a silence broken only by the sounds of their footsteps and the wind. Then Sarah began to hear other noises: saws scraping across branches, shovels plunging into hard earth, hushed voices.

"We are here," said Tellurak. "Please, wait a moment while I find Miss Lucy."

Tellurak disappeared. Samuel lowered the ice chest to the ground. To her right, Sarah watched as two men wearing hard hats with built-in flashlights carried a sawn log down a hill and disappeared into a thicket of miraculously unburned trees. A moment later they were followed by two dwarves pushing a wheelbarrow full of football-sized stones.

"What are they doing?" asked Sarah.

"Rebuilding," said Samuel. "The aenimos people who live here lost their homes and gathering places to the fire. Many of the Sentinels across Texas have volunteered to spend their nights here, helping the survivors rebuild."

Survivors. The word carried a weight that pressed Sarah's heart into the pit of her stomach. "How many were…" Sarah's voice cracked, and she swallowed. "How many were killed?"

"It is impossible to know for certain yet. Some fled, so some may still return. The last I heard, thirteen were missing. Seven bodies had been identified."

Sarah hung her head and fell to her knees. Fresh guilt crashed over her like a wave. She may not have started the fire or sent the hunting dogs, but both were done because of her. Sarah closed her eyes for several minutes and tried to shut out everything around her. When she looked up again, Duke was there, licking her face with one paw on her leg, and Samuel had knelt and laid a hand across her back.

"I found her," called Tellurak when he returned a few minutes later. "Come with me."

Samuel rose, opened the cooler, lifted Ced's body from the ice, and handed him to Sarah. He was cold and rigid. The blood and burned fur had been cleaned away, but his leg was badly mangled, and teeth marks were visible along his chest.

Tellurak led them around a clump of burnt trees to the top of a small, grassy hill where a group of a dozen aenimos people stood around a small bonfire in the cool night air. When they reached the group, Samuel knelt and bowed before a teary-eyed badger.

"Miss Lucy?"

"Yes," she said and sniffed.

"On behalf of The Sentinels of God, I wish to thank you for your bravery and for the care of our agent, Miss Aubrey Dvorak. She is recovering beautifully, and we owe that to your swift and effective treatment. Thank you."

The badger managed a trembling smile through her tears but did not speak.

"And since you are the only remaining relative of your valiant cousin—"

At this, Lucy began to sob.

"—it is my great and solemn privilege to present to you, on Mr. Cedric's behalf, our highest honor: The Flaming Heart of Heroism." He pressed something into Lucy's hands. "Whenever you look on this, I pray that it will remind you of the selfless and courageous sacrifice your cousin made. As it has been written, there is no greater love than to lay down one's life for another. We are grateful beyond words for the love Mr. Cedric showed this morning."

Sarah's eyes filled with tears. Tellurak touched her shoulder and led her around the crowd to a small casket on the far side of the bonfire. She laid the badger inside and stepped away.

One by one, the others crossed in front of the casket, placed a paw, hand, or beak inside, and then moved on. Sarah saw Barnabas, Thomas, and Frankie. Last of all, Lucy approached the coffin, and Sarah thought she saw her leave The Flaming Heart inside. Then a jack rabbit and a fox closed the box and two large badgers hefted it onto the bonfire. Everyone stood and watched, teary-eyed, for what seemed a very long time as the flames consumed the casket.

Sarah followed the others at a distance as they walked down the hill to where a picnic awaited them, spread across a long green cloth embroidered with a golden lion and illuminated by half a dozen oil lanterns.

There were berries and leaves of various sorts in clay dishes. Sarah thought she also saw breads and cheeses. Some of the aenimos (Lucy, for one) did not eat, but most did, and as they ate, they told stories about Cedric. Despite Ced's claim that Lucy was the best medic they had, many described him as Rancho Alvarez's primary physician, and they praised his resourcefulness when supplies had been insufficient or non-existent. He had been known to treat not only sick and injured aenimos, but also any earthling animals that he happened to find. Barnabas called Ced a peacemaker and a loyal friend. The largest rat Sarah had ever seen told a story of how Ced had stood guard over her son, protecting him from a pack of coyotes by dousing them with a reserve of skunk spray he had stored up for reasons nobody seemed to know. She laughed and said that Ced had smelled so badly afterward that nobody would visit him for three full weeks.

There were plenty of tears from the aenimos who had known him, but there were also lots of smiles and laughs. Sarah kept to the shadows. To her relief, the funeral guests seemed happy to ignore her.

But then Frankie the cougar cleared her enormous throat—causing several of the aenimos to shriek with fright—and spoke. "Most of you probably know," she said, "that I was there when Cedric breathed his last. What you may not know, however, is that he died saving my life."

Sarah gasped. *No*, she thought, *he died saving* my *life.*

Frankie continued. "I was surrounded by a pack of highly trained and fierce Rhodesian Ridgebacks—hounds that were bred to hunt lions—and I was losing. Our dear Cedric had the presence of mind and the bravery to attack one of the dogs over and over until it left the pack to chase him. Miss Lewis," she nodded toward Sarah, "followed his lead and did the same. I owe my life to them both." She bowed her head to Sarah until her nose touched the ground.

There were gasps and murmurs. Sarah tried to shrink further into the shadows.

"In the past," Frankie continued, "I have harbored ill will for The Sentinels. I confess that I even begrudged this human and her Taborian friend their safety when I saw that they had brought danger upon us. But before you make the same error in judgment that I made, let me tell you what changed my mind. This child, a mere cub herself, when she was moments from safety, turned and fought the dogs to defend our dear friend, Cedric, even though he had already ordered her to run. I saw her kill the hound that had attacked him and then join Cedric in defending me. Had she done as she was told—as any of us would have expected her to do—I would be in a coffin alongside dear Cedric, and the dogs may have gone on to kill others when they had finished with me. But she did not. She was true to the mission of The Sentinels, and I for one am honored to count her a friend—as I am honored to have called Cedric the same." Once again, she bowed to Sarah.

For a long moment all was silent. Then Lucy stood. Her fur was still wet with tears, and she said nothing, but, staring straight at Sarah, she stood and bowed low. Slowly, the others joined her until the whole crowd was bowing before her.

Sarah did not know what to do or to say. She wished more than anything that she could make herself invisible. But no. If she backed away now she would lose the chance to say what she needed to say, and she would regret it for the rest of her life. So instead, she walked across the grass, knelt, and threw her arms around Lucy. "I'm so, so sorry, Miss Lucy."

The two held each other and cried for what felt like an eternity and not nearly long enough all at once. And in that moment, hugging a talking badger and sobbing, Sarah made up her mind: if this is what it meant to be a Sentinel—to watch over and protect people like these who lived their whole lives hiding from the very humans their ancestors had defended—then she wanted nothing else but to be a Sentinel. For the first time, she did not want only to save Grandpa Kirk, but to spend her life advancing the cause to which he and her parents had given their lives.

29

PLANS

The ambulance arrived before daybreak the next morning. Aubrey and Boarsmash were placed on stretchers and taken away. An hour later, a Cadillac with darkly tinted windows arrived for Fred and Tellurak. Finally, around mid-morning, Father Stephen escorted Samuel, Sarah, and Duke to the rear of the church where he helped them into a hearse and personally drove them to Austin.

They arrived at an old office building at lunchtime, and Sarah was glad to glimpse a stack of pizza boxes through the tinted glass front door. Samuel bowed to Father Stephen, and they all shook his hands and said goodbye with many thank-yous.

Once inside, they were greeted with cheers and applause by the science team, Bonk, those who had arrived from San Antonio earlier, and several people—humans by all appearances—that Sarah did not recognize. Samuel greeted several people quickly with bows and handshakes and then crossed the room to speak with Michael.

Everyone wanted to know if Sarah was all right. Benjamin seemed particularly moved at the sight of her and gave Sarah an awkward side-hug. "We were quite worried about you," he said. He checked her burns and cuts despite her assurances that they had been treated already. "Now," he said once he was satisfied, "let's get you something to eat."

Sarah piled a paper plate with pizza. Then she plopped into a chair next to Duke, handed him a steaming slice of pepperoni, and crammed a second into her own mouth. Sauce dripped down her chin, and she closed her eyes, relishing the moment of familiar comfort.

The large conference room had been cleared away to make room for the science team's new laboratory. Wooden crates, cardboard boxes, and pallets stacked with equipment had been piled along one wall. A long wooden table had been pushed against another. Swiveling office chairs and metal folding tables were scattered around the empty space.

Both Aubrey and Boarsmash felt well enough to sit up and eat with the others. They laughed and told stories of the past two days' adventures. When Aubrey told her version of how she and Sarah had fought Arabella Minot, the Les Luminaires shifter, she attributed most of the heroics to Sarah. And when she told everyone how Sarah had escaped from Rancho Alvarez "through the flames," she included a half-dozen more dogs and made Sarah sound much braver than she had actually been. Sarah tried to correct her, but Aubrey accused her of being too humble.

"No," Sarah said. "It wasn't like that. I was just trying to not get killed."

"The way that cougar spoke," said Tellurak, who had just entered the room, "it seems you must have done a bit more than that."

Sarah blushed and looked away.

Then Samuel appeared—she had not seen him since she started eating—and put a hand on Sarah's back. "Now, now," he said to the room, "we are all very proud of Miss Sarah. And I am pleased with you all. But enough of what has already happened. We must now decide what to do next, and quickly, before opportunity escapes us. A reliable source," Samuel glanced knowingly at Sarah, "said that we should look for Les Luminaires to make a move today. It is for this reason that we are reunited."

In an instant, the atmosphere transformed. Plates were set aside. The room hushed. All eyes were fixed on Samuel.

"First things first. Dr. MacPherson has spoken with Mr. Carraway at headquarters. He was, in turn, able to confirm the location of Dr. Drake's Berlin laboratory with a field team in East Germany. All is just as Dr. Allen said it would be. This information is not all we have learned from the search of Mr. Blackwood's memory, of course, but if it were, it would be more than enough to justify the experiment."

"And has the German team begun surveillance?" asked Boarsmash.

"Aye," said Michael. "Though, I don't know who's leading it or how many they've got."

"That is quite all right," said Samuel. "Thank you for your diligence, Dr. MacPherson. I will speak with the council soon. If they are able to confirm Dr. Drake's presence, I suspect they will approve any resources required to extract him."

Sarah glanced at Benjamin. He was chewing his thumbnail and staring at the floor.

Then Samuel turned to Tellurak. "Were you able to reach your contact on such short notice?"

"Yes, sir," replied Tellurak. "She said Mr. Kirk was sighted in Oklahoma City less than an hour ago."

Sarah gasped.

"She wanted to call sooner, but she did not know how to reach us," Tellurak added. "How did you know that we should call her today?"

"Nevermind that," said Samuel. "What else did she say?"

"They moved Mr. Kirk from the building where he was last seen into an armored bank vehicle. It is heading south now with a convoy. The Red River division has dispatched a full scale surveillance team. They will not let you down, sir. My friends will keep a close eye on the vehicle and will let us know of any changes in its course. For now, it is heading south, toward Dallas they think, and there is no reason to believe Les Luminaires know they are being watched."

"Thank you, Mr. Tellurak," said Samuel. "Let us hope they are correct."

"But why are they backtracking, sir?" asked Bonk. "Why take him to Oklahoma for a few days and then bring him back to Texas?"

"That is an interesting question, Mr. Bonk," said Samuel, "and I admit that I do not know the answer. If our intelligence is correct, however, their next move will be to transport him to Berlin. In that case, they may be headed to an airport." He thought for a moment. "I do not believe they would attempt to drive onto DFW airport. We have too many friends there, and they know it. Les Luminaires have been known, however, to utilize a private jet that is kept in a hangar at Love Field. Perhaps they are headed there now. Mr. Bonk, would you please telephone our office in Dallas? They will be able to tell us if the hangar in question is currently occupied, and if so, I believe they may be able to arrange some flight delays."

Bonk stood, bowed, and hurried out of the room.

"Miss Martinez," Samuel said to one of the humans Sarah had not met, "do we have an airplane or a helicopter here in Austin that could carry myself and a companion or two to Dallas within the hour?"

"I…" she stammered, visibly nervous. "I don't know. I can make some calls and find out."

Samuel nodded, and she left the room.

Then Samuel cleared his throat, put his hands behind his back, and addressed the room like a king sending his troops into battle. "Friends, the time for action has come. In a few short hours, unless we stop them first, Mr. Kirk will be on an airplane bound for Berlin. Once it has left the ground, our rescue efforts will become much more difficult. We need a plan. Who has an idea? Any and all suggestions will be heard and evaluated."

For several minutes, nobody spoke. Then Tellurak said, "What if we asked the Red River team to arrange a road block in the vehicle's path. They could attack and take Mr. Kirk while Les Luminaires are unable to drive away."

"No," Samuel replied after a moment. "The vehicle is armored, so it would require significant force, and there will be too many people. We cannot risk injuring bystanders or being exposed."

Another minute passed.

"Could we…" Boarsmash started. "I mean, might it be time we involved the human authorities?"

"I'm afraid not," answered Benjamin.

Samuel nodded and explained. "One of the things Dr. Allen

learned from Mr. Blackwood's memories is that Les Luminaires have recruited or paid off high ranking officials in strategic locations. As likely as not, any police involvement would put Mr. Kirk in more danger than he is in already."

Again, nobody spoke for several minutes. Then, suddenly, a door flew open and Bonk entered. "The plane is not at Love Field, sir," he said.

Everyone fell to murmuring and whispering.

"Maybe," said Bonk, "they aren't taking him to an airport after all. We might have more time than we thought."

Samuel took a deep breath and looked up at the ceiling. "It is more likely that we have mere minutes," he said gravely. "They may not be going as far as we thought. There are many small air strips south of Oklahoma City that they might use."

"But they would need a large jet to get to Berlin," said Duncan. "They don't keep airplanes that big at little air strips."

"No. You are correct. But they might plan to use a smaller craft to connect to another, larger airport. In any case, Mr. Bonk, please alert Miss Martinez. We may not require air transport after all. It may be too late already."

Bonk bowed and left.

"If you are right, sir, then we must act now," said Tellurak. "Let me call my home division."

"And what'll they do?" asked Fred. "Unless your people have something Les Luminaires wants more than Mr. Kirk, anything they try is likely to end in…" Fred caught himself. "We just can't risk it."

"Then what?" snapped Tellurak. "Should we just sit here and let them go in peace?"

"Of course not," said Fred. "We just need a better option."

"Like what?"

One of the men from the Austin team spoke up. "I have a thought. Could we have a team ready to intercept them when they land in Berlin?"

"Perhaps," said Samuel, "but it is dangerous—much more dangerous than it would be to intercept them here. You must remember that the headquarters for Les Luminaires are in Berlin.

225

Their power and influence are much stronger in that country than here."

"Are there any Les Luminaires people or comrades or whatever-they're-called here in Austin?" asked Sarah.

"Yes, of course," answered the man who had suggested the German ambush, "but what good would that do?"

"Well," said Sarah, "I know one thing they want more than Grandpa Kirk: me. What if—" Sarah did not get to finish her sentence.

"No way!" shouted Aubrey. "You can't!"

With that, the room was in an uproar.

Samuel silenced them all with a gesture. "Please," he said, "Miss Sarah is more aware of what is at stake than most of you. I share your caution, but her ideas deserve to be heard as much as anybody's. Let us hear her out before we reach a verdict." He nodded at Sarah.

"All right," she said. "Well, like I said, they'd rather have me than Grandpa. And you know the story of the Trojan horse? What if I was the horse? We have the oubliette right? We could put some of you in the oubliette and I could put the controller in my pocket, and then somebody could offer to exchange me for Grandpa. Once I'm in and Grandpa is safe, I could let everyone out. We'd take them by surprise and escape."

Every eye in the room watched Samuel's reaction. For a long time he sat with his eyes closed. Then he looked at Sarah and said, "No, little one. While it is the best idea anybody has presented yet—or rather, it could be with some changes—we cannot risk it. You are too valuable. And we do not yet know if the oubliette is safe for our agents."

"What do you mean?" asked Sarah. "Blackwood was in there, and he was all right. Wasn't he?"

Samuel raised an eyebrow and looked at Benjamin.

"Well, yes, he was, in a manner of speaking," said Benjamin. He nibbled his thumbnail. "But unfortunately for him, it seems the experience was not as pleasant as we had hoped. I wish I did not know how painful it was for him. Indeed, I wish I did not know much of what I learned in that tortured mind." He trailed off for a moment. "Besides, he's human, and our agents are not. We have never put an otherworlder in the oubliette. In theory, it should be no different for them than for a human, but—"

"I could do it," said Aubrey.

"You want to go into the oubliette?" asked Benjamin.

"No," she said. "I could be Sarah."

30

BOXES

"No way," said Fred. "You're still recovering from the last time you played that role. I'll do it."

"You haven't practiced! I have!" argued Aubrey. "I've been studying Miss Sarah for months. Even your girlfriend bought it when it mattered!"

That stung, and it showed on Fred's face. "Look," he said, "it's not that you aren't good enough, Sis. But you're hurt, and...and it's my fault. I can't let you get hurt any worse. You're all the family I have, you know."

"Then you should understand why it's so important to do this right—to rescue and protect all the family Miss Sarah has left. I'm the best one for this role, and you know it. Let me do my job. I'm well enough now."

The siblings argued for several minutes. A few of the others weighed in as well. In the end, it was decided that Aubrey, not Fred, would impersonate Sarah; Fred would impersonate Arabella Minot. The distress on Fred's face was apparent, though whether it had more to do with Aubrey risking herself or him having to impersonate his now deceased girlfriend, Sarah could not tell. But it was a good plan, and he did not object. Aubrey had already successfully masqueraded as Sarah, after all, and Fred was the only Sentinel who knew Arabella.

Somebody would need to hand Aubrey over to Les Luminaires, and this gave Fred the best shot of staying with and protecting his sister. Fred—or rather *Arabella*—would reach out to a contact Benjamin had discovered while searching Blackwood's memories. Her story would be that, after being knocked unconscious by Sarah, she had awoken and hitchhiked to safety, and that she had used her Sentinel contact (Fred) to discover Sarah's location and capture the girl on her own.

Once they believed they had her, It was a safe bet that Les Luminaires would either stop what they were doing to bring Sarah (Aubrey) and Grandpa Kirk together right away or that they would fly both to Berlin. They would use the two against each other—torturing (or at least, threatening to torture) one to make the other talk. After all, both were merely means to a more desirable end: the capture of Sarah's father. And in either case, two Sentinel shifters would get close enough to Grandpa Kirk to attempt a rescue.

Fred and Aubrey would take the oubliette, but nobody would go inside, though Tellurak and Boarsmash both volunteered. It was too dangerous. Instead, the shifters would take what weapons they had on hand and whatever else could be cobbled together in the next half hour. Their movements would be tracked by aenimos spies, and an extraction team would be assembled to help if they got into real trouble, but once they were behind closed doors, they would be on their own.

As soon as the plan was finalized, Fred and Aubrey shut themselves in a side room to discuss strategies and to get their story ironed out. Boarsmash and Bonk were sent to round up all the local aenimos spies they could muster in the time they had. Samuel and Tellurak telephoned their contacts.

Sarah and Duke followed Benjamin around the would-be laboratory as he, Michael, Duncan, and several members of the Austin team quickly assembled gadgetry they thought might be useful to the shifters. Sarah did not understand most of what they said, but she did catch that Fred would wear a "wire." Anything he said or heard would be transmitted to a receiver with a range of up to one mile. Being a shifter, Fred could cause the mic and transmitter—along with the oubliette controller—to be invisible to others. A metal detector or x-ray machine, however, would give it all away, and it was possible that he might encounter either or both of these if he were forced to pass through a high security checkpoint. The team agreed that this was a risk they would have to take since the wire would allow The Sentinels to monitor the mission from a distance.

"But if that happens, they'll find the oubliette and the controller too, right?" asked Sarah.

"Well, no," said Benjamin in a shaky, nervous voice. He had seemed anxious all afternoon. "Both are made entirely of otherworld materials encased in plastic. There's no metal, and they would just look like plastic toys under x-ray. He shouldn't have any trouble if he's careful."

"Then why couldn't he just put the wire in the oubliette with everything else?"

"He could," answered Benjamin, "and that might be a good way to get through security if he can manage it. It wouldn't exist while it was in there, so it wouldn't be detectable. Of course, it also wouldn't transmit anything. We'd be cut off."

"What do you mean, it wouldn't exist?"

Benjamin smiled at Sarah and then looked questioningly at Michael, eyebrows raised.

"Go on," said Michael. "It's going to be a long one for this lassie. Give her something else to think on, then, will you? We can take it from here."

"Come with me," said Benjamin, clearly relieved at the excuse to leave the chaos. "Let's continue that science lesson, shall we?" He walked to a corner of the room away from the others and sat in an office chair. Sarah sat next to him. "I'm not a physicist, but I'll try to explain as best I can. Best to keep our minds occupied, if you ask me."

Sarah nodded.

"When something goes into the oubliette, you might also say that it's going out of Cosmos—outside of reality. Or, at least, it goes outside of space-time as we perceive it. It's still accessible, of course; we can retrieve anything we put in there, but the thing itself doesn't technically exist until it comes out again—not in a way that makes sense, at any rate."

Sarah looked at Benjamin with a puzzled expression. "But didn't you say that Blackwood—"

"Ahh yes. Now, that is troubling. I don't know how to explain it, but he knew," Benjamin paused, "*something*. It felt like…" A distant, pensive expression fell over Benjamin's face. "Well, like I said, I don't know how to explain it. It was like waiting a very long time except that nothing happened. No time actually passed. He should have felt as if he were standing on your grandfather's lawn one moment and then found himself standing in the Alvarezes' library the next. For him, there should have been nothing at all in between. All our experiments with atomic clocks and the like have shown that no time passes inside the oubliette. And it only makes sense. Time is just another dimension of space, you see. If you go outside of space, you also go outside of time, and you shouldn't experience anything at all until you return. Somehow, though, he felt it. I know he did," Benjamin's hands shook as he remembered. "It was awful."

Samuel burst into the room—Sarah had never seen him move so quickly. He opened the door to the side room where Aubrey and Fred were planning, and said "It is time. Ready yourselves. Dr. MacPherson will brief you on the way." Then he turned and shouted, "They must be equipped and traveling within three minutes."

"Oh!" said Benjamin, standing, his face flushed. "Right then. I'm afraid I'll have to leave you now, Miss Sarah. We're going to lock Blackwood in an upstairs room, and I've…well, I've volunteered to stand guard."

"Blackwood is here?" she asked.

"Of course," said Benjamin as he walked backward toward the stairwell chewing his thumbnail again. "He's in the oubliette. Time has come to unbox the scoundrel and pack the toys." A nervous grin spread across his face. Then he turned and rushed up the stairs at the back of the room.

Sarah stood, caught up in the excitement of the moment, but she soon realized she had nowhere to go and nothing to do. She put a hand on Duke's head and watched busy Sentinels hurrying and shouting and trying to ignore the shouts of others while they worked.

Everyone, it seemed, knew what they were supposed to do except Sarah.

Moments later, Samuel opened the outside door and the shifters flew through it followed by Michael. "Duke," called Samuel, "have you made a decision?"

Duke barked.

"Very well then." He paused a moment and then said in a warmer tone, "If all goes well, Miss Sarah, you may see your grandfather in a few hours. We will do all we can to make that happen. I promise." Then he turned and disappeared into a hallway with Duncan and two of the Austinites.

And with that, the room was empty and quiet.

This was it—the moment Sarah had been waiting for. They were finally going to rescue Grandpa Kirk, and she had been left out. She understood why, of course, but she still felt helpless, useless. So she slumped down onto the floor with her back against the wall.

"I hate this," she mumbled. "It's my family, you know. You'd think they'd at least let me hang out in the control room or something."

"TRUST," said a robotic voice in Sarah's mind as Duke pressed his nose against her shoulder.

She had forgotten she was wearing the earrings, and the sound startled her. Sarah turned to Duke and scratched behind his ear. "Thank you. Thanks for staying with me. I know you didn't have to."

Duke licked her cheek.

"Well, what are we going to do now? I'll die if we don't do something."

"TRAIN." Duke hopped up, jogged to the other side of the lab where Sarah had left her things, and returned with her backpack.

"All right then," said Sarah. "Pizza wasn't enough for you?" She unzipped the backpack and began unpacking it, looking for the little bit of beef jerky that was left. When she pulled out her mom's diary, though, Duke barked and pushed it toward Sarah with his nose.

"What do you want me to do with this?" asked Sarah. "It's just—"

Duke barked again.

"All right, all right!"

But before she could crack the cover, Duke shoved his head into the open backpack and started pulling out the rest of its contents. When he found the wooden box Samuel had given Sarah as a blessing at the end of her oath ceremony, he set it on the floor, whimpered, and clawed at it.

The box was stained a deep brown but had no special markings. A simple latch held it closed. Sarah unhooked the latch and opened the lid.

Inside was a gem that reminded Sarah of the ruby on Samuel's turban except that it was clear as water. Sarah lifted it and gazed in stupefied wonder. It was heavier than she had expected. One side was concave and smooth like a lens; the other was cut into dozens of geometric facets. Even in the fluorescent light, it seemed to reflect a million different colors as it turned and sparkled.

"Wow!" Sarah was awestruck. "It's the most beautiful thing I've ever seen." Sarah held the gem and marveled at it, hardly able to breathe. "What am I supposed to do with it, I wonder."

Duke nosed at the diary again. "LOOK," said the robotic voice.

Sarah set the gem back into the open box and picked up the diary. Maybe her mom had included instructions on how to use it or what it was for. She laid down, using Duke as a pillow, and flipped open the diary to the first page.

"STONE," said the voice.

"Yeah, I'm looking fo something about it."

"NO. USE STONE. LOOK."

Sarah picked up the gem and held it to her eye like a monocle. "Like this?"

Duke wagged his tail enthusiastically.

Sarah peered through he gem and examined the first diary entry. It was like looking through a kaleidoscope. Her mother's handwriting and doodles were broken into a thousand tiny, repeating pieces. She turned the gem a little and watched the patterns spin and rearrange themselves. It was enchanting, but if there was a point to this, Sarah didn't know what it was. She flipped to the next entry.

"So you knew my mom?" she said after a moment.

"YES."

"Samuel said she made these earrings. Pretty amazing, huh? I mean, I guess I always thought she was smart, but in a mom sort of way, you know? Not like a scientist or an inventor." Sarah sighed. "I wish she was here now."

Sarah's mind filled with memories of her mother: helping her cook dinner, lying in her lap as she told stories at bedtime, listening to the sound of her singing when she thought nobody was around. She imagined her mother as a Sentinel, working on secret projects with her dad.

Then it happened. As Sarah absent-mindedly rotated the gem between her fingers, a three-dimensional lion's head suddenly formed out of the bits of ink on the page and leapt toward her.

31

THE CAPTIVE ESCAPES

Sarah gasped and slammed the diary shut. Duke's ears twitched as he looked at her, concern in his eyes.

"It's okay, Duke," said Sarah, clutching her chest. "I'm all right. I thought I saw something in there. It surprised me. That's all."

Once her pulse had slowed, Sarah cracked the cover again and flipped the pages until she found the one that she had last inspected. Slowly, she lifted the gem to her eye. Nothing.

Sarah breathed a sigh of relief. "Must have been in my mind," she said, shaking her head and looking up. But as her eyes left the page, the lion formed again. Sarah's gaze snapped back to the diary in an instant, but it was gone, replaced by a meaningless kaleidoscope of black ink on yellowing paper.

Sarah set the gem down and rubbed her eyes with her fists. "I need a break. How about some of that jerky?"

Sarah had just slipped the gem back into its box and shut the lid when she heard a commotion from the direction of the stairs. Duke leapt to his feet.

"No need to be so rough, you…Oof! I'm coming!" said Benjamin, his voice choked and strained, as two sets of struggling feet appeared in the stairwell.

"Not another word!" This voice was familiar. Snarling. Terrifying.

It had frequented Sarah's nightmares since she had first heard it calling for her in the dark. She trembled.

Duke barked and rushed toward the stairs.

"You make him back off, brainiac, or I'll kill you here and now!" said Blackwood. He pressed the blade of a pocket knife into Benjamin's neck, and blood trickled onto his hand. "Now!"

"Stop, Duke!" shouted Benjamin. "Please! He'll kill me!" His hands were bound behind his back. One eye was swollen shut and his nose was bloody.

Duke stood and snarled.

Blackwood was taller and broader than Benjamin, and he dragged his hostage easily toward the door. "That's right. Nice doggy. No surprises now. Just you stay there, and—"

He saw Sarah.

"You!" Then, to Benjamin, "You didn't tell me the girl was here!"

"I didn't—" Benjamin choked under Blackwood's tightened grip.

"You're coming with me," he roared at Sarah. "Right now!"

Sarah couldn't speak. She just shook her head.

Blackwood took a step toward Sarah, but Duke jumped in front of him and growled, teeth bared, hair on end.

"Keep the mutt under control, or so help me—" said Blackwood.

"I...I can't," squeaked Benjamin, gasping for air. "He'll...He'll let me die...long before he lets you touch...Miss Sarah. God's honest...truth."

"Well, I guess that's just a risk we'll have to take," said Blackwood. Then he lifted Benjamin off the ground and heaved him at Duke. Sarah heard a loud thud as Benjamin's head slammed into something hard, but she didn't see what it was. Blackwood was half-way across the lab already.

The next few seconds passed in slow motion. Sarah bolted, screaming, but Blackwood was too fast. Just as she reached the entrance to the hallway, he caught hold of her tee shirt, and then she felt a calloused hand grip her wrist and yank her backward. She spun and saw Blackwood's expression change from one of rage to one of agony as Duke, who must have dodged Benjamin's fall, sank his teeth into Blackwood's thigh. Sarah kicked and flailed, but the more she struggled, the more Blackwood's grip tightened. Then, while his head was turned to shout curses at Duke, something from Sarah's training with Aubrey came back to her: she jumped toward Blackwood, pulled his hand to her mouth, and bit as hard as she could. Involuntarily, Blackwood's fingers relaxed and she pulled her wrist free.

Sarah sprinted down the hallway, screaming for Samuel and pounding on doors all the way. The sounds of barking and yelling behind her told Sarah that she was not being chased—not yet, anyway. Still she ran. She rounded a corner and kept running. A series of other corridors branched off to her right. She slowed at each, screamed for help, and ran to the next.

Finally, she heard a door fly open and footsteps running. She turned to see who it was. Samuel appeared from a corridor just behind her, followed by Tellurak. "Hurry!" Sarah shouted. "It's Blackwood! He's got Benjamin!"

"Wait here, little one," said Samuel as he flew back down the hallway toward the lab.

A moment later, Duncan and a few people from the Austin team appeared. Duncan ran to Sarah, stooped down, and asked, "Are you hurt, Miss Sarah?"

"No. I'm fine. But Blackwood, he's got Dr. Allen!"

"Is he all right?" asked Duncan, panic in his voice.

"I don't know," said Sarah. "Don't worry about me. Go!"

A FEW MINUTES LATER, SARAH SAT ON THE FLOOR AND STROKED DUKE'S head while a woman in a white coat checked him for broken ribs. He had been pinned beneath the heavy table that had been overturned in the struggle.

"Blackwood is gone," said Tellurak, breathing hard as he reentered the lab. "There are fresh tire marks in the parking lot where somebody peeled out. I don't know if he stole a car or forced someone to drive him or what."

Duncan cursed. Duke barked loudly.

"No, Duke," said Samuel. "Our situation is grim indeed, but we will not violate the treaty over one escapee." Then he kicked a folding chair. It bent, slammed into a wall, and fell to the floor. He turned and began to pace, rubbing his temples with his fingertips.

Everyone froze. Sarah had never seen Samuel angry before. He seemed dangerous, and it was terrifying. She remembered that her mother's diary had alluded to stories Grandpa Kirk had told about Samuel. She had said that he sounded like a warrior giant out of an old legend.

"And Dr. Allen? Is he injured badly?" asked Samuel.

Duncan hesitated a moment and then said, "He'll live. His nose is broken, and he was knocked unconscious. We'll have to watch him a bit to be certain he hasn't received a concussion, but he'll live."

"Who here has a vehicle?" asked Samuel.

Several of the Austinites raised their hands.

"Spread out and check every convenience store, hotel, and pay phone you can find nearby," said Samuel. "Blackwood will not go far before he calls for help. If you find him, do not pursue or engage him. Find a telephone and report his location."

Immediately, everyone whose hand had been raised began scrambling for their keys.

"The rest of us must leave immediately," said Samuel.

"But the operation!" said Duncan. "We can't abandon Fred and Aubrey to—"

"We don't have a choice," said Tellurak. "The Watcher is right. Blackwood will alert Les Luminaires that Miss Sarah is here as soon as he can get to a phone. Our position is compromised."

"Gather what you can," said Samuel. "We depart in five minutes. Mr. Tellurak, please contact Red River before we leave and let them know about our situation. They must adjust accordingly. Dr. Connolly, pack up the control room and destroy anything we must leave behind. I will make travel arrangements to take us to Berlin. We must arrive before Mr. Kirk and catch them off guard. We will take back our own." He walked toward a door and then stopped. "Sarah, you stay with me. So help me God, I will not allow you to leave my sight again until we have dealt with Les Luminaires sufficiently that they dare not touch you." He paused. "And Miss Martinez?"

"Yes?" said the Austinite nervously.

"Miss Sarah needs a disguise, and it needs to be convincing. If Blackwood had not recognized her here, we would not now be in such a dangerous and unfortunate position. It must not happen again. Here. Take this." Samuel pulled a handful of folded bills from within his tunic and held them out to her. "Purchase dye for her hair, makeup for her skin, new clothing—anything you can think of to hide her identity. Meet us at the regional office in one hour. Thank you. Go now."

Sarah crawled on the tile floor and gathered her things. The box with the gem had been knocked behind a cabinet, and it had taken Sarah several anxious moments to find it. She slipped the box into her backpack, which had been spilled, and then reached for her mother's diary, open and face down on the floor. She picked it up, brushed away the dust, and flattened the folded pages before closing it and checking the cover for damage. There, on the back, she noticed something she had not seen before—four lines written in silver ink in her mother's elegant cursive near the bottom:

> *Unravel the riddle,*
> *Piece the puzzle,*
> *Stab the dark,*
> *And see.*

She picked it up to read the lines again, but they were gone.

32

FLYING & OTHER FIRSTS

Sarah had never flown before. She had never even left Texas. Now she was watching the tops of cotton candy clouds, pink in the setting sunlight, drift beneath her through a tiny window in the second airplane she had boarded that day: a mostly empty private jet that would take a little more than ten hours to carry her across the Atlantic.

Her red hair was black now. It had been cut short (just above her shoulders), and had been straightened and then crimped. Her eyebrows were dyed to match. She wore a black beret, makeup, a dangly gold necklace, dark sunglasses, pleated black pants, tall black boots, a short black jacket, and a white striped cotton shirt over a stuffed push-up bra—a far stretch from her usual tee shirt and jeans. She hated it all. Perhaps this was how girls dressed in Austin or Atlanta or Berlin—all cities she would have visited by the end of the next day—but Sarah felt as conspicuous as a pig in a hen house.

That's how Grandpa would have said it, anyway. Sarah Ann Lewis's Grandpa.

But she was no longer Sarah Ann Lewis. Her new name—the one printed on her passport next to a photo that looked nothing like her—was Emilia K. Johnson. In public, she was not to speak more than was necessary, and then quietly. She had been escorted through the

Atlanta airport by a tall, dark haired shifter she had never met. His real name was Thomas, but she had called him "Daddy." Those were her orders.

She wondered now if she would ever see her real father again. What would she say to him if she did? *Thanks?* She knew now why he had done what he had done, but it still hurt. She was still angry. And she missed him terribly. Sarah sighed and slid the window shade shut. She leaned onto Duke, who sat in the seat next to her, and ran her fingers through his warm, white fur.

POOR DUKE HAD BEEN CAGED UP IN THE CARGO AREA WITH EVERYONE'S luggage during their first flight—a commercial flight from Austin to Atlanta. This had seemed horribly unfair and undignified to Sarah. He was, after all, a high psuchamora of the pentrafax. But The Sentinels had not been able to charter a private flight out of Austin on such short notice, and the airline did not allow dogs in the cabin. Duke had not complained, though, and Sarah had tried not to worry. If Sarah was honest with herself, the thing that had bothered her most about Duke's exile to the luggage compartment was that she could no longer hear his comforting machine voice telling her to "BE CALM" and "TRUST."

BUT THAT'S EXACTLY WHAT HE WAS DOING NOW. THE AIRPLANE BEGAN to shake, and the captain's voice announced over the intercom that they were experiencing some mild turbulence. "DO NOT FEAR," said Duke. Sarah scratched behind his ears and then sat up and glanced around the cabin at the others.

Samuel was across the aisle on the same row as Sarah. His enormous frame did not easily fit into the space provided by his seat, and Sarah almost giggled at the sight. Samuel caught her eyes and smiled. In the airport, Sarah had not been allowed to make eye contact or speak with him, though he had never been out of sight.

"You look quite different, little one," he said.

"You look uncomfortable," replied Sarah. "Are you really going to stay like that the whole time?"

"I plan to lie down in the aisle in a little while," said Samuel with a half-grin. "These airplanes are too small for me." Then, when the plane shook again, "I do not enjoy flying."

A couple of rows back, Duncan was telling Benjamin—whose nose had been bandaged—that, no, he would not be allowed to sleep yet and that he'd better suck it up and get used to the idea. Duncan agreed that Benjamin probably did not have a concussion, but he was not willing to risk it.

"Then at least let me have my flask, won't you?" said Benjamin. "Lord knows I need a stiff drink after the day I've had."

"What you need, lad, is coffee," said Duncan, "but unfortunately they won't serve it while we're being jostled about, so you'll have to settle for some water and my company until this turbulence stops."

"Oh, won't that be just—" started Benjamin.

"Would you two shut up already?" said Michael from behind them. "You're like an old married couple. Now quiet. I'm trying to read."

Before they had left for the airport, Benjamin was forced to retell the events that led to Blackwood's escape at least a dozen times. Benjamin told them that he had started his guard shift watching Blackwood through the small window in the office door. Blackwood was unconscious, slumped over in his chair—the tranquilizer the Sentinels had given him at the Alvarez mansion was still in his system. But after a few minutes, Blackwood awoke. He groaned pitifully, and Benjamin said he looked every bit as miserable as he sounded. But while Benjamin admitted that he had, indeed, felt sorry for Blackwood, he insisted that he would never have opened the door out of pity alone. It was just that Blackwood seemed too sedated to be dangerous even if he hadn't been tied to a chair—and he was, in fact, tied to a chair. So when Blackwood begged for water, Benjamin had mercy on him. How was he to know what a foolish decision it would turn out to be? So he filled a cone-shaped paper cup at a water cooler and took it to him. But as soon as he had lifted the cup to Blackwood's lips, though, Blackwood headbutted him. Benjamin, apparently, blacked out. When he came to, Blackwood was dragging him downstairs. The rest Sarah had seen.

Nobody had openly blamed Benjamin for the mess they were in, of course, but the fact that Blackwood had freed himself so quickly and with no assistance—well, that had raised a few eyebrows. Benjamin had no explanation to give.

THE AIRPLANE DIPPED AND SHOOK AGAIN, AND SARAH GRIPPED THE armrests so tightly that her fingers hurt. *Is this normal?* she wondered. Nothing was *normal* anymore. She was overcome with the realization that everything and everyone she had ever known, every place she had ever been was behind her. An open and uncertain horizon lay ahead.

"WAKE."

Sarah opened her eyes. The plane's cabin was darker than it had been, and the only sound was the hum of the engine. Duke nudged her shoulder.

"What's wrong, Duke?" she whispered.

"ALL SLEEP. TRAIN NOW."

Sarah looked for Samuel. His seat was empty. *He must be on the floor,* she thought. She glanced back at the others. He was right. Everyone was asleep, even Benjamin. "Train?" she asked Duke.

"GEM. DIARY."

"Now?"

"YES."

Sarah groaned and stretched. She reached down and pulled her backpack from beneath the seat in front of her, unzipped it, and extracted the small wooden box and her mother's diary. "I don't know what's so important that it can't wait," she grumbled under her breath.

Duke looked at her with stern eyes and wiggled his jaw for a long time. Then she heard, "YOU ARE NEXT WEAVER. YOU MUST TRAIN. SECRET."

"But my dad—" she started. "Besides, I don't even know what I'm doing."

"TRY."

Sarah nodded and held up the book and the box. "All right," she said. "I'll try. But there's something else I want to check out first."

There had been words written in silver amidst the scribbles and doodles on the back of her mother's diary, words she could not always see but that had appeared when she wasn't looking. It had just happened, the same as when she had seen through the disguises of shifters. If she was going to find the words again, she knew that concentrating and focusing would not work. At least, not the way she had concentrated and focused before. Somehow, she had to do something different. She laid the diary in her lap, face down and closed. Then she took a deep breath and closed her eyes. *Just relax,* she told herself. *Let it happen.*

For a while, Sarah allowed her thoughts to wander freely. A picture of Tellurak drifted into her mind. He was waving goodbye as they drove away from the regional office in Austin—so much warmer than he had seemed in the basement of the Alvarez mansion just two days before. She pictured Boarsmash standing on a milk crate to teach, and she smiled. She thought of Benjamin and the awful things he had been through before The Sentinels rescued him. Then she remembered how Blackwood had dragged him across the laboratory in Austin and thrown him at Duke. This memory scared her, and she put it out of her mind only to find it replaced by worry for Aubrey and Fred. She wondered whether they were hurt, whether they were still alive. Nobody had heard anything from them since they had arrived at the house in Oklahoma where the armored car had stopped. Sentinel spies had watched the shifters arrive, and they watched the armored car leave again and drive to a private airport, but nobody knew who was in it.

No, she thought. *This isn't helping.* So she focused on her mother— imagined her working in a laboratory, talking to Duke, preparing secret messages that Sarah would find someday. She saw her mother's face. Her smile was warm and gentle and perfect. She remembered the sound of her singing, softly, *You are my sunshine, my only sunshine...*

Sarah opened her eyes and let them fall onto the diary, dimly illuminated in the dark cabin. She did not try to look at it, exactly, but rather to *see* it without looking. It worked. There, on the back cover, were the silver words she had seen before:

> *Unravel the riddle,*
> *Piece the puzzle,*
> *Stab the dark,*
> *And see.*

It was strange to use her eyes this way. Unfamiliar. Instinct and habit fought against her will for control of her vision, but Sarah resisted. This was not seeing as she knew it; it was the gift Samuel had told her about, *sight beyond sight*, and it came with a new way of looking. For several seconds, she held on, reading the lines over and over, committing them to memory. Then she closed her eyes and exhaled. Sarah had not even realized that she had been holding her breath.

She reached into the backpack and pulled out her own diary, flipped it open, and wrote the lines on a blank page.

"What do you think this means?" she whispered to Duke, showing him the page. "It's written on the back, but I can only see it when I'm doing…whatever this is."

Duke looked. "ELIZABETH," he said.

"Yeah, it's my mom's handwriting for sure," said Sarah, "but what does it mean?"

Duke said nothing for a moment, then, "TRY GEM."

Sarah took the gem from the box and held it in her hand. She opened the diary, held the gem to her right eye, and spun it. A picture came into focus.

This time, above where the silver words had been, jumping off the page and formed from scribbled lines of ink, she saw the forms of a box covered in swirls and lines, a cube made of many smaller cubes, and a dagger with a swirl etched into its blade.

Sarah gasped. "The riddle! It's written on the box Dad left for me. And the puzzle is the cube. I should have known. And I guess I'm supposed to stab something with the dagger? I don't know."

"WHAT DOES RIDDLE SAY?" asked Duke after several seconds.

"I don't remember. The box is in my suitcase. So is the dagger. But I think I have the cube. Hold on a minute. I have an idea."

Sarah placed the gem back into its box and dug around in her backpack until she found the black cube at the bottom. "Here it is."

As before, the rows and columns could be rotated up and down or left and right. Well, some of them could, anyway. Some would move one direction but not another. Some moved with difficulty. Some moved easily. Some would not move at all.

Again, Sarah closed her eyes and took a deep breath. Then she opened her eyes and looked at the cube again using her newfound gift. Now the symbols glowed different colors. Protruding from several points were what looked like luminescent crystals of various lengths and colors. Some were touching, preventing the rows from swiveling one direction or another. Some were gridlocked. Her hands moved freely through all of them and felt nothing. Sarah twisted and turned the blocks. She noticed that crystals of the same color would block one another while those of differing colors might or might not. Some color combinations created resistance but eventually passed through each other.

On a whim, Sarah grabbed her mother's diary. She flipped it open to the first entry and looked beyond what she could see with her natural eyes. The words she had seen before were the same, but beneath these, new words now appeared in silver: *Solve the cube to a single blank side. From this starting position, the diagrams outlined within will solve it for patterns we've discovered so far.*

Sarah dropped the diary and went to work on the cube. It took more than an hour to arrange all the blanks on one side. More than once, she found herself at an impasse where further progress was blocked by interlocking crystals, and she was forced to back up and try another solution. But eventually, she did it. One side was comprised entirely of blank tiles. No blanks showed on the remaining five sides, and no crystals protruded from the blank side of the cube.

Now she picked up the diary again, lifted the gem to her eye, and flipped through the pages, spinning the gem as she did, until a lion's head leapt toward her. This time she paid more attention.

Surrounding the lion were a series of letters, numbers, and symbols. There was an outer circle comprised of swirls, lions, men with swords, jagged circles, smooth circles, and stars. But there was also an inner circle of smaller but more familiar characters:

$$\begin{array}{cc} & A \downarrow 3 \\ 1 \leftarrow 3 & 2 \rightarrow 2 \\ G \uparrow 2 & 3 \leftarrow 1 \\ 1 \rightarrow 3 & 4 \leftarrow 1 \\ C \downarrow 2 & G \uparrow 2 \\ 7 \rightarrow 3 & 1 \rightarrow 3 \\ & G \uparrow 2 \end{array}$$

"A code!" she exclaimed a little louder than she intended.

Duke looked at her with questioning eyes.

"Hang on," she said. "There's something else."

She examined the outer circle. There was a pattern. Four of the symbols were larger than the others. At the top was a man with sword, on the right was a swirl, on the bottom was a star, and on the left was a jagged circle. Between these were smaller circles and lions.

Sarah picked up the cube. The five sides that were not blank were a mishmash of symbols with no apparent pattern.

"I don't know," said Sarah. "There are all these numbers and letters and pictures, but it doesn't make any sense. Here, I'll show you."

Sarah grabbed her pen and transcribed the letters, numbers, arrows, and symbols into her diary. Then she held it up to show Duke. "Does this mean anything to you?"

Duke looked at it for several seconds. Then, without a word, he jumped down from his seat and disappeared into the aisle. A moment later, he returned with Samuel.

Sarah handed Samuel the cube and the open diary. "I found this code in my mom's diary using the gem you gave me. I think it's supposed to help me solve the puzzle cube, but I can't figure it out. Do you know what it means?"

Samuel's gaze moved from the diary to the cube and then to Sarah. "Was the cube like this when you received it?"

"What do you mean?" asked Sarah.

"All the blank tiles are on one side. Were they in this position already, or did you do this?"

"I did it. It took a while, but the first page said to start here and then—"

"Then he has done it," said Samuel. His eyes were wide.

"What?"

"Your father. Do you remember when I told you he that could not solve this on his own? *This* is what he could not do. And now *you* have done it. Do you understand what this means, little one?"

"No."

"He has passed on the rest of the birthright blessings to you. *You,* Miss Sarah, are the Weaver. Right now. Your father—for reasons he believes best, I am sure——has chosen to put the gifts out of his own reach."

"Does that mean he—"

"I do not know what that means for him. I am not certain I want to know."

33

CUSTOMS

Sarah had never thought much about traveling to another country, but she had always assumed that if she did, she would be on vacation, seeing new sights and visiting new places. It would be nothing but fun, relaxation, and excitement. This, however, was no vacation.

The sky was overcast and dreary when they touched down in Berlin. The sun had not yet risen in Texas, but here, the captain told them over the plane's intercom, it was almost lunchtime. Samuel fastened a leash to Duke's collar, and Benjamin clumsily removed their carry-on items from the overhead bins, handing each to its owner and dropping bags more than once. As soon as the captain opened the door, they hurried off the plane. Nobody spoke much. Sarah was glad. She didn't feel like talking.

The floors and walls of the airport were drab shades of white and gray. Everything was cold. The air was filled with the sounds of travelers speaking half a dozen languages Sarah did not understand and an instrumental version of an American pop song she was sure she had heard somewhere. *Never gonna give you up...*Those were all the words she could remember.

While they were picking up their suitcases at baggage claim, Samuel whispered, "I will usher Duke through customs. There will be some paperwork to complete. Please stay near to Dr. Connolly, Miss Johnson." Sarah did not realize whom he meant by *Miss Johnson* until she remembered that Emilia Johnson was the made up name on her counterfeit passport. Her heart raced. What if the customs agents realized the passport was a fake? What if they did not believe she was the girl in the photo? She wasn't, after all.

But before she had time to process these questions, Sarah found herself in the line for customs. Since they had been the only passengers on their flight, the wait was short. Benjamin went through first without any problems, followed by Michael. Then Duncan sent Sarah through ahead of himself while Samuel and Duke waited to go through last of all.

Sarah held her breath. The woman behind the counter scanned the forged passport and the form Sarah had completed on the airplane without glancing up. She asked in broken English if Sarah had anything to declare as she rifled half-heartedly through Sarah's backpack. Sarah shook her head. The agent stamped the passport and waved Sarah on. She joined Michael and Benjamin on the other side and exhaled with relief.

"Now see, lassie, that wasn't so bad," said Michael. "Nothing to worry—" He stopped, eyes fixed on the customs agent.

Sarah turned and saw that the woman was holding Duncan's arm and speaking into a walkie-talkie. Duncan looked back at Michael and shrugged. Beyond Duncan, Samuel watched, but he appeared unconcerned.

"Wait here," said the customs agent.

A moment later, two men wearing all-black combat gear and carrying assault rifles arrived. They spoke to the woman in whispers. She held up Duncan's form and said something Sarah could not hear. Then she pointed at something on the form and spoke to Duncan. Duncan shook his head, held up his hands, and shrugged his shoulders. One of the armed men spoke to Duncan in German. Again he shook his head and shrugged.

"Bugger!" said Michael. "What has he got himself into now? Likely checked the wrong box."

But then the two armed men turned and approached Samuel, their guns pointed his direction. One of them shouted an order in German and motioned for Samuel to step toward the wall. The other snatched Duke's leash from Samuel's hand. Duke growled, but Samuel spoke calmly to the men in German as he handed them his passport and papers followed by his carry-on bag, which they immediately unzipped and emptied onto the floor.

Duncan shot a panicked look at Michael and Benjamin and mouthed the word "help." He turned and started toward Samuel, but the customs agent put a hand against his chest and said, "Nein!"

"Ey! Now just you wait one bleedin' moment," said Michael as he approached the counter.

All was confusion. The customs agent was arguing in broken English with the two Scottish scientists. The armed men were pointing their guns at Samuel and shouting as he removed his turban for their inspection.

"Can you understand them, Dr. Allen? What's going on?" asked Sarah.

Benjamin was fidgeting nervously with something in his pocket. "I don't really speak German, but it appears they believe Samuel is carrying something dangerous," he said in a cracking voice. "They're asking something about Duke too."

"What do they want?"

"You can ask him later," said Benjamin. "Right now, Miss Sarah, I think you and I had better move along. It's probably nothing, but just in case."

"Right," said Sarah. The two slipped away and rushed toward the noisy concourse.

Sarah asked if they should find a place to hide out and wait for the others. Benjamin said that Samuel and the others could take care of themselves and would know where to find them, but that right now, he needed to find a telephone so he could alert headquarters to what had happened at customs.

After several minutes of searching, they arrived at a row of pay phones. Benjamin pulled some coins and a scrap of paper from his pocket with a shaking hand and dialed.

"Hallo? Ja. Das ist Benjamin Allen. Ja. Nein. Ja." He hung up, then said to Sarah, "They've sent a car for us. You and I are to go right away."

"I thought you didn't speak German," she said as he took her arm and whisked her across the concourse toward the doors.

"Just a bit," he said, looking back over his shoulder.

Outside, they found a large man with a dark beard holding a cardboard sign with the words "Benjamin Allen" written on it. They approached. Benjamin whispered something to the large man. He nodded and opened the door to a black sedan. "Willkommen, Dr. Allen," he said and laughed.

Sarah left her bags with the man who held the door and stepped inside. The car's back seat was a leather bench, and a tall, slender man sat at the far side. Sarah slid to the middle and dug for a seatbelt as Benjamin crawled in and sat next to her. She found the seatbelt, snapped the buckle into place, and looked up.

Then she saw him. He was the last person she expected to see: Mr. Litchfield—the substitute math teacher who had been escorted from Sarah's school by police, the man who had kidnapped Grandpa Kirk and set their house on fire. He was sitting in the front passenger seat wearing a triumphant expression and pointing a handgun at her forehead.

"Well, hello, Miss Lewis," said the familiar, nasal voice. "Trying out a new style are we? I must say, it doesn't suit you."

Sarah gasped and turned to look at Benjamin.

"I'm so sorry, Miss Sarah," said Benjamin. "I—"

"Shut up," Litchfield shouted. "Stefan, the chloroform."

A moment later, the slender man was holding the back of Sarah's head tightly with one hand and pressing a wet rag over her face with the other. She struggled and kicked, but however she fought, she could not get free. For a moment, she felt as if she would drown or throw up or both. Then the world began to spin and she felt very sleepy. Everything faded to black. The last thing she heard was Benjamin whispering, "I'm so, so sorry!"

THE NEXT THING SARAH SAW WAS A FLICKERING FLUORESCENT LIGHT attached to the wall. It seemed to be spinning. She couldn't tell for sure. The world was blurred at the edges through her squinted eyelids. Her head throbbed. She closed her eyes and tried to focus her thoughts. No, she realized, it wasn't the wall she had seen; it was the ceiling. She was lying flat on her back. Beneath her was a cold, hard surface. And now she realized that there were other people nearby. She could hear voices arguing.

"I don't believe it," said a gravelly voice with a thick French accent. "Look at her. This is not the girl."

"I swear it!" said another panic-stricken voice. This one belonged to someone Sarah knew—or at least, someone she thought she knew. "They disguised her," squeaked Benjamin, "but she's—"

"Lies!" said the first voice. "The Weaver's daughter is on her way here now in the care of some of our own. By your own admission, you are in the employ of The Sentinels. Do you take us for fools?"

"Now, Monsieur," interjected a third voice, deep and smooth and distinctly British, "Dr. Allen was my colleague. I knew him quite well at one time—well enough to know that, while he may be many things, he is no liar. He's no good at it. If he says this is the young Sarah Lewis, then I for one believe him."

"Then you are a fool, Drake," growled the first. "Not that it matters; we have your Weaver already. We have no use for the girl now."

Drake, thought Sarah. Where had she heard that name before? She repeated it in her mind, trying to place its significance. *Drake. Drake.*

Benjamin gasped. "You have Mr. Lewis? Here?"

"Indeed," replied Drake. "He was found in Frankfurt two days ago, and our agents brought him in. A bit anticlimactic, I thought. Though, I must say, he has been less than cooperative since he arrived." He paused. "And that, Monsieur, is where I believe young Sarah might prove useful. Perhaps we should try a new tactic? Hmm? I can think of no better subject to read a man's memories than his own child. We can operate on both girls if you like. Whichever is the true daughter will know how to find his secrets. And what father could refuse his little princess? It will be easy for her. Given all the trouble the pair of them have caused us, it seems almost poetic, don't you think?"

Sarah began to panic. *Drake. Memories.* It was all coming together. *The man Benjamin knew, the one who was stealing memories and had been recruited by Les Luminaires—what was his name? Was it Drake?* She had to get out of here. She struggled to move.

"Sir," said a new voice, "she's waking."

"More chloroform, Stefan."

Sarah woke to something buzzing near her left ear. *Why is my head wet?* She wondered. Now that she thought about it, her whole body was cold, but especially her head, as if she had stepped out of the shower into a cold room. Something was scraping against her scalp. And still, she could hear the buzzing.

She opened her eyes and immediately squeezed them closed again to shut out the bright light.

"Ahh Sarah," said Drake. "Just in time."

Sarah tried to move, but she couldn't. Her arms seemed to be tied down. She squinted again and tried to lift her head. It too was held firmly in place. Something soft brushed against her foot, and she realized she was no longer wearing socks or shoes. She squirmed and fought to move her legs, but she found that they too were restrained. Worse still, she realized that she was naked beneath what felt like a thin sheet. "What are you doing to me?"

"Me? I'm standing here talking with you. My assistant, however, is shaving your head." Sarah jerked in a vain attempt to look at her own head.

"Please don't struggle. You'll only wear yourself out, and we can't have that," said Drake. His gaunt, clean-shaven face and dark eyes came into view, obscuring the bright light above him. "Now, as I was saying, you are waking just in time. We have a custom here that I did not want you to miss. Before our subjects undergo the procedure, we like to give them one last chance say anything they like. Some shout obscenities. Some beg for mercy. Some confess hidden sins or unspoken love. Some cry to their gods for forgiveness or help. Some, like your father, say nothing at all, and that's most unfortunate, I think. It's the last chance you'll ever have to think and speak of your own free will, Sarah. So I beg you, choose your words wisely."

Sarah glared at him for a moment. Then she spat in his face and clenched her mouth shut.

Drake lifted the white sheet that covered Sarah's naked body and used it to wipe his face. "You may proceed, Doctor," he said and disappeared from Sarah's view.

"Count backward from thirty, if you please," said a voice.

Sarah grunted defiantly and did not open her mouth.

"Very well, then."

A mask was pressed over Sarah's nose and mouth, and she was unconscious again within seconds.

34

A THIEF IN THE NIGHT

The sand was hot beneath Sarah's bare feet. From behind, she heard the calls of exotic birds and animals. The wind blew through her short, thick hair, and it felt strange.

"No," said a voice in her mind, "not here."

For a moment the world seemed to slip away. A familiar fragrance filled her nostrils. Perfume. Sarah's mother's perfume. She was holding a piece of paper to her nose. As she lowered it, Sarah glimpsed her mother's signature. Affection and longing and sorrow filled her heart, and she thought she might cry. She folded the letter and slipped it back into her coat pocket.

Hang on, she thought. There was something she needed to remember. *What was it?* The memory hung on the edge of her mind, just out of reach. *Water. I was going swimming,* she remembered.

The beach returned. She felt herself wade out into the breakers up to her waist, and then she dove. The sensation of the saltwater against her skin was different than anything she had ever felt; it seemed to pull at her in places as if she were wearing a loose shirt. But she wasn't wearing a shirt. Why wasn't she wearing a shirt? And how was she able to swim so fast and so deep? She looked through the greenish blue water and caught sight of her arm. It wasn't her arm. It was longer, more muscular, and covered in black hair, like her father's arm.

"Stop!" said the voice.

SARAH SIPPED UNSWEETENED BLACK COFFEE AT AN OUTDOOR CAFÉ. She was wearing sunglasses, and her heart raced. She had to appear calm, relaxed. Two men across the street were pretending not to watch her. But she knew they were watching. She wanted them to watch, to find her, to catch her. It scared her to death, but she had to do it.

A waitress appeared and asked in German if she wanted anything else. She understood the German. And she replied in German: "Nein, danke." Her voice was deep and masculine. She did not sound afraid, but she felt it.

She glanced across the street again. The men were approaching. One had his hand inside his coat. He was armed. She intentionally knocked a salt shaker from the table, making it look like an accident, and bent over to retrieve it. While she reached for the salt shaker with her left hand, she slipped her right into her own coat and, with one smooth motion, disengaged the safety on the Ruger 9mm pistol that was hidden in the shoulder holster against her ribcage.

No, no, no, she thought again. *I've got to remember.* She didn't know why, but she felt it was somehow vital that she remember whatever it was she had forgotten. This other scene, this memory, was just a distraction. She cleared her mind and thought back to the ocean.

AGAIN SHE SWAM. AHEAD AND ON HER RIGHT, SHE SAW SAMUEL through the hazy water. His long muscular legs made him a fast swimmer. She veered to the right a little and followed him.

BOOM!

Something like thunder stole her attention. The sound was clear and airy. She realized she was dry now. The ocean was gone. For an instant, she was aware of her cold feet and a terrible itching sensation in her scalp. Voices were shouting, but she could not understand the words. Then the voices faded, and she felt herself slipping once again into the memory she so badly wanted to relive.

SHE EMERGED FROM THE WATER INTO A DARK CAVERN. FRESH AIR FILLED her lungs. It stung, but it was so wonderful to breathe again that she didn't mind. Sarah pushed herself up onto a rocky ledge inside and stood.

"It has been long, my friend," she heard Samuel say. She turned and saw him standing beside her. He wore swim trunks and held a canvas bag. He did not seem as tall as she thought he should. The rippling muscles in his bare shoulders and chest seemed surprisingly familiar. And now she saw that he had a tattoo on his forehead, just behind where the jewel on his turban normally sat. It was a flower. *Primrose*, she thought. It was a primrose. She knew it, though she did not know how.

They climbed a stair of rocks deep into the cave until they reached a flat place. *The dais*, she thought.

"No!" screamed a voice in her mind. "Stop!"

SHE WAS BACK AT THE CAFÉ. THE MEN HAD REACHED THE FRONT DOOR. She heard one of them request a table on the patio in German. Again, she understood perfectly. Her heart beat hard in her chest. This was the plan, she told herself. She could not panic. Not now. She took a deep breath and began to silently recite the twenty-third Psalm:

The Lord is my shepherd; I shall not want...

The men appeared in the doorway to the patio. She sensed them in her periphery, but she forced herself not to look. Instead, she took a sip of coffee and continued her mental recitation.

The waitress led the men to a table near the street. They ordered coffee. The waitress left.

Yea, though I walk through the valley of the shadow of death, I will fear no evil...

The man with his hand in his coat was now standing directly behind her. She forced herself to breathe slowly.

"Hello, Jacob," said the man in perfect American English. "Keep your hands on the table where I can see them. Good. Now, turn slowly and come with me."

"Ich spreche kein Englisch," she replied with the same deep, calm voice she had used with the waitress.

"You're not fooling anyone, Weaver," said the man, "and if you wish for your daughter and your father-in-law to live, I suggest you drop the act and come with us. Now. No fight. No funny stuff. Nobody gets hurt. All right?"

Sarah thought her heart would leap from her chest. But no. There was no reason to be afraid. All was arranged. Everything was going according to plan. She was prepared, she reminded herself.

Yea, though I walk through the valley of the shadow of death, I will fear no evil...

"Okay, okay. I'll come," she heard herself say. "Just swear to me that you'll leave my family alone."

BOOM!

There it was again. Now her scalp didn't just itch, it burned. The sounds of shouting voices were distant. Nearer, she heard another voice mumbling. It seemed familiar.

SARAH WALKED OUT OF THE CAFÉ. SHE WONDERED WHETHER SHE WOULD need to use the gun tucked beneath her left arm, and if so, whether she would be able to reach it in time.

A black car was parked ahead. A large man with a beard stepped out and opened a door. He seemed familiar.

I will fear no evil...

BOOM!

The voice mumbled something again. She couldn't make out the words, but the accent...

Remember! Remember! Remember! Sarah told herself.

THE FLOOR OF THE CAVE WAS SMOOTH AND COOL. ON HER LEFT, something glowed. It was the Weaver's Key, she knew, but she was not looking at it now. She was looking at the puzzle cube. She had to send a message first. Colored crystals emerged and glowed as she twisted it this way and that in her hands. She knew exactly what she was doing.

"One more turn," she heard herself say, "and there."

Suddenly, everything aligned perfectly, and a whole new set of bright objects emerged from nowhere, bending in ways that defied logic, entangled with the familiar crystals. Heat radiated from the cube as she lowered it to the open metal box at her feet.

"NOOOO!" the voice in her mind screamed.

SHE WAS IN THE CAR. THEN TIME SKIPPED AHEAD, AND SHE WAS standing in front of a brick and steel building guarded by men with automatic weapons. She knew that her pistol had been confiscated. But it was going to be all right; she still had—but no. She would not allow herself to even think about it.

I will fear no evil...

BOOM!

There was a sob and more mumbling.

Sarah forced her eyes open. "Dr. Allen?" she said. "Is that you?"

"Miss Sarah?" said Benjamin. "How are—"

"What were you saying?"

"Nothing. Just a litany. From Dune. I thought it might help with the…" He paused. "How are you awake?"

"I…I don't know," said Sarah. "Am I awake? What are those noises? Why does my head hurt? Why can't I move?" Then, as her own memory returned to her, "What did you do?!"

35

CONFESSION

"Oh, God forgive me. I've made a mess of things," Benjamin groaned. "We're in it now, Miss Sarah. All of us. And it's all my fault."

Sarah tried to sit up, but she could not move anything below her neck, and her head was held in place by something she could not see. Anger welled up in her chest. "What did you—"

"I'm so sorry, Miss Sarah. I'm so, so sorry," said Benjamin, his voice trembling.

BOOM!

Sarah heard panicked voices shouting somewhere far off. Then there was a reverberating clanking noise, and all became silent except for the whirring of machines and the sound of Benjamin's continued groaning.

"What's going on?" asked Sarah. "Where am I?"

"Oh, God forgive me. You don't even know." Benjamin took a deep breath. "I've given you up, Miss Sarah. I've handed you over to Les Luminaires, to Drake."

Sarah fumed with anger. "How could you?" she shouted. "After everything they've done? After what Drake did to you? After the way Blackwood hurt you just yesterday?"

Benjamin grunted. "The way I *let* Blackwood hurt me, you mean."

"What?"

"I'm so sorry, Miss Sarah." Benjamin's voice was soft and mournful. "I let Blackwood out. It was all my idea. Gave him the knife, told him I'd help him get away and find your dad. He was supposed to take me, not you, but then..." Again, he groaned.

"What is wrong with you?!" demanded Sarah.

"I..." he started. "I *had* to do it."

Sarah tried to bang her fist on the table and found that she could not. For all her effort, she only managed to move her pinky finger a little. The helplessness only added to her frustration. At last she simply asked "Why?"

Benjamin stuttered and struggled for a bit before he finally said, "Do you remember the letter in your lunch tin, Miss Sarah? The one from Desjardins?"

Sarah did not reply. Instead, she strained to move her body. A sensation like a thousand tiny pin pricks began to creep inward from her toes and fingertips.

"I dug through your things the night your grandfather was taken. I'm sorry. I had no right. I was suspicious, and, well...Do you have any idea who Desjardins is?"

Silence.

"No, of course you don't. Nor do I. Nor do any of The Sentinels. You see, Dr. Connolly and Dr. MacPherson built a device—well, it's just a dot-matrix printer, really, connected to a photon receiver by some advanced fiber optics they were working on back at Southampton. 'The future's in quantum entanglement,' they said. 'Instantaneous data transmission across any distance at all,' they said. 'And if we can entangle photons across space, what's to say we couldn't someday entangle them across time as well?'"

Sarah cut him off. "If you're going to talk, could you at least use words I understand?" Her feet itched and burned now almost as badly as the top of her head.

"Oh. Right. Sorry. I'm rambling. I'll get to it. Their idea was to enable communication between two points in time. Mankind will likely never travel through time, of course. There are so many problems with it that are simply ignored in movies and books. And not just paradoxes and—"

"Is there a point to this?"

"I'm sorry, Miss Sarah. I suppose I don't really want to admit to what I've done, now it comes to it. I'll get to the point.

"Dr. MacPherson and Dr. Connolly believed so strongly in the idea of someday being able to send messages back in time that they built a machine to receive data from their future selves or descendants. They set up a log to record the receiver's exact location, operation times, and other vital data, and they locked it away. Then they turned the device on. And right away a message came through. Only, it was addressed to me, not to either of them."

"I don't see what this has to do with anything," said Sarah. Her patience was wearing thin.

"I'm coming to that. But just think with me. If you were going to send a message back in time, wouldn't you address it to yourself? I would. But I don't think it could be me for several reasons. For starters, why wouldn't I sign it with my own name? Why call myself Desjardins? I'm not even French."

"So?"

"So we don't know who sent that message! Or any of the messages since. There have been many. And they weren't kind little notes like the one you received. Oh no. There were specifications and blueprints for machines that have not yet been invented. How do you think we came to create the molecular printer and the brain scanner? Desjardins sent the plans. To me. Not to the two physicists. To me.

"It made no sense. I didn't like it. I felt we were treading on ground that wasn't ours to tread. We don't know what agendas this person might have. Why shouldn't Desjardins be an enemy from the future? Or perhaps, an enemy from another universe? Perhaps the Obsinders themselves have been sending signals through the tiny gap in the gateway and using personal secrets and the promise of advanced technology against us. But the others wouldn't hear of it. They were convinced it was their future selves or perhaps an heir or colleague giving them a leg up on the real baddies. So, I determined to put a stop to the whole thing on my own. I started sneaking into the lab at night and burning the transmissions from Desjardins before anyone could read them.

"That was all well and good, of course, until you showed up. When I found the letter in your tin, I was furious. I hid the whole thing—pretended I lost it. What with the laboratory being relocated, I thought that would be the end of it. But then we got to San Antonio, and—wouldn't you know—Dr. MacPherson set up the blasted thing again. And what comes through but another letter from Desjardins? Only this time, it's addressed to the Watcher, and it's written in some sort of code. Well, that was too much for me. I sent Dr. Connolly to fetch the Watcher, and then I pulled the plug. Told them it malfunctioned."

"What does any of this has to do with kidnapping me?" Sarah tried to look at Benjamin. She strained her eyes as far as they would go, but she could only see the ceiling.

"I read Blackwood's memories that night, and when I saw what I saw in his mind, I felt my deepest fears had been confirmed." He was breathing harder now. "I can still see it. I'm in a dark room. There are men in hoods holding torches all around me. There are candles on the walls. My heart is beating out of my chest. I kneel, and one of the men cuts my arm with a strange sword. He says something I don't understand. Then he places the sword into this...this thing, and, and well, something tears open in the middle of the air. Everything goes cold, and through the tear I see a massive eye, bright and golden-green, and the most beautiful and terrible voice I've ever heard starts speaking straight into my mind, like some sort of god. It tells me that they're coming. The Obsinders are coming to Earth. They're going to kill everyone—humans and otherworlders and halfies alike—and there's nothing we can do to stop it unless we let this whatever-it-is through to fight for us. The Obsinders do not sleep, it says. They do not forget. They cannot be fooled, and they cannot be defeated without it's help. It says that already, the Obsinders have scouts in our world. It says their coming will mean long, slow, torturous deaths for everyone I know and love unless I obey its orders exactly.

"And I believed it, Miss Sarah. I believed it deep in my bones. I know it was Blackwood's memory, of course, not mine, but somehow it spoke to me, not him. I've seen other memories, Miss Sarah. I know how that feels, as I'm sure you do now. Believe me when I say this was different. It told me *my* secret thoughts, uncovered fears I had forgotten since childhood. It said that I was right about Desjardins. It was all a plot by the Obsinders. They were trying to gain our trust, to use us to build what they needed for their invasion. It told me the others would not believe me and that I must say nothing to The Sentinels. It talked about you, Miss Sarah, and how you were the key to your father. It said I had to bring you to Dr. Drake myself. It said I was the only one who could do it. And then it showed me my little daughter back in London. Did you know I have a daughter? I haven't seen her in years. She lives with her gran now that her mother's gone, and I'm not allowed to see her. But I still love her, Miss Sarah, fiercer than anything. And this creature, this lovely, awesome, terrifying creature, it showed me how she would die if I failed."

"And you believed this, this *thing*? Some crazy monster shows up in Blackwood's head, and you take orders from it?"

"Well, at first I tried to change the plan. Offered to let Blackwood take me instead of you, told him you weren't there. But then he saw you, and well, I had to go along. Don't you see? There was nothing I could do. I came so close to failing, and seeing what that would mean for my own little girl."

Sarah was speechless. A thousand questions raced through her mind, but she could not give them a voice.

"I couldn't stop thinking about it. So I set it all up before we left, and then I scribbled a note in German on Dr. Connolly's customs forms when he wasn't looking. Implied that the Watcher had contraband in his bag. It worked. Bought the few minutes I needed to get you away from the others.

"And now look what I've done. Your head is covered in little metal ports like mine. Only you've got more of them than I have. Upgrades, I suppose. They've made you like me—turned you into a reader and forced you to dig up your father's memories."

Sarah's breath caught in her chest, and she squeezed her eyes against the tears that were welling up.

Benjamin sighed. "Your father. Now there's a real Sentinel. He wouldn't tell them how to find the Key. Oh no, of course he wouldn't. So they've used you to pry his secrets out of him against his will. He might have resisted another mind—he's been training against this sort of thing ever since he first learned what happened to me, after all—but how could he resist you, his own daughter? It's impossible. There's too much love in the way. You have too much access already." Benjamin groaned. "And Drake saw it all, no doubt. He's got exactly what he wanted all along. And now that he has it, they're going let the devils come and bring all of Hell with them."

"Devils?" asked Sarah. Benjamin was frightening her.

"The Obsinders. I was wrong, Miss Sarah. Bought the lie. Drake told me all about it. It's no benevolent god that he and his superiors serve. That's just a part it plays it to manipulate the weak—a costume it wore to fool me. Drake and the others, they know they're dealing with a vicious snake who wants nothing more than to wipe us all off the planet. They worship it like pagans—blood sacrifices and all. And they believe they've earned its good graces. They've been promised positions of power in exchange for their treachery against the Earth. They think they'll get to rule what's left of this world when all's done. They believe the Obsinders will reward them. They really do. The fools. God help us."

He made a noise that might have been a pathetic laugh or a whimper, Sarah could not tell which. "What a mess I've made. And for what? We're all going to die the moment they open that gate. All because I was a coward."

36

REPENTANCE

"Hang on a minute," said Sarah. "They can't open the gate—"

"Oh, but they can," Benjamin whimpered pathetically. "Thanks to me. Why was I so stupid?"

"Oh, shut up!" Sarah shouted. She'd had enough of all this whining from a grown man, from a scientist, from a traitor. She needed to get out, and she couldn't do it on her own. She needed Benjamin's help whether he deserved her trust or not. "Pull yourself together! There's always a better use for your brain than reliving a failure. That's what Grandpa says. Now come on. This isn't over yet. Yeah, you screwed up, okay, but right now you're all I've got. So I need you to focus. Maybe we can still figure out a way to fix this."

Benjamin took a deep, stuttering breath. "Yes. Of course, you're right. I'm sorry, Miss Sarah. For everything."

"Yeah, you've apologized enough. It's not helping. What would help is if I could get out of here."

"I'm afraid I can't help with that," said Benjamin. "They handcuffed me to a pipe so I couldn't interfere."

"Why can't I move?"

"Well, you've been drugged for the reading—a syringe full of chemicals meant to keep you unconscious and cooperative—and that after they'd already knocked you out for the surgery. I can't understand how you're awake at all."

"Does it matter?" Sarah squeezed her eyes shut. Her head burned, and she couldn't think straight.

Benjamin took a deep breath and began mumbling to himself. "The drugs must have begun wearing off before…No. That's much too quick." He paused and looked at the ceiling. "They started the surgery, what, six, seven hours ago? And finished within three hours? Two-and-a-half? Incredibly efficient team Drake's got, I'll give them that. And it's only been an hour or so since they brought her here and gave her the second injection. Two, maybe? I've lost track of time. Either way, that dose would keep a normal person under for…but wait. Ha! That's it, isn't it? She isn't normal. Of course! You're a ginger, Miss Sarah!"

"A what?"

"A redhead! Nobody knows why, but people with red hair seem to show a peculiar resistance to anesthesia! Of course! I should have known. My cousin's a ginger, and he woke in the middle of having his tonsils out. But Drake's anesthetist wouldn't have known you were a ginger at all because you'd dyed your hair. Ha! Can you move at all?"

"Yeah, a little. I'm tingly all over."

"Wonderful! Keep moving. Get your blood flowing. And take deep breaths."

Sarah obeyed. She was still angry, her head ached horribly, and her whole body itched and burned, but it felt good to be doing something besides lying down, helpless. "How long do you think it will be before I can get up?" she asked.

"I can't say," said Benjamin.

Sarah flexed her fingers and toes. "And what did you mean when you said they could open the gate? I thought only the Weaver could do that."

"As I understand it, the Weaver can open the gate because he can see how aligning the elements in the Key affects the gateway beyond what a normal person's sight would allow. There's nothing else magical about it. So if someone else studied the Weaver's motions while operating the Key, the sequence could be memorized and repeated—like the difference between a safe cracker and someone who simply knows the combination." He paused. "When you were inside your father's memories, you saw the Key, didn't you? And how to open it?"

"I—" said Sarah, "I don't think so. No."

"Are you certain? They would have used hypnotic suggestion to make uncovering memories of the Key your primary objective."

"No, I'm sure. I tried to see it. I felt like I *had* to remember it. And I did see where it was, but I never got a good look at it. Every time I started to remember, there was this voice in my head that said 'no,' and then the memory would switch to something else."

"Ha! He resisted! It worked! There's still a chance!"

"But even if I had seen it, who would know? I didn't tell anybody."

"Dr. Drake," said Benjamin. "He gave me a tour of the whole facility while you were in surgery. Wanted to rub it in, I suppose—show me what I missed when I refused his offer all those years ago. He's turned this place into a network of subjects and readers. And at the center of the whole thing, the psychopath's built himself a hub. He plugs himself into it so he can spy on his readers and see what they see. If you think my head is gruesome, you should see what he's done to himself!"

"Do you think he knows I'm awake? Where is he now?" Sarah could move her ankles a little, but most of her body was still paralyzed from the anesthesia. If somebody came looking for her, she would be at their mercy.

"Still plugged in, I'd have thought. He left me here with a couple of armed lackeys so I could watch you suffer and uncover The Sentinels' most precious secret. Then he went to—"

BOOM!

The loud noise made Sarah's head throb. "What was that?" asked Sarah. It had been several minutes since she had heard it last.

"I don't rightly know," said Benjamin. "But judging from the way everyone's disappeared, I'd say there's a good chance it's The Sentinels trying to break in and rescue you. There were a handful of technicians working in here earlier, but they all slipped away after the guards left. You should have seen their faces."

BOOM!

Sarah's heart leapt in her chest despite the increasing pain. "Do you really think—" But she stopped. There was another sound now. A loud creaking. Then Sarah heard distant voices shouting.

"Shhhh!" whispered Benjamin.

One of the voices sounded like Drake. There was a clanking noise, and the voices stopped.

"What did they say?" Sarah whispered.

"I couldn't make it out, but you'd best lie still and shut your eyes."

Sarah closed her eyes and froze.

"Breathe slowly," whispered Benjamin. "And wiggle your eyes a bit. It'll look like you're dreaming."

A moment later, Sarah heard quick footsteps approaching. The door swung open. Someone came close and stopped.

"Oi! You! Tubby!" said Benjamin.

"Shut up," said a man's voice. He sounded American. "I've got work to do."

"Oh? You've work to do, have you? I thought you'd all gone on holiday."

"Watch your mouth, pretty boy, or I'll shut it for you."

Sarah felt a strange sensation in her scalp. The man must have moved the cables that were attached to the ports in her skull.

"Ahh, noticed the connection problem, have you?"

The man grunted.

"Well, I can see your problem from here. Noticed it straight away. It's obvious, really."

"Yeah? You some sort of electrical engineer?"

"Not at all. Neuroscientist. But even a child could see something this plain."

"Well, spit it out then."

"Tell you what," said Benjamin. "I'm thirsty. You bring me a glass of water, give me a drink, and I'll help you with your problem."

"Not a chance," said the man, and Sarah again felt the strange sensation of cables rotating in the ports on her head.

"Right then. Have it your way." Benjamin broke into a loud rendition of *God Save the Queen*.

"Would you mind?"

"Me? Here I am, minding my own business, tied to a wall, slowly dying of thirst, and the same bloke who won't bring me a glass of water has the nerve to complain about my singing. Of all the—"

"Just shut up."

"God save—" Benjamin sang again, even louder.

"Oh for…If I bring you some water, will you shut your trap?"

"On my honor, kind sir. And what's better, I'll show you the problem with your connection."

"Fine then," said the man. Sarah heard his footsteps fade into the distance.

"What are you doing?" she whispered.

"Getting us out of here. Well, trying anyway. It worked so well for Blackwood in my cover story, I thought I'd give it a go myself."

The footsteps drew close again.

"All right, songbird, here's your water."

Sarah heard slurping. Then Benjamin said, "Ahh. Thank you. Now, look right there and you'll see the problem."

"Where?"

"I can't exactly point. Right there, just below the…Crouch down here. You can see it better from this angle."

"I don't see anything wrong"

"Lower. Can you see that blue cable there, beneath the table?"

The man grunted. "I see it. What's the problem?"

WHACK!

"The problem is she's awake, you stupid prat."

BENJAMIN STOOD OVER HER, BROKEN HANDCUFFS STILL HANGING FROM his wrists. Slowly and carefully, he removed each wire from its port in Sarah's shaven head. Then he helped her sit up, keeping one hand on her shoulder for support.

All around her, Sarah saw glowing screens and tall, whirring machines covered in blinking lights and little white dials. She was wearing a plain white gown that stopped at her knees, and she was sitting on top of a thin mattress that had been wrapped in a white cotton sheet. On the white tile floor, she saw a man in a white lab coat lying in a heap.

"What did you do to him?" she asked.

"Headbutted him," Benjamin said as he examined her scalp. "Aimed for his temple. Not sure where I hit him, exactly, but it seems all that titanium Drake put into my skull has made it excellent for bludgeoning." He smiled stupidly. "It felt good, I can tell you. Really good."

Sarah stared at him in wonder. "And the handcuffs?"

"Wire cutters. Bloke had them in his coat pocket. Now," he said, looking into Sarah's eyes. "I suppose we should find somewhere to hide you before he wakes or Drake sends someone else. Then I'll go and look for your father."

"*We* will look for my father. But first, do you know what they did with my bags?"

"Your bags? Yes. They're locked up in a closet near the operating room, but—"

"We have to get them first."

"No, it's too far. Safer to—"

"Benjamin!" Sarah took a breath and softened her voice. "I mean, Dr. Allen. Please. This is really important. There are things in my bags that we can't let Les Luminaires find."

"Like what?"

She looked at him suspiciously for a moment, then said, "A training thing for the Weaver. Some old Weaver artifacts. Codes that might have something to do with the Weaver's Key."

"Blimey! Why on Earth would a junior agent have all that?"

"Because I'm not just a junior agent. I'm the Weaver."

37

KNOCK, KNOCK

Benjamin stared into Sarah's eyes for a long moment. First confusion and then doubt crossed his face. "All right, Miss Sarah," he said at last with a sigh. "Can you sit up on your own?"

"I think so," said Sarah.

BOOM! The sound had returned.

Benjamin glanced toward the ceiling, then back at Sarah. "Good," he said. He lifted his hand cautiously from Sarah's shoulder, and when he was satisfied that she would not fall, he turned and crouched next to the unconscious man.

"You don't believe me," said Sarah. The pain made it difficult for her to focus her eyes.

Benjamin said nothing. He rolled the man over and pulled his arms free of his lab coat sleeves one at a time.

BOOM!

"Well, it's true," she said. "Dad passed it all on to me before he came here."

Benjamin cut a bundle of wires loose from a nearby machine. There were sparks, and a screen went dark. Then he flipped the unconscious technician onto his back and began tying his wrists together. "Your father may have left you a few trinkets, but…" He stopped, took a deep breath, and looked at Sarah. "I won't argue.

Whatever you say." He finished his knot and moved on to the man's ankles.

BOOM! The sound was coming regularly now. It had almost a rhythm to it. And it hurt.

"What do you mean by that?"

"Who am I to disagree with you after all I've put you through?" Benjamin stood, slipped his own arms into the lab coat's sleeves and began to dig through the pockets. "Ahh, there we are," he said and held up a roll of cloth adhesive tape.

"So you don't believe me, but you're just going to go with it because you feel guilty?"

BOOM!

Again, Benjamin did not reply. He knelt next to the technician and placed a length of tape over his mouth.

"It's because I'm adopted, isn't it?" Sarah said.

Benjamin looked at her with a startled expression. "I…I didn't know you knew. The Watcher told us not to—"

"I know *now*," said Sarah. "And I also know that the Weaver's gifts aren't—"

BANG!

That was a different sound. Somebody far off screamed. Benjamin and Sarah stared at each other.

"Was that a gunshot?" asked Sarah.

"Sounded like it," said Benjamin.

Sarah strained her ears. There were more noises: frantic voices, running footsteps, doors slamming.

Benjamin ran to the door, turned the handle, and peeked out through the crack for a few seconds. He pushed it shut. "There are two armed guards coming this way, looking into every room they pass."

Sarah gasped. "Can you lock it?"

Benjamin patted his pockets and then ran back to the man on the floor. In a front pocket of the man's pants, Benjamin found a large ring of keys. He sprinted back to the door and tried one. No good. He tried another.

BOOM!

The voices in the hallway grew louder.

"Hurry!" said Sarah.

"I'm trying!" Benjamin tried a third key and a fourth. "Blast!"

Now Sarah could hear footsteps. A man's voice shouted, "Try that one."

Sarah felt dizzy. For a moment she thought she might fall.

"Got it!" whispered Benjamin.

Sarah heard the tumblers snap into place as Benjamin turned the key.

"Did you hear that?" said a voice beyond the door.

"Yeah," said the voice she had heard before. "It came from over there."

BOOM!

Benjamin stared at Sarah, frozen with fear.

Footsteps.

The handle jiggled. Then something pounded against the door.

"Who's in there?" shouted the man on the other side.

Benjamin was silent.

"Open up," the voice demanded, "or we'll tear the door down!"

BOOM!

Sarah saw Benjamin trembling. Her own heart was racing, but she was not petrified. Her father's words came back to her: *I will fear no evil.* She took a deep breath and repeated the words in her mind.

"All right, have it your way."

THWACK!

Something hit the door hard. It shook with the impact but held.

Sarah caught Benjamin's eyes. "Do something," she mouthed.

BOOM!

Benjamin swallowed hard and nodded. He walked around the room, trying cabinet doors and peering under desks. Then he disappeared for a moment behind a tall machine. When he reappeared, he held a computer keyboard, the attached cable dangling to the floor.

"What are you going to do with that?" whispered Sarah.

Benjamin pantomimed hitting someone in the head with it. The cord flailed and clacked against the tile floor. Benjamin shrugged. "Got a better idea?"

Sarah shook her head without thinking. Her neck was stiff, and her brain seemed to slosh against her skull with the movement.

THWACK!

Still, the door did not open.

The man on the floor made a muffled groaning noise.

"He's waking up," whispered Sarah.

"Hey! Who's in there?" demanded the voice from outside.

Benjamin tucked the keyboard under one arm and lifted Sarah from her bed. He carried her to the other side of the tall machine and set her on the floor, out of sight from the door. "Stay here and don't say a word," he said. Then he lifted the keyboard over his shoulder like a batter at the plate and tiptoed back to the door.

"I can hear you in there. Open the door!"

Sarah heard the technician trying to shout through the tape over his mouth.

"N…not on your life, ye loonie Lumie," Benjamin stammered, his accent even thicker than usual.

All was silent for a moment. There was another BOOM from high above.

"Who's there?" the voice demanded. "Do I know you?"

"Break the door down and find out, why don't you?" taunted Benjamin. He still sounded nervous despite his brave words.

"Oh, get out of the way," said the other voice beyond the door.

CRACK!

Sarah heard the door fly open. There was a shattering sound that must have been Benjamin's keyboard slamming into something hard. Shoes scuffled and slapped on the tile floor. Men's voices grunted.

"Stop that!" said the man's voice, clearer now that he was on this side of the door.

"Let go of me!" shouted Benjamin.

"Stop fighting me, Dr. Allen! It's me, Fred!"

"And Aubrey!" said the other voice.

"Fred? Aubrey? Oh, thank God!"

The door slammed shut. Sarah's heart leapt. "Aubrey!" she said and struggled to crawl.

"Sarah?" said Aubrey, now in her own voice.

"And who's this on the floor?" asked Fred.

THE SHIFTERS WERE HORRIFIED WHEN THEY SAW SARAH'S BALD AND studded scalp, and they demanded to know everything that had happened. Benjamin started to recount his story, but Sarah cut him off and said that the details didn't matter. They had both been captured by Les Luminaires, she said. Then she gave a quick recount of her surgery, how she woke from trying to steal her father's memories, and how Benjamin had knocked out the technician and freed himself before disconnecting Sarah from her wires.

In turn, Fred and Aubrey explained that their plan to impersonate Sarah and Arabella had gone very well. Nobody had suspected that Fred was not the shifter they knew. He had recounted Aubrey's and Sarah's battle with Arabella in such detail and with such venom in his voice that they could not help believing that he was really her. And when somebody mentioned that another comrade had identified Sarah at a Sentinel laboratory earlier that day, Fred said that it had probably been one of The Sentinels' shifters acting as a decoy. Arabella had, after all, seen them do just that. The band of Les Luminaires comrades bought it hook, line, and sinker, and their leader (a woman named Katrina) rushed to phone headquarters about their victorious find.

Fred and Aubrey had planned to retrieve their weapons from the oubliette and make their escape with Grandpa Kirk at the first opportunity, but then Katrina returned, livid from her phone call, and said that some idiot had already notified headquarters that he had Sarah in his possession and was on the way to Berlin with her at that very moment. And so, fearing that someone might have captured the real Sarah, Fred and Aubrey decided to risk the trip to Berlin. At first, Katrina had wanted to leave Arabella (Fred) behind, but Fred insisted that, since Arabella had been the one to successfully capture Sarah, she would be the best person to vouch for Sarah's identity if it came to a dispute.

They must have arrived around the time Sarah was coming out of surgery. Aubrey's impersonation of Sarah had been so convincing that Drake admitted he might have performed surgery on the wrong girl, and he immediately ordered his team to prepare for a second surgery. But when Aubrey reached the operating room, she shapeshifted, overwhelmed the entire medical staff single-handed, injected each of them with their own cocktail of drugs, took on a nurse's appearance, and walked out unquestioned.

Shortly after that, the booming sounds had begun, and guards everywhere went into a frenzy. Fred (in the form of Arabella) had been ordered to help the guards deal with the trouble upstairs, but he shapeshifted into the form of a lab assistant when nobody was watching and went looking for Aubrey instead. He found her fighting a couple of the guards who had been left to defend Drake's underground facility, and when she had dealt with them, the two shifters assumed the guards' appearances, took their guns, and started making their way through the halls looking for Grandpa Kirk and taking out any remaining guards as they went.

"But instead of Mr. Kirk," explained Aubrey, "we found you two."

"Well, there are two more Sentinels around here somewhere," said Benjamin, "and Miss Sarah says she has some artifacts that need retrieving."

38

TRUST

In the few short minutes he was gone, Fred managed to find all of Sarah's things and several bottles of medicine with German labels. Then he took up a sentry post in the hallway and left the others to tend to Sarah.

Benjamin examined the pills, selected two bottles, and held them out to Sarah. "This one will only take the pain down a notch, but it will have no other side effects. The other will—"

"Will it make me loopy?"

"Yes. And sleepy. We'd have to—"

BOOM!

"No." Sarah closed her eyes and gritted her teeth. "Just give me the first one. I need to be sharp."

Sarah swallowed the pills without water. Then Aubrey took her to the far side of the cabinet and helped her change into a tee shirt and jeans from her suitcase. Sarah put her mother's earrings into her earlobes and slipped the color-changing ring onto her finger, facing her palm, the way her father used to wear it. With Aubrey's help, she slipped her belt through the loop on the dagger's sheath and tightened it around her waist. Then she dug through her suitcase until she found the sample of L-421. It had saved her life during the fight with

Arabella Minot, and somehow it felt lucky. She shoved it into her front pocket.

"So you're the Weaver now?" said Aubrey as she pushed a clean sock over Sarah's foot. "Whoa. I mean, I can't...but this explains so much. When do you think, you know, it happened?"

BOOM!

Sarah winced at the noise. "You mean, when do I think Dad passed the blessings on to me?"

Aubrey nodded.

"I don't know," said Sarah. "Maybe the night we fought that shifter."

"Arabella." Aubrey slipped a sneaker over Sarah's toes and struggled to force her heel into it.

"Yeah. You were wrestling for her gun, and suddenly you were both different," Sarah took a deep breath and tried to relax, "like you were both smaller somehow. Younger. She was really scared. I could feel it. Almost like I was in a trance or something."

"But you could see things before that, couldn't you? I mean, you knew it was me earlier that same day when I was imitating Samuel. And you'd seen through my disguises even before that."

"Yeah, but I think that was just from my mom's half of the blessings. It wasn't as—"

"Your mom's half?!"

BOOM!

Sarah groaned, trying to ignore the pain in her head. "She was...I mean, my dad...It's hard to explain." She reached up and ran her fingers across the top of her head.

"Does it hurt to touch it?" asked Aubrey.

"My whole head hurts whether I touch it or not. Like I ate ice cream too fast. Up here it mostly itches like crazy.

"The pills will help a bit with the pain," said Benjamin. He was pointing the gun Aubrey had stolen at the technician lying on the floor. "I'm afraid the itching will stick around a while, though." He sighed. "I am truly sorry, Miss Sarah."

Aubrey shot a questioning look at Sarah, but Sarah did not answer.

BOOM!

Sarah moaned.

Aubrey finished tying Sarah's first shoe and moved on to the other foot. "Almost done."

"Great. Now we have to figure out where we're going. I don't guess you have any idea where they've taken Grandpa Kirk?" Sarah asked.

BOOM!

"Not a clue," answered Aubrey. "I haven't seen him since we arrived."

"And what about you, Miss Sarah?" asked Benjamin. "Did you happen to see anything in your father's memories about it?"

BOOM! BOOM!

"No," squeaked Sarah, wincing. "Nothing."

BOOM! BOOM! BOOM! CRASH!

Sarah could hear distant gunfire from somewhere high above, and she squeezed her aching skull between her hands.

The man lying on the floor began to whimper. Benjamin gave him a warning kick, and he was quiet again.

"Sounds like the fight is coming to us," said Benjamin. "It won't be long now."

"We have to find Sarah's family before they get here," said Aubrey. "If he's cornered, Drake might...we just have to get to them first."

Sarah nodded in agreement.

"Let's think," said Aubrey, now tying Sarah's second shoe. "Mr. Kirk could be anywhere, but Mr. Lewis must be plugged in somewhere. Right?"

"Right," said Benjamin, "but that doesn't narrow our search much. The whole place is wired."

The technician mumbled nonsense through the tape over his mouth.

"Oh, shut up," said Benjamin, fixing his gun on the man's torso. "I thought I told you to be silent. We've no time for your—"

"No, wait," said Sarah. "Maybe he knows something."

The man nodded.

"I don't trust him, Miss Sarah," said Benjamin.

"Me neither," said Aubrey. "He's probably hoping we'll take that tape off his mouth so he can call for help."

The man shook his head urgently.

"Or send us into a trap," said Benjamin.

Again the man shook his head.

Sarah closed her eyes and rubbed her temples. They were probably right, she realized. But the memory of Duke's voice came to her mind: "TRUST." There was no time to debate. She opened her eyes and crawled toward him. "He might know something. Let's just ask."

"Miss Sarah, I don't—" started Benjamin.

"Dr. Allen," interrupted Aubrey. "If she's really the Weaver, then technically she—"

"She outranks us. I know," said Benjamin. "But—"

"Just trust me," Sarah interrupted. "Please."

Then to the technician, she said, "Look at me. If we take this tape off your mouth, will you promise to be quiet and tell the truth?"

The man nodded.

Sarah looked at Benjamin and then at Aubrey. Aubrey nodded.

Benjamin sighed and said, "Look here, mate, if you so much as breathe too loudly, I'll—"

"Dr. Allen," said Sarah, "give him a chance." Then she reached out and pulled the tape from the man's mouth.

"Ow!" he whispered.

"What's your name?"

"Stephens. Robert Stephens."

"Okay, Mr. Stephens. Do you know what they did with my dad, Jacob Lewis? Or my grandpa?"

"Look, I'm just a technician here," he said. "I swear, I had nothing to do with any of this."

"That's not was she asked, you git," snapped Benjamin. Then to Sarah, "Shall I tape him up again?"

Sarah held up a hand to Benjamin. "Mr. Stephens, I'll ask again. Do you know where my dad is?"

The man eyed Sarah and then shot a dirty look at Benjamin before he answered. "Yes. Okay? I helped set him up. But I was just doing my job. They want him for some ceremony, and…but listen, if I tell you where he is, I want you to guarantee my safety, because I'll be writing my own death warrant. Got it? I don't know what's going on upstairs or who you're with—they don't tell us much—but I can see the writing on the wall. Drake's about to get what's coming to him for all the people he's messed up, and that's just fine with me." His eyes went from face to face, a frightened, questioning look on his face. "I'm done with him. With all of it. I swear. I've seen and heard enough of this insanity to last a lifetime. So when you all get out of here, I want to go with you. I'll defect. I'll swear allegiance to you or to anybody. Just don't leave me here to die. Please."

"Why should we—" started Benjamin, but Sarah shushed him.

"Okay. It's a deal," she told Stephens. "We can hide you and take you with us if you'll tell us where to find my dad." Sarah turned and mouthed the word *oubliette* to Benjamin and Aubrey. Then she looked Stephens in the eyes, took his still-tied hand in her own, and shook it. "I promise."

"All right then," Stephens said and took a deep breath. "Out this door, to the left, maybe a hundred feet down, there's a black door with a red dragon on it. The lock is computerized. It uses a code, but it's easy enough. Just type J419 on the keyboard mounted to the wall. Got that? Then hit enter, and the door will unlock. You'll go down a long spiral staircase. At the bottom is a…well, it's sort of a dungeon. You'll see when you get there. I hate it. Drake's into some weird stuff, and I'm not sure you'll want to see what they've done to your dad. But you'll have to go that way if you want to find him. There's no other way in or out. No elevator, even. And let me tell you, carrying a grown man down all those stairs was a real pain in the—"

"We get the picture," said Benjamin.

Stephens nodded. "There's my end of the deal."

Sarah nodded. Then to Aubrey, "Do you have it?"

"Sure thing." Aubrey produced a small device from somewhere the others could not see. She flipped a switch on the thing in her hand. There was a flash of darkness, and the contents of the oubliette (a pair of walkie talkies, two handguns, a couple of survival knives, some matches, a first aid kit, Aubrey's black baton and another like it that belonged to Fred) fell to the floor. She tossed the controller to Benjamin and began distributing items between them.

Stephens swore. "How in the—"

"No time," said Aubrey. "Just be happy and try not to think about it too much. This is your ticket out."

"Oh, no you don't!" he said. "No way—"

"Oh, shut up," said Benjamin as he placed Sarah's backpack and suitcase near Stephens's feet. "Now just you hold still. You won't feel a thing." He began to count: "One."

"No, please!"

A grin spread across Benjamin's face. "Two."

Roger Stephens opened his mouth to scream, but he was swallowed up by a sphere of darkness that appeared and disappeared before the sound could escape his lungs.

"Three."

Benjamin tossed the controller back to Aubrey and watched it disappear from sight. "You know," he said, "I think I've seen that place Stephens described. Or rather, I think Blackwood saw it. I might have an idea."

A MOMENT LATER, THE DOOR OPENED, AND A TALL, BLACK-HAIRED guard emerged leading two prisoners: a thin man in a white lab coat and a young girl with a bald head studded with titanium ports who hobbled as best she could on weak legs. A second, mustached guard appeared behind them as they marched toward the black door with the red dragon.

39

THE SACRIFICE

They found the black door moments later, and it was just as Robert Stephens had described it. Aubrey entered the code the technician had given them, and the tumblers clacked in response. Fred pushed against the red dragon. The door swung into the darkness beyond, and they were greeted by the dank fragrance of mildew.

"Do you hear that?" Fred whispered.

Sarah strained her ears and heard the faint sound of distant chanting. She looked at Aubrey with a curious expression, and Aubrey shrugged her shoulders.

"There's no telling," said Fred as he stepped through the doorway. "Let's go." Aubrey followed her brother, and Benjamin and Sarah brought up the rear.

The stairway on the other side led them down through a narrow concrete-walled cylinder. Small buzzing lights were mounted to the wall every few feet, but these gave off so little light that Sarah could barely see each step before her foot found it. She held tightly onto Benjamin's arm. Her strength was returning with each passing minute, but the steps were steep, and her legs were still wobbly. The top of Sarah's head itched worse than ever, but—whether from the pills she had taken or the adrenaline or both—the pain had dwindled. The air grew cooler and mustier as they went, and the chanting grew louder, though not loud enough to cover the pounding of Sarah's heart in her ears.

"Stop right there," she heard someone whisper when they reached the bottom. "What do you think you're doing?" A warm glow was visible on the wall ahead, revealing a narrow passageway.

"What does it look like?" Fred replied in a whisper as he motioned toward the others. "I've got orders from Drake to bring them here."

"Well, I have orders from Drake to let nobody past this point."

"All right," Fred said. "Have it your way."

He struck quick as a snake. Sarah heard a slapping thump, then some gargled grunting and the scraping of boots on stone, and finally a squashy thud.

"Well that was fun," said Fred with a wry smile when he had finished. "Man, it feels good to be on a real assignment again." Sarah had not seen him smile since the meeting at Flatland Hall. A spark of that Fred, cocky and bold, was in his eyes now. "Come on, Sis," he said to Aubrey. "There will be more of them before it's over. If you're lucky, I'll save you one or two." He chuckled. "And it sounds like they've got live music. Not my style, exactly, but still. We shouldn't keep our hosts waiting."

They tiptoed through the passageway, quiet as shadows, the glow on the walls brighter and the chanting louder with every step. Then Fred stopped and held up a hand. "Found the honor guard," he whispered. "Showtime."

Benjamin held his wrists together behind his back, and Fred led him around the corner, a hand on the back of his neck and standing close enough to hide the broken handcuffs. Aubrey grabbed Sarah's arm and followed.

"Look what I found lurking in the shadows," Fred announced.

A moment later, they were surrounded by twenty armed guards just inside the arched doorway of a circular stone chamber, fifty feet across. An ornate platform was built into a section of the wall, and high candelabras held a dozen white, half-spent candles along its curvature.

Beneath the candles stood eleven adult-sized figures. They were statue-still and wore hooded black robes that obscured their faces and hung to the floor. Each held a flaming torch in both hands and droned mysterious words that Sarah did not understand.

Slumped on the far side of the room sat a white-haired old man in dirty, tattered clothing. His wrists and ankles were chained. His skin was bruised and hung ragged from his bones, and his eyes were downcast. Grandpa Kirk was thinner than Sarah had ever seen him, but she recognized him at once. She gasped and felt unwanted tears well up in her eyes.

In the middle of the room lay two men in white robes, stretched on long, low tables. A box covered in blinking lights and white dials sat between them. The wires that dangled from the men's heads were gathered into bundles near the place where they disappeared into the box. Sarah could not see either man's face from where she stood, but she recognized the one by his frame: her father. The other man, she guessed, was Drake.

On the far side of her father's unconscious body stood a lone figure, cloaked in red. One of his hands held an ancient-looking leather-bound book. The other swept along the edge of the table where her father lay, out of sight. Then he stepped back, lifted his arm, and revealed a long, slender sword, red with blood. At his feet, thick liquid dripped slowly from the table and pooled onto the floor, dancing in the flickering torchlight. Sarah felt as if she might vomit.

Fred cleared his throat loudly. "Sorry to interrupt, gentlemen, but I've got a delivery for Dr. Drake. Anybody know where I might find him?"

The chanting stopped, and the candles all seemed to flicker. The man with the sword turned slowly to face them, but he did not speak. In the silence, Sarah heard Drake's voice quietly murmuring, "Stop fighting, Mr. Lewis. That's right. Just show me."

Grandpa Kirk looked up, his eyes wide with surprise. "Dr. Allen?" he croaked. Sarah's heart sank. He had recognized Benjamin, but not her.

The nearest torch bearer threw back his hood and stepped toward the intruders. "What is the meaning of this?!" he demanded. His voice was gravelly, full of fury, and carried a thick French accent.

"Meaning?" said Fred. "It means I deserve a reward."

"Why you insolent—" began the Frenchman.

"Whoa now, Monsieur," said Fred, "I'm just following orders! Drake said I should bring these two down to join your little party if they got out of line. So here I am. You're welcome." He bowed.

The Frenchman gasped. "How dare you!" He slapped Fred. "I'll have your skin for this, you—"

"Peace, Gaspard," said a hoarse, hissing voice. "Thank these men for supplying us with such a fine young sacrifice, and send them on their way so we can complete the ritual." The man in red lifted a snow-white hand and made a dismissive gesture.

Sarah felt a chill shoot through her spine. She could not bring herself to look up, so she stared down at her feet and fidgeted with the ring on her finger instead. The others must have felt it too because, for a long moment, nobody moved or spoke.

"Watch your forked tongue, Fourteen," snapped the Frenchman. He held out a hand toward Benjamin. "I'll take this one. You may go."

Fred did not move.

Another of the torch bearers approached, grabbed Sarah roughly by her elbow, and yanked. Aubrey held tight. "Hands off," she snarled in the deep, masculine voice of the guard she played.

The man spit on Aubrey's shoe. "Who do you think you are, boy?"

In response, Aubrey growled and transformed before his eyes. In an instant, she was a towering woman, tall and fanged, beautiful and terrifying. Her skin was the pale gray of a winter sky. Her hair, white as snow. Her eyes glowed a fiery red. She was clad in black strips of cloth that floated as if weightless in the air around her. And when she lifted the robed man off the ground by his throat with one hand, it seemed to require no effort at all. Aubrey held the hooded face close to her own and whispered, "I am no boy. I am a Sentinel of God. And you, little man, are hurting the people I've sworn to protect." Then she raised her head and let loose a terrifying scream before slamming her victim to the floor.

The guards stood in terrified silence.

"Well, that's new," said Fred, a stunned expression on his face. "Nice one, Sis!" Then he transformed himself into a hulking, black-furred man-beast with sharp claws and the head of a panther. "Monsters it is!" he growled.

"Taborians!" shouted the man in red. "Kill them!"

The room exploded into chaos. Both shifters produced their batons from nowhere and sent hooded men and armed guards flying before them. Benjamin ran for the machine in the center of the room, dodging robed men as he went, wire cutters in hand. A gun fired, and the bullet ricocheted off the curved wall, knocking a candelabra to the floor. Someone shouted, "Don't shoot, idiots! You'll kill us all!" but the command was lost in the noise of the fight. A moment later, another ear-splitting gunshot sounded, and Sarah heard a man cry out in pain. She did not look. There was no time. She limped as quickly as she could toward her father, dagger in hand, dodging fallen bodies along the way. Aubrey had offered Sarah a handgun before, but she had declined. It was too heavy for her, and she had never used one. Now she wished that she had taken it.

Sarah had almost reached her father when a new voice thundered above the din. "SILENCE!" it roared, and in its wake, a chorus of clone voices whispered other words into Sarah's mind. "Don't move," they said. "Stop fighting. You're pathetic. You can't win. You're too weak and helpless." She felt the words in her bones. She *was* utterly vulnerable, she realized, and her body was so tired. Fighting was useless. "And don't bother calling for help," the voices commanded. She was suddenly certain that she could not speak if she tried. "Nobody will help you. Nobody will come for you. Nobody cares about you." It was true, she thought. She was not important. She had no family left except the two men in this room who would die with her. The other Sentinels would be right to abandon her.

The moment passed, and the whispers stopped, but the feeling of hopelessness remained. All was silent. Nobody was moving, she realized. Nobody was fighting anymore. Sarah stood, wide eyed, and searched the room. Guards and chanters lay motionless in every direction. Only Fred and Aubrey still stood, but they had shrunk, it seemed. What was happening? Had everyone else heard it too? Sarah could not think straight.

And then she saw something that filled her heart with fresh dread:

hovering above the stone platform was a huge, green, slitted eye, peering through what seemed to be a tear in the air around it. "Do you dare come to me empty handed, abomination?" said the voice. "I require a sacrifice."

"You shall have your sacrifice, Great One," said the man in red.

He stepped from where he stood next to the eye and walked toward Sarah. His sword, she saw, he left behind, protruding from something on the platform: a shiny black box, roughly the size of the red and gold one she had left in her suitcase. There was something else in the box too: a black cube sitting just in front of the sword.

"We have brought you a double sacrifice tonight," the red-robed man continued. "One you shall have now, and the other you shall have as soon as he has given up the last of his secrets."

Sarah felt the panic rise within her to a pitch she had never before experienced. Her body was frozen with it. It stabbed at her fingertips and clenched her chest. Her ears rang. She could not breathe. Her thoughts raced in confused circles. "This is it," said a voice in her mind. "This is the moment you die." And with that, the panic hardened into a thick, tangible despair.

A hand, cold and rough, gripped her forearm just above the wrist and jerked it upward. It was still tender where the hound had bit her, and Sarah winced.

"I'll have that now, if you don't mind," snarled the man in red as he pried the dagger from Sarah's fingers with one hand while he kept a firm grip on her wrist with the other. Then, as he examined the blade he said, "My, what a pretty thing this is. Why, I do believe the dagger of Ammon the Bold has come home to its brother." He waved toward the sword. "What luck. For me. How did you come by this, child?"

Sarah did not answer. She was about to die. Why should she bother speaking? So instead, she stared blankly at her now empty hand and felt all remaining hope drain from her heart. The ring on her finger looked as melancholy as she felt. The normally pearly gem had faded to a dull, pathetic gray. Her eyes fell to the boney hand squeezing her wrist. It was a lifeless white, covered in jagged scales. Sarah paid it no attention. Nothing mattered now.

"Answer me!" the man hissed.

His face was close to hers now. She could see pale, scaled cheeks and green, slitted eyes reflecting the dim light of the torches scattered across the floor. Still, Sarah said nothing. And still, nobody moved.

The man growled in frustration. "Come!" He jerked her forward, toward the eye.

Sarah would have followed the man in red to her death right then and there if not for one thing: Jacob Lewis began to speak. He could not move, but her father had not given up. His voice was only a strained mumble, but Sarah recognized the words:

"Yea, though I walk through the valley of the shadow of death…"

Something sparked then in Sarah's mind, a faint glow in the darkness.

"I will fear no evil," she whispered.

The man in red spun and looked at her. "What did you say?"

"I will fear no evil," she whispered again, a little louder.

"Shut up, you fool," said a chorus of voices in her mind. And she almost obeyed. But then Grandpa Kirk took up the recitation:

"I will fear no evil: for thou art with me…"

"Shut up!" shouted the scaly man, and he slapped her. "Both of you!"

Grandpa Kirk ignored him and continued. From behind her, Sarah heard Aubrey's voice join her grandfather's:

"Yea, though I walk through the valley of the shadow of death, I will fear no evil: for thou art with me…"

In her mind, Sarah could hear the accusing voices screaming for attention, but she ignored them.

"Stop it, I say!" shouted the man in the red robe.

"SILENCE!" bellowed the eye.

But The Sentinels' voices only grew stronger. And now Fred had joined in. Sarah's eyes darted around the dark room, looking for him. Instead, she found Benjamin, crouched on the floor next to the blinking machine, snipping wires one at a time. "I will fear no evil," said Sarah again, staring straight into his eyes. Benjamin smiled back at her and mouthed the words silently. "I will fear no evil." Life seemed to return to Sarah's veins.

She took a deep breath. Her mind cleared, and flashes of memory suddenly joined together like pieces of a puzzle: the gray stone in her ring, the scaly white hand. This thing in red robes was no human. But what was it? A shifter? Sarah shut her eyes for second and channeled her gift. Then she opened them again and gazed at the creature's face, no longer hidden by earthly shadows. Its nose was square and wide. Its tongue was forked behind its teeth. And in its eyes, a black fire burned cold. No, this was no shifter; this was something else—something that turned her ring gray, not the red of the Taborian banner.

Just then, something bright and beautiful caught Sarah's eye. She was snapped out of her thoughts when she realized what it was: her own dagger, a piercing rainbow of light in the monster's hand. Seven different blades protruded from the handle into seven different dimensions. Each was as elegant and deadly as the next, though each had its own unique shape and length. It was breathtaking.

Sarah came to herself then and realized that she was no longer afraid. Despair and panic had evaporated. She felt her strength return, and with it, hope. "I will fear no evil!" Sarah shouted and shoved her hand into her pocket. An instant later, she removed the scrap of otherworld metal that had saved her life once. But before she could wield it, she was interrupted.

BOOM!

The great, green eye flickered for a moment, like a television with bad reception, and dust fell from the ceiling at the shock. The sound came from above as before, but now it was closer. Louder. More real.

"End this!" said the eye.

The thing in the red robe tensed his grip on Sarah's arm and jerked her toward her father. Out of the corner of her eye, Sarah saw Fred and Aubrey standing with their hands raised over their heads. Half a dozen guards stood nearby with handguns pointed at their heads.

Sarah held up the piece of Luxephorian alloy and stared at it. She could see the jagged outline of a broken shield. She turned it so that it seemed to be parallel to her body and clutched it to her chest.

In a wretched, hissing voice, the creature screamed at her father, "Lewis! You hear me? This girl is going to die because of your stubbornness! Your foolish loyalty! Your secrets!" Then he turned and raised Sarah's dagger to strike. Sarah squinted and lifted the shield defensively over her head. The dagger plunged toward her, slammed into the invisible shield with a screech and a flash of light, and flew from the creature's hand.

Without taking time to think, Sarah punched the arm that still clasped her wrist with the edge of her shield and watched the bone break in two before her eyes. The white creature screamed as he fell backward in pain.

"Well done!" shouted Benjamin.

"That's my granddaughter!" shouted Grandpa Kirk.

"YOU WILL ALL DIE FOR THIS!" said the voice from the eye.

Sarah spun to face it. For a moment, she trembled against her will. But then she saw the box pulsing with red light, the sword that pierced it glowing like her dagger, and hundreds of glowing, translucent crystals protruding from the black cube. That was it, she realized. The sword was holding open the tear. It was letting that monster speak.

She ran toward the platform. But before she had landed her third step, something caught her ankle. She fell and dropped the bit of L-421.

BOOM! The ground shook.

Sarah glanced back and saw a white hand clutching her blue jeans and angry green eyes staring at her. She kicked, but she could not get free. "I've still got one good arm," the monster spat. "And you'll pay for the one you broke."

"KILL HER!" said the eye.

"No! The sword!" screamed Sarah. "Dr. Allen! Get the sword!" But she could not see him. The thing stood and lifted her by one ankle. Sarah wriggled and jerked in vain. Then she felt her body flail helplessly as she was flung into the air. Her head slammed into the stone floor. Pain shot through her whole body, and searing light blinded her eyes. She tried to stand, but she was dizzy and disoriented, and she fell. Blood dripped down her face. She searched the floor, but she could not find her shield.

A moment later, the room darkened.

"NOOOO!" screamed the white monster.

Sarah looked up and saw the thing running, one arm dangling

awkwardly at its side, toward where Benjamin stood holding the sword, still red with her father's blood. The great green eye was gone.

"I think you've done enough damage for one day," Benjamin said as he ran to meet his opponent, the sword lifted over his head. But before he could land his blow, there was another BANG!

A gun had fired, but there was no ricochet this time. Benjamin fell to his knees as a red stain bloomed in the chest of the stolen white lab coat he wore. Beyond him, a guard stood, his gun still raised.

"No!" screamed Sarah.

Chaos erupted again. Aubrey snatched up the guard who had shot Benjamin and sent him flying across the room before she ran back to Fred's side. Guns fired and bullets ricocheted. Sarah ignored it all and ran to the man who had betrayed her and saved her life all in one day.

"Sarah," said Benjamin when she reached him, his voice cracking. "I'm so sorry."

"Stop it!" she said. "Don't apologize. You brought me right where I wanted to be. You gave me the chance to see my dad and Grandpa Kirk again. Don't apologize for that!"

Benjamin smiled a weak smile. "Then go to them. Go to your family."

Tears filled Sarah's eyes. "No," she gasped.

"Shhh," he said. "It's all right. I am not afraid. Fear—" He did not finish the sentence. Dr. Benjamin Allen fell to the floor and spoke no more.

BOOM! CRACK!

A thunderstorm of feet and voices filled the air as an army of Sentinels flooded into the circular chamber, injured and worn from the battle above, but fierce nonetheless. The few Les Luminaires guards who remained dropped their weapons and surrendered. Someone shouted, "They're in here! Send for the Watcher!" and a moment later, Samuel appeared, towering above the rest. The crowd parted to make way. He seemed to have grown even more enormous than usual. The jewel in his turban blazed with red light and he held a flaming warhammer in his hand. At the sight of him, the scaly white creature in the red robe shrieked and ran into a narrow passageway at the other end of the room. Samuel sent two shifters after him, but when they returned much later, they were empty-handed.

Sarah stood next to her father, her hands soaked with his blood. Grandpa Kirk had helped her tie a strip of fabric torn from her own shirt around her dad's arm as a tourniquet, but the blood still dripped. Sarah called for help, and her dad woke for a moment at the sound of her voice. His eyes opened just long enough to look at her, smile, and whisper "Sprinkles," before he passed out again.

Dr. Absalom Drake also roused for a moment, and saw his own defeat. There was a flash of black, and for an instant, Robert Stephens appeared on the floor, tied up and trying to scream. A moment later, he was gone again, and so was the table where Dr. Drake had lain.

"THERE YOU ARE," said a robotic voice in Sarah's mind. She lifted her head, wiped the tears from her eyes with the cleaner of her two sleeves, and called out for Duke. The great white German Shepherd appeared, tongue out and tail wagging as he limped around the goat-legged man who was wrapping Aubrey's arm in a sling.

A few seconds later, Sarah was huddled on the cold floor with Grandpa Kirk's arms wrapped around her shoulders, crying into Duke's warm fur, as Sentinel medics carried her dad away on a stretcher.

They had done it, she thought. Her heart ached for Benjamin, and she worried for her father, but they had won. She had her family back.

40

THREE DAYS LATER

Sarah and Grandpa Kirk sat at the top of a low grassy hill watching the sunrise. Behind them stood the beautiful English manor that had served as The Sentinels' headquarters for more than one-hundred years. Birds chirped and flitted around a huge willow tree below. Grandpa puffed on a new pipe that Dr. Connolly had given him (briar wrapped in tawny stitched leather) and stared into the distance.

"Grandpa," said Sarah, "do you think Dad will ever wake up?"

Grandpa Kirk chewed the stem of his pipe thoughtfully, then said, "I can't tell the future, Princess."

Sarah picked a blade of grass and twirled it between her fingers.

"He's a fighter, though," Grandpa said after a moment. "You get that from him, you know. I wouldn't give up on him yet."

Sarah nodded. He was right. She had given up on her dad before, when she thought he had abandoned her, but she would not repeat that mistake now. She needed him. She needed him to be there, to teach her what he knew, to hold her, to sit with her and watch television in the comfort of their own home. But of course, a home was not something she had anymore.

Sarah wondered how differently things would have turned out if she had never snuck out of her room, had never seen the letter from

Desjardins, whoever that was. Nobody seemed to know, and that scared her. The mysterious messenger was responsible for so much that had happened, whether for the better or for the worse. She feared that Benjamin had been right about him all along and that she now found herself homeless with no idea what her future held because of a note from a stranger.

"What are we going to do, Grandpa?" she asked.

Grandpa Kirk raised an eyebrow. "First thing we're gonna do," he said, "is find some breakfast. They've got something called 'proper bacon' around here that I've never tried, and I intend to remedy that situation."

Sarah stared at him. She knew he was just trying to cheer her up, but it wouldn't work. Not today.

He sighed. "Then we'll get dressed and go to Dr. Allen's funeral. You can wear that wig the council gave you if you want."

She frowned. The wig was ridiculous. It made her look like a shorter version of Ronald McDonald. "No thanks. And that's not what I meant. After that. Where are we going to live? We can't stay here forever."

"No," Grandpa agreed, "we can't." He paused a moment and then laughed. "Maybe they'll send you and Miss Aubrey to steal back more stolen artifacts! She's getting pretty good, I hear. Impersonating an imagined form is some advanced shapeshifting." Then, in a whisper, "And you got that old sword back, after all."

"Finding that sword was a lucky coincidence," said Sarah, though she didn't really think it was lucky at all. She hated the sword. She would have given it away if she could have. It had spilled the blood of someone she loved. But Samuel and Duke had insisted that it belonged with the Weaver, so she kept them, hidden and secret in her room as instructed.

"Coincidence?" said Grandpa. "Do you really think there's any such thing?"

Sarah eyed him curiously but didn't reply.

Grandpa smiled. "No, I don't think they'll send you to hunt down any more lucky coincidences. I imagine that, since you went and enlisted in The Sentinels without asking first, you'll be due for some basic training. Sentinel school."

"What about you?" she asked.

He laughed. "Me? They'll probably force me to retire. And who'd blame them?" Then he caught the look on Sarah's face and added, "As long as I've got you back, I won't mind. You're all the family I've got, you know. You and your dad."

"And Duke," said Sarah.

"And Duke. But if you ask me, Duke's the one you need to worry about. Well, him and Samuel both. They broke a few rules getting us out of that dungeon, you know, and the council ain't too happy about it."

Sarah smiled. "As if any old council could keep those two away."

Grandpa smiled back. "Come on, kiddo," he said, standing. "The day's getting on and we're missing it. Can't let any adventures happen without us!"

Sarah sat at the desk next to the window in the tiny room that had been reserved for her by the council. The door was locked and the curtains were drawn. Throughout the rest of the manor, people were sleeping. But she had been startled awake that night, the same way she had been every night since the escape, by Duke's insistent voice in her mind. "TRAIN NOW," he had said, as clearly as if he were sitting next to her, though she knew he was locked up in another part of the manor while they awaited the council's verdict.

And so she trained. Sarah twisted the black cube in her hands, eyes closed, and worked the pattern from memory: first column down three quarter-turns, second row two turns to the right, third row left one, and so on. After a few more twists she was finished. Sarah opened her eyes and saw the columns of light aligned perfectly. She had nailed the Narinaelia pattern without looking. She should be excited, she thought, but she wasn't. She had opened that portal already, two days ago, and she hadn't liked what she had seen: nothing but ice wherever she looked. Not a single sign of life. Then last night she had unlocked the Fodinaran window. Utter darkness and silence. It broke her heart to think what Boarsmash would say if he knew.

But tonight she was thinking of another pattern, one she hadn't yet tried. She had only found it this morning, as she was working the cube by sight while she waited for a turn to shower. When the crystals had aligned, they formed a new structure, greater than the sum of its parts. But this pattern was not written in her mother's diary, and she was uncertain what would happen if she tried it. She was not sure she should.

Finally, her curiosity won out. She returned the cube to its starting state, flipped to the note she had made in her diary, and repeated the pattern she had discovered. It was more than thirty steps. This one would be much more difficult to memorize.

When she had completed the sequence, she set the cube on the desk, pulled the gold and red box from beneath the pile of dirty laundry next to her suitcase, spun the letters on its top until it spelled "SPRINKLES," opened the lid, and set it down next to the cube. Inside was a flat platform with a wide slit and a square pocket, just the right size. She lifted the black cube, turned it so that the crystal column pointed straight down, and lowered it carefully into position. Warmth and light began to radiate from the box. *It's just a little interdimensional friction*, she told herself, her heart racing. Then she pulled the dagger from her backpack and inserted it into the slit in the platform next to the cube.

Nothing.

Sarah sighed and pulled the dagger back out of the cube. It made no sense. Every other combination she had found had opened a little window into one of the other dimensions. Sarah sighed and set the dagger onto the desk. She was about to remove the cube when another thought struck her. It was not an idea that she liked, but she had to try.

Reluctantly, Sarah withdrew the sword of Ammon the Bold—the same sword that had been used to cut her father in Drake's laboratory—from beneath her mattress. She slipped it carefully into the slot where her dagger had been and held her breath. Again, the box began to glow and heat up, but this time there was also a faint ripping sound.

A few inches above the sword's hilt, Sarah saw an opening in time and space. Through the portal, she glimpsed a world of blues and greens, bright light, and shiny objects that did not make sense to Sarah's eyes. All was silent. Nothing moved. None of the signs of life she had so hoped for. She slumped in her seat and sighed.

"Oh well," she said and reached up to remove the sword. But before she touched it, something caught her eye from beyond the portal. She stared for several minutes, hoping to see what it was. Nothing. She reached again for the sword, and the room filled with blinding light.

"Hello, Sarah," said a voice. "I have been expecting you."

TO BE CONTINUED

HELP THE SENTINELS!

The Sentinels need you.

Here's how you can help spread the word about this book and help Sarah and The Sentinels.

—

Tell your friends!
Recommend this book to your friends.

Leave a Review!
Let other readers know what you thought of this book by sharing your thoughts on your blog or YouTube channel, Amazon.com, Goodreads.com, BookBub.com or the review site of your choice!

Ask your local library or bookstore to stock it!
Librarians and book sellers can order this book through Ingram at a great discount, and even return it if it doesn't sell.

Want more of The Sentinels?

Joshua C. Carroll is working hard to get the next book in this series written as fast as possible. In the meantime, how about a **FREE ebook** to hold you over?

What would happen if a pentrafax (like Duke) took over a human rather than an animal?

Sign up (or have your parent sign up) for Joshua C. Carroll's mailing list, and **get a FREE ebook** copy of **The Bahushnovat**, to find out.

JoshuaCCarroll.com

PRONUNCIATION GUIDE

There are a few tricky words in The Adventures of Sarah Ann Lewis and the Memory Thieves, and it may not be clear how to pronounce them when you're reading. But fear not! Here's your guide:

- **Aenimor / Aenimos** – EYE • ni • mor / EYE • ni • mose
- **Almast** – ALL • mast
- **Arabella Minot** – air • uh • BELL • uh • MY • not
- **Aravatis** – are • uh • VOT • tiss
- **Aureulis** – are • ay • YOU • liss
- **Boarsmash** – BORE • smash
- **Desjardins** – day • zhar • DUH
- **Dvorak** – duh • VOR • rack
- **Fodinara / Fondinaran** – foe • din • NAR • ruh / foe • din • NAR • run
- **Obsinder** – ub • SIN • dur
- **Oubliette** – oob • lee • ET
- **Les Luminaires** – LAY • loo • min • AIR
- **Lumovitae** – LOO • moe • vit • tay
- **Malemorphos** – mal • lay • MORE • fose
- **Murik** – MYOOR • rick

- **Narinaelia / Narinaelian** – nare • rin • NAIL • yuh / nare • rin • NAIL • yun
- **Pentrafax** – PIN • truh • fax
- **Psuchamora** – soo • kuh • MORE • ruh
- **Samuel Bin Perelderoth** – SAM • mule • BIN • purr • RELD • dur • roth
- **Tabor / Taborian** – TAY • bore / tay • BORE • ree • yun
- **Tellurak** – TELL • your • rack
- **Vaelhala / Vaelhalar** – VILE • ha • la / VILE • ha • lar

For an updated list and audio samples, visit
JoshuaCCarroll.com/sarah-ann-guide

ABOUT THE AUTHOR

Joshua C. Carroll is an author, a dad/foster dad, the founder of Dads Who Read, and a creativity addict. When he isn't hanging out with his family or writing, he makes music, shoots photography, cooks food, and builds software. He lives in Fort Worth, Texas with his wife and kids, his dog, a wall of musical instruments, and an overflowing bookshelf. Learn more at JoshuaCCarroll.com.

facebook.com/JoshTellsAStory
twitter.com/JoshTellsAStory
instagram.com/JoshTellsAStory

Made in the USA
Columbia, SC
15 July 2019